Pastor and Patient

Pastor and Patient

A Handbook for Clergy
Who Visit the Sick

EDITED BY

RICHARD DAYRINGER

NEW YORK   JASON ARONSON   LONDON

ISBN: 0-87668-437-1

Library of Congress Catalog Number: 80–70247

Manufactured in the United States of America.

Contents

Foreword   xi
Preface   xiii

PART I
THEORY OF PASTORAL CARE FOR THE SICK

1. Reading the Message of Illness   3
   Robert B. Reeves, Jr.
2. Initiative in Pastoral Relationships   11
   Daniel DeArment
3. Ministering to the Woman Patient   21
   Dorothy Faust
4. Depressive Reactions and Pastoral Care   29
   Joe Boone Abbott
5. A Dynamic Concept of Praying for the Sick   39
   James T. Hall
6. Justification by Faith as a Concept in Pastoral Care   49
   Murray S. Thompson
7. Some Theological Implications of Illness   59
   Richard Dayringer, Eugene Mendenhall

PART II
PASTORAL CARE FOR PATIENTS

8. Ministering to the Presurgical Patient   71
   Dennis Saylor

9. Crisis Intervention in Orthopedic Surgery   87
   John L. Florell

10. Ministering to Kidney Dialysis and Transplant
    Patients and Their Families   97
    W. Noel Brown

11. Ministering to Persons with Drug Dependency
    Problems   111
    E. W. Belter

12. Balm for Burned Patients   119
    Claude V. Deal, Jr.

13. Implications of the Psychosomatic Approach
    of the Clergy   133
    David Belgum

14. Pastoral Care of the Patient with
    Gastrointestinal Complaints   141
    Robert B. Lantz

15. Pastoral Care in the Intensive Care Unit   149
    David M. Hurst

16. Ministering to Cancer Patients   159
    Leroy G. Kerney

17. Pastoral Care of the Stroke Patient and his Family   167
    Rudolph E. Grantham

18. Ministry to the Unconscious Patient   179
    Alquinn L. Toews

19. Ministering to the Dying   185
    Carl A. Nighswonger

PART III
PASTORAL CARE FOR CHILDREN

20. To Touch a Child   197
    Robert Wedergren

21. Establishing Rapport with Hospitalized Children   205
    John Schaefer
22. Ministry to Hospitalized Children   209
    Harold W. Butler
23. Pastoral Concerns for Children in Hospitals   221
    Palmer C. Temple
24. Pastoral Care for the Dying Child and His Family   225
    Carl Rabon Stephens

PART IV
PASTORAL CARE FOR THE AGING

25. Aging with Meaning   237
    David F. Freitag
26. Pastoral Care to Geriatrics   245
    C. Raymond Probst
27. Ministry in Extended Care Facilities   253
    John Patton

Index   263

To

the Reverend Carl A. Nighswonger, Ph.D.

(1933–1972)

and

All those who visit the sick

in the name of the Lord

Foreword

Pastors interested in improving their ministry to hospitalized persons from childhood through aging will find this book a valuable tool. Written by a group of ministers who speak out of their unique experiences in a wide variety of healing situations, it is a well-balanced mixture of the theory and practice of pastoral care of the sick.

The busy pastor will find help in ministering to those patients whose life-threatening illness make heavy demands on pastoral resources for intense understanding, support, and acceptance. Especially welcome are the sections on the pastoral care of hospitalized children and of aging persons.

The chapters of this book direct attention to the spiritual implications of illness and health and reflect the role of the pastor in ministry to the sick. As he gains insight into the spiritual and social aspects of illness and health, the pastor will see the significant contribution he can make to the new thrust in modern medicine and health care—an emphasis on health and on illness prevention.

I am grateful to Richard Dayringer and each of the authors for their contributions to this book, which is a significant addition to the body of literature on pastoral care. Each author has demonstrated a generous spirit in assigning his share of all royalties from the sale of this book to The College of Chaplains. Their sense of fulfillment will be achieved from the realization that those who read the book will become more effective pastors in caring for persons experiencing the crisis of illness.

Charles D. Phillips
Executive Director
College of Chaplains
Schaumberg, Illinois

Preface

Today's pastor spends a good portion of his work week visiting the sick at the hospital and in their homes. His people expect this, and he usually enjoys doing it.

I served as pastor of a church in Kansas for six years and found myself drawn increasingly into this ministry. Somehow I felt wanted and needed by the sick. I hadn't had any training along those lines then and wasn't sure I was doing the "right" things, but it was wonderful to feel so useful.

The pastor's role at the hospital and with the sick is still somewhat elusive. Owen Brandon[1] discussed the minister as servant, interpreter, learner, teacher, guide, theologian, priest, pastor, and professional. I think he is all these things at different times to different people: the questions are when, how, and to whom. Many of the answers are to be found in this book. There can be a "positive use of the minister's role."[2] I think Heije Faber[3] suggests an intriguing metaphor when he presents the minister as being like a clown in a circus. He reaches the patient, family, doctor, and nurse not by his versatility and expertise (though I think he should have both), but by his humanity.

Many pastors have had the opportunity to take seminary courses in pastoral care to the sick or, even better, clinical pastoral education; some have not. This book is designed to meet the needs of pastors who have had either a little or a lot of such training. It is written by the only real specialists in the field of pastoral care to the sick—hospital chaplains. The authors of these chapters have dedicated their lives to a ministry to the infirm. They all have had at least a minimum of one full year of clinical pastoral education after completing college and seminary. Moreover, they know about the pastor's workaday world because they have served a congregation as pastor for at least three years (and some for many more). More than half of them are chaplain supervisors in clinical pastoral education. Several hold faculty positions with theological seminaries or universities.

Unfortunately, chaplains don't have many opportunities to share the fruits of their experience with pastors. This book is one attempt to do so. These chapters were written out of a special interest and expertise in the subject. Originally they were presented as workshop papers at meetings of the College of Chaplains. With the authors' collaboration, I compiled them into one volume because they discuss important topics that pastors must frequently confront.

The book is designed as a handbook for the pastor who wants to improve his ministry by learning to do or say the most appropriate thing at the proper time, for a specific individual with a particular problem. Some of the chapters are quite technical, and in others the authors have a very personal approach to their subjects. I think pastors will find themselves referring to the book again and again. If, as a result of the publication of this book, pastors become more proficient in their ministry to the sick and patients are comforted, our purpose will have been achieved.

ACKNOWLEDGMENTS

I am grateful to Dr. Glen W. Davidson, Phyllis Shaw, and Nancy Pistorius for invaluable editorial assistance and also to Dorothy Floweree and Peg Moehle for typing the manuscript.

Notes

1. Owen Brandon. *The Pastor and His Ministry.* London: S.P.C.K., 1972.
2. David C. Jacobsen. *The Positive Use of the Minister's Role.* Philadelphia: Westminster Press, 1967.
3. Heiji Faber. *Pastoral Care in the Modern Hospital.* Philadelphia: Westminster Press, 1971, pp. 68–94.
4. A knowledge of the fundamentals for visiting the sick such as those mentioned by Bill Justice in his book *Don't Sit on the Bed* (Broadman Press, 1973) is assumed.

Richard Dayringer, Th.D.

PART I

*Theory of
Pastoral Care
for the Sick*

Reading the Message of Illness

Robert B. Reeves, Jr., S.T.M.

Chaplain
Presbyterian Hospital
New York, New York

Among the most useful questions clergy can ask a patient is, "How do you see your sickness? What do you make of it? Does it tell you anything?" We ask almost everyone else the meaning of illness: physician, psychiatrist, sociologist, moralist, theologian; but the patient is the one who is sick—why not ask him or her? We tend to dismiss the patient's interpretation as distorted or uninformed, when it may be in fact be of great diagnostic and prognostic value.

I have been asking patients this kind of question. The initial response, more than often not, is a shrug and "I guess it's just one of those things that happen," an unhappy accident of life, in Hamlet's words, one of "the thousand natural shocks that flesh is heir to." But while most patients are likely to give something like that as a first answer, I find that very few are content to let it rest there. Almost always, if you will listen, they go on to say a great deal more. And that "more" usually indicates that they read a message of some kind in their illness. The message comes through at various levels, and not all patients will start at the same level; nor will all follow the step-by-step readings that I am about to describe. Occasionally, however, a patient does go through the whole process; and whether he does so or not, it is almost always the case that the longer a pastor lets him talk, the deeper a level of awareness is revealed.

Disassociation

At the level of his first response to your inquiry—"It's one of those things that happen"—the patient seems to be aware simply that something has happened *to* him that interferes with normal work and play. It may have been something alien; a car that hit him, some food that disagreed with him, a malignant invading agent of one kind or another. Or it may have been some one of his organs that quite perversely and independently acted up: his ticker, stomach, or bowel. Or some congenital condition had caught up with him. Whatever it was, it was something he apparently had nothing to do with. He disassociates himself from any involvement. It happened to him. And a great many medical practitioners support him in this attitude, for that is the way they also like to think of disease: as an invading enemy that they can stomp out, without themselves having to become involved with the patient as a person.

For the patient, this is the easiest way to answer your question, the quickest way to get rid of you if he feels you are not really interested, the least revealing and the safest when he is insecure.

But if you listen and let him talk some more, he is likely to reveal another level of awareness. Instead of locating the source of his trouble "out there," in a balky organ that he has nothing to do with, or in his heredity, he may begin to tell you how in some particular way *he* is not functioning properly. He may say such things as, "I picked up a virus," "I slipped and fell," "I noticed a lump," "I was losing weight." Here is the first hint that he reads a message in his sickness: he sees a signal that something *in him* is out of kilter, he is involved, he cannot disassociate the something from himself.

Disharmony

Let him keep on talking. Usually very soon he moves from the particular dysfunction, or injury, or pain to another level, where he discloses that it is not simply in an organ or organ system that he is out of kilter, but in the way he lives. Beneath his awareness of dysfunction is an awareness of disharmony. Beneath the symptom, he discloses stress. He is somehow at odds with life. He may say it in any number of ways: "I've been going too hard," "Things haven't been right for a long time now," "I've been very unhappy in my work," "I just can't seem to take proper care of myself," "I'm all out of whack," "I've kind of fallen apart." From a segmental awareness the patient has moved toward a global awareness. He conveys a sense of disaffection or alienation, a loss of meaning, direction, or integrity, a bewildered groping for a selfhood that seems lost. The message he reads is that his way of life is out of tune.

Responsibility

Keep listening. He is not through yet. At a deeper level still may be an awareness that in one way or another he is responsible for his condition. In effect he says, "I have brought this on."

GUILT

He may not say it in so many words at first. He may try to fight it off and put the blame on God: "It's hard to understand how God can let things like this happen," "I have faith, but sometimes I wonder why I have to suffer," "It doesn't seem right, but if it is His will, I must accept it." If at this point the minister gets trapped into defending the ways of God, he may succeed in shutting up the patient, but his usefulness is *ended.* If, however, he holds his peace, he may not have long to wait before the patient turns the finger of blame from God upon himself. Almost always, blaming God is a kind of rear-guard action against yielding to an insistent sense of guilt.

Now, the patient begins to tell you how he has been careless or negligent or outright sinful. He has put the wrong things first and the right things last. He has been dishonest or unfaithful or arrogant or selfish. He has hated his work and pretended to like it. He has hurt people that he loves. He has failed the trust of wife or husband, son or daughter. He has been running like mad to avoid facing himself. He is no good, deep down inside. He is in the wrong, and he himself is to blame. He sees his sickness as a judgment he deserves, and he may sometimes grovel in guilty self-abasement.

Here the minister can fall into another trap. He may try to assuage the patient's guilt, tell him that sickness does not come as punishment, or insist that he is not to blame. In effect the minister may say that sickness *is* "just one of those things that happen," and miss the real significance of this confession of guilt. For what the patient is saying underneath his words is that his *sickness is a consequence and expression of his way of life. It is his doing. He is responsible.* And that is a great deal more than to say it is a judgment for his sins.

If the pastor shies away from, or tries to talk him out of, his guilt, he closes the door on the possibility of getting at this deeper message, and may as a result lose the surest clue to what is at the root of his sickness. Instead of helping him to understand it, the pastor forces him into silence where he must deal with it hopelessly alone, and so, in effect, he negates what might be a lifesaving moment of truth.

This feeling of the patient (that he is to blame for his sickness) should always be explored, no matter how fantastic or far-fetched it appears to be. It may turn out to be unfounded or inappropriate, and in such cases the pastor can help the patient sort out the true from the false. For instance, disease may result from external influences. Many environmental factors are at work such as bacteria and viruses in the air, infections passed from hand to hand or mouth to mouth, poisons, falling bricks, stray bullets, and wildly driven automobiles.

Some ills are inherited. As a species we are in many ways at odds with nature. Ecological imbalances and wayward genes can harm an individual who has done nothing specifically to bring it on. As members of humanity we are, in a large sense, of course responsible, but, it is hardly appropriate for an individual to say, "It is all my fault." Such things should be sorted out.

Also to be sorted out are the exaggerations of guilt which are part of the regression toward infancy experienced in some degree by every person who is sick. With weakened controls, the patient tends to fall back on the emotional patterns of his early years, when his security depended upon his parents' favor by being "good." If he lost their favor, as evidenced by things going badly for him, it must have been that he was "bad." Some of the guilt that a patient reveals may represent a reawakening of such long-forgotten experiences of childhood.

BEYOND GUILT

There will probably remain, however, after all the sorting is done, a residue in the patient's self-accusation that is relevant—evidence of desires, ambitions, deceptions, habits in which he was wittingly or unwittingly inviting trouble. It is necessary to get at these particulars, if the meaning of the message is to be understood and if the patient is to understand what his sickness has to say about his way of life. If we do not give him opportunity to see in what ways he may have been preparing the way for his sickness, and if we content ourselves with merely ridding him of inappropriate elements of guilt, we leave him where he was before this bout of sickness. His life may go on as it did before, with underlying problems still untouched and possibly building until he is sick again.

So we need to explore with him what he is doing in this sickness, whether or not he is following a pattern, and how he may be using it to serve hidden needs. For instance, what does his ulcer say about the way he habitually handles anger? When do the migraine headaches come, and what do they prevent—or save—him from doing? The bad back, the arthritis, the cardiac arrhythmia, the spasms of emphysema—with what kinds of threat, danger, or crisis are they associated, and what do they accomplish? What alterations in style of life does this radical surgery imply, and which is the cart, which the horse?

We need to be especially alert for possible connections between the form the patient's sickness takes and the state of his intimate relationships. Most sickness is in some degree a sign of a sick relationship, and the form of the sickness, or the organ that expresses it, may sometimes be a clue to what is wrong between the patient and those close to him. Where sustaining relationships are damaged or broken, a sickness may be the patient's way of trying to cope when other ways have failed. Is his sickness, for instance, the kind that will excuse him from sexual relations with his wife and secure her mothering instead? Does the care of his colostomy provide an organizing focus for a life that has no other center? Does the attention he gets as a cripple compensate for the neglect he suffered when he was well?

The tighter and better organized a person's control over his conscious life, the more likely it is that his sickness will point to basic relationships that have gone askew. Because his ego strength keeps him from falling apart emotionally, he may have no choice, when his problem is more than he can cope with, but to somaticize, to unconsciously make use of the bacteria under his fingernails, the virus in his lungs, the constriction of his blood, or the looseness of his bowels. The message he blocks out of his consciousness gets expressed in his illness. With a weaker ego, he might become neurotic or psychotic, and the nature of the damaged relationships might be more readily recognized. It is the apparently adequate, competent, coping person that fools you: he/she seems to have everything well in hand. But he/she is just the one to look out for.

Redefinition

There is still another level in the reading of the message of illness. When the patient's awareness of responsibility has moved from guilty self-reproach to an understanding of his disease as an expression of himself, he is ready for the last and most important message his illness can convey—the message of reevaluation, redirection, redefinition, the righting of the wrong. "I see how I must change my way of life."

Many times, of course, the damage has gone too far to be reversible, and the patient faces the prospect of living with his or her ailment, or of dying with it. A disease like cancer, that expresses inner meaninglessness, once it spreads to vital organs may be beyond all curing, no matter how well the patient recovers his selfhood. As in suicide, there may be a point of no return, even though the person undergoes a radical change of heart. And many other illnesses, where bugs or breaks or heredity have been a factor, may leave a person permanently damaged. There are no "mind-over-matter" miracles.

But many troubles can be caught in time, and a redefinition of the self achieved, such as to alter the patient's response and affect the total situation. This deepest reading of the message of illness can bring new understanding, new relationships, new selfhood, and new life. It must be the patient's reading of the message, and not something imposed upon him by his doctor's edict or his pastor's admonition. The changed way of life must be an expression of himself. It must be his doing. The same principle applies here as in the conversion experience, whether it be under evangelical auspices or Alcoholics Anonymous. Life is renewed and redirected effectively, only when a person himself accepts the responsibility.

A person recovers from sickness only when he/she is able to redefine his or her life-style so that he/she no longer needs to be sick. Sickness is a crisis in selfhood. It is cured only as the person is cured and is helped to find himself anew. That is the message.

Suggestions for Further Reading

Arnold Arluke, Louanne Kennedy and Ronald C. Kessler. Re-examining the sick-role concept: an empirical assessment. *Journal of Health and Social Behavior,* 20: 30–36, 1979.

John F. Miller III. The pastorate and the new age of healing. *Pastoral Psychology,* 27 (2), 1978.

Paul W. Pruyser. *The Minister as Diagnostician: Personal Problems in Pastoral Perspective.* Philadelphia: Westminster, 1976.

Jacques Sarano. *The Hidden Face of Pain.* Valley Forge: Judson Press, 1970.

Aarne Siirala. *The Voice of Illness.* Philadelphia: Fortress Press, 1964.

2

Initiative in Pastoral Relationships

Daniel DeArment, Th.M.

Director and Chaplain Supervisor
Department of Pastoral Care and Education
Presbyterian University of Pennsylvania Medical Center
Philadelphia, Pennsylvania

One of the most exciting discoveries I made, during the time that I was beginning to learn to "do theology" in the pastoral field, was that the word "responsibility" could be seen in down-to-earth, person-to-person encounters as meaning "able-to-respond." A responsible person was one who was able-to-respond to the messages of another person or group.

This discovery of the meaning of a word arose partly from a preacher's tendency to see the homiletic opportunity and partly from a more basic feeling about the importance of honest, open, and sensitive human relationships. So I became more sensitive to others' signals and to my own. I learned to *respond* in a variety of nondefensive ways.

But always in my mind was a distinction (sometimes fuzzy) between what I did *in response* to someone else and what I did on my own initiative. Through the last ten years I have been reading most of the journals in the field of pastoral care, and I have yet to see an article or a book on initiative in pastoral care.

Seward Hiltner's work on precounseling as it relates to *Pastoral Counseling*[1] and *Preface to Pastoral Theology*[2] is, broadly speaking, a treatment of this subject from a different angle and using a different word. (Incidentally, I asked him about this, telling him of my plans to present this paper, and he told me though he "did not use the word *initiative* in his book *Pastoral Counseling*," much of it was about that.) Nevertheless, I think the time has come to create an outline around this word, and perhaps to formalize a dimension of pastoral relationships which have been in effect for a long time.

I really mean an "outline" on initiative because, as I began to write my accumulated thoughts in this area, I realized that I was dealing with much more than could be contained in a brief paper— in much the same way that ten or fifteen years ago one might have tried to write about "response" in pastoral relationships.

To put the matter in as broad a fashion as possible, I would propose to begin with a phenomenological study of initiative in pastoral care as a stance, a particular aspect of relating which *in itself* contains *healing power*.

Let's begin with a brief verbatim account of a conversation. The chaplain had been called on the phone by the director of one of the departments in the hospital:

Director: Chaplain, I would like to see you for a few minutes—today, if possible.

Chaplain: Well, John, I could see you now for a "few minutes" but I have a conference in about ten minutes with the rest of the chaplains.

Director: Fine, I'll be right down. (He appears almost immediately, comes in, closes the door, and begins to tell a story about a relative in another city who is in trouble, how he has always "bailed this relative out," and goes on and on.)

Chaplain: John, I'm going to stop you, since it seems that what you want to talk over with me is going to take longer than 5–10 minutes, and I don't want you to feel rushed, or me to leave others waiting. (The Director nods and waits.) Can you come back at 3:30, and then we can take an hour, if need be, to deal with the whole issue—as it does sound complicated?

Director: Great. I guess I am pretty upset. I'll be here.

The chaplain's initiative was clearly seen in his saying (1) "Stop," (2) There is more than I have time for (and you were able to recognize), and (3) Let's set a time to pursue this as soon as we can.

One way to look at this exchange is by asking: Was this a client-centered stance for the chaplain? I would say "Yes!" emphatically. If we ask: Was this a "nondirective" response?—"No!" It was almost totally directive, but not entirely. The client was given some freedom of movement. (Corresponding with Hiltner's belief that in precounseling the client needs to have a chance to say yes or no.) So, we can define pastoral initiative as a word or move which (1) acts on behalf of the client, (2) is not in response to his expressed feelings or ideas, yet (3) allows the client optimum freedom in the given situation.

The word which best defines this particular phase of pastoral initiative is: *structuring.* The chaplain structured time for himself and his client. He did this, not because he failed to hear the panic in the man's voice but because he picked it up (he might have been sharp enough to hear it on the phone but this would have meant doing the same thing earlier). Nor did he structure time because he was avoiding the feelings. Rather, he wanted to give those feelings ample chance to be expressed. And finally, he structured time in terms of who he was, and the commitments he had made to other people.

This "structuring-on-behalf-of-the-chaplain" is critical. The structuring needed to be a clear ego act, set free from any rigid and compulsive need to meet his schedule; he could express initiative toward the client only when he had enough time to hear the man outright. He could then express initiative toward the group of students by saying to them, "Something has come up. You go on without me." In other words, he had to deal with time as an existential limit, realistically assessed (he could not allow the man to continue and himself get to the meeting on time), and yet as a limit within which he would build and break structures for his benefit, and the benefit of his clients, students, co-workers, etc.

"Structuring" is a positive-initiating act, reflecting creative decisions which are in response to real (space-time) limitations. Notice that I have used initiative and response in the same sentence, because they really are closely related. The word "response" asks the minister to consider the internal frame of reference of a person, so that the client is the stimulus, and the minister is the ego-directed, decision-making responder.

Whereas, when the Gestalt or the field is broadened to include all significant persons in the pastor's life, and all demands on his time, then he can best be described as an ego-directed free agent, if he considers himself not as a responder but as an initiator.

Behind Semantics

This entire discussion could be seen as splitting hairs over the issue of two words: initiative and response—except for the crucial issue of how the minister feels about himself in relation to these two words. This leads us into a consideration of fundamental psychological questions.

Let me state several observations which I think are central to this discussion:

1. Human growth, both developmentally and therapeutically, can be described as turning the "passive into the active." The passive infant soon begins to learn how to control his or her environment and moves throughout life along this continuum until in death he/she again becomes completely passive. The client or patient who is dysfunctional is usually aided to realize his or her own potential for decision, change, and growth, rather than to see himself/herself as the passive victim or impotent recipient of life's "slings and arrows."

2. Many would-be helpers are attracted to "educative" (responsive) counseling and thus misuse it as a "nondirective" technique because they are more comfortable with a passive role than they are with the active one seen in an effective, client-centered, initiative-taking style. In other words, many helpers are "turned off" by client-centered work because they misconceive it (often through being clients of dilettantes) as essentially passive.

3. Initiative comes from the life instinct (as in Freud's Dual Instinct Theory), but passivity is from or on the side of death. Since we are all inwardly conflicted between these two instincts, we often confuse initiative (opportunities) for initiative (expressions of aggression) rather than creative acts of love. And, to make it even more confusing, at times we believe we are initiating from the active principle of love, when we are really being hostile.

Erik Erikson, writing on the psychosocial development of man, sees every child passing through a state in which the primary tension of life is initiative vs. guilt.[1] As the child grows in energy and achieves autonomy he begins to undertake, to plan, to attack. Action and achievement become necessary. But being a child, he inevitably undertakes a task he cannot complete, he "bites off more than he can chew," and guilt emerges. Erikson's full treatment of this subject is worth reading, but for our purposes I would like to call attention to one sentence. Speaking of "the inner powerhouse of rage" which is submerged in all of us at this stage, "as some of the fondest hopes and wildest fantasies are repressed and inhibited," he says:

> The resulting self-righteousness—often the principal reward for goodness—can later be most intolerantly turned against others in the form of persistent moralistic surveillance, so that the prohibition rather than the guidance of initiative becomes the dominant endeavor.[2]

I think it is neither twisting Erikson, nor caricaturing the ministry, to paraphrase this to read:

> In a profession which places a premium on being good and being right, self-righteousness (sometimes in the form of humility) is often intolerantly turned against others and against oneself in the form of persistent moralistic surveillance, so that the prohibition rather than the guidance of initiative becomes the dominant endeavor.

In a footnote to his chapter on "The Eight Stages of Man," Erikson adds that there are some essential strengths "which evolution has built into the ground plan of the life stages and into that of man's institutions."[3] The basic virtues, which he sees deriving from a favorable ratio of initiative vs guilt, are direction and purpose. Since Erikson has ventured to use the word "institution," I cannot help but wonder if there is not a pathetic but profound correlation between Protestantism's recent history of "persistent moralistic surveillance" and "prohibition rather than guidance of initiative as dominant endeavor" and our present lack of direction and purpose.

My own experiences looked at through the various techniques of clinical pastoral education would confirm what Erikson is telling us, that initiative in adult life is one aspect of a complicated process of child psychosexual and psychosocial development. Anyone who would take seriously the task of exercising more creative initiative in the ministry must be ready to undertake a personal program of ego strengthening and whatever other measures of training and analysis are necessary and possible.

The meaning of these observations, as they pertain to pastoral theology and to your work and mine, is partly historical. Freudian-Rogerian-dominated styles of pastoral relating came as a necessary corrective to moralism, imperalistic evangelism, and other dehumanizing tendencies in the Church through the last thirty years.

Now the times call for a new corrective (pioneered outside the Church by active therapies, such as Transactional Analysis, Gestalt, Rational Emotive, and Reality techniques) in which the pivotal word will be, I think, initiative, just as it has been response in the recent past.

The inherent distortions of too heavy an emphasis on response patterns were passivity and loss of self in the pastor. The inherent distortions of an exaggerated emphasis on initiative are —to name a few—manipulation, superficiality, and compulsiveness; but such is life and involvement in the dialectic of pastoral theology.

Going one step further, beyond what has happened to pastors in their thirties, forties and older, I think that the emerging generation of clergy needs to hear less about response patterns and sensitivity to others, and more about pastoral initiative in relationships. Perhaps it is because the entire person-centered movement has been so effective, perhaps because of other factors—but as I work with young ministers and theological students today, I find them more naturally able to respond, yet at a considerable loss of feeling comfortable with initiative and the corollary structuring of life about which I have spoken. A gross caricature of this point of view is in the uptight, middle-aged conservative who says of modern youth: "They know how to tear down and attack the establishment (or depersonalize values), but they have nothing to offer in its place."

Theological Underpinnings

In further outline fashion, I would like to point toward some theological-biblical roots of initiative in pastoral work. The most obvious affirmation is that God Almighty, as revealed and known in the Hebraic-Christian faith, is a God of initiative. To be sure, He hears His people, but He seldom, if ever, does what they want. (Neither does the good client-centered counselor.) Rather He is always summoning prophets who initiate comments and dramatic moves, showing the people what they are doing. He sends His Son in the grandest of all moves of Divine Initiative, and Jesus said to His disciples—"You did not choose me. I chose you."

INITIATIVE AND GRACE

Nowhere is the theme of initiative as clear as in our understanding of Grace. The father of the prodigal son ran to greet the son, "while he was yet far off." The father had loved him and reached out to him always. Men and women who are seized by the Grace of God always testify to the fact that God came to them—in many ways, sure—but they have felt that the forgiveness and acceptance they know came first. This has long been a focus in Christian dogmatics, centering around such questions as the Pelagian controversy, and leading to some rather near theological hair-splitting terms, such as "preconvenient grace," the grace which allows us to say "Yes" to God.

INITIATIVE AND CREATIVITY

The original creative act of God—as the Genesis story goes—tells of creation *ex nihilo*. The Creator brought into being some things, some animals and some persons who were not present before. He did not respond to a need; He did not follow any of the rules of cause-effect; He created: down with Newton—up with Michelangelo: Creation and the creative act are always filled with initiative. Fanita English, Philadelphia's "mother figure" in Transactional Analysis circles, has pointed to the innate creative potential in man as residing in his Child ego state. She found here (and hopes we all can find in ourselves) the first quality of creativity to be *curiosity*. Those of us who have experimented with various *structures* in counseling, group work, and patient care know that effective work with people involves a lot of creative work, of creation *ex nihilo*, of initiating.

Again, I see a logical movement from initiative and creation to the subject of initiative and sexuality. For a long time, the male was supposed to be the active, pushing person in his sexuality and the female was to be a passive recipient and hence always more a woman if more passive. Women's Liberation has begun to free us from these stereotypes, and we know now that initiative in love-making (as in all of love) is a thrilling and creative step, one which too long has been relegated to half the human race.

Conclusion

One of the eye-opening discoveries I made while in my first year of pastoral work was that it didn't matter much where or when I went into people's homes. I was always welcome. Oh sure, if I intruded on a dinner party, or caught the woman in the middle of house-cleaning, or the man taking his car apart, I sensed the inconvenience. But that is not what I mean. What I usually found was that with stranger, church member, unchurched, Protestant, Catholic, or Jew, young or old, the announcement "the pastor from the Church is here" was a signal which at least lowered mistrust, and raised curiosity (why are you here?), and frequently produced a warm response, "Come on in; glad to see you." People generally assume that we are not there to take, or to threaten, but to bring some message of hope, faith, or love.

No other professional in the entire range of helping persons in our society has this kind of prerogative with people. We can take the initiative in going to people, and hardly anyone bats an eye. Whereas the doctor, the psychologist, the lawyer wait for the symptoms to produce a chief complaint—then comes a knock on his door. (Some social workers are trained in "aggressive case-work" but most are responders to human need.) Even nurses go to patients to "fulfill the doctor's written orders or because the patient calls her." (The best nurses know the power of initiative in a visit where they say, "Mr. James, I always seem to come to see you with pills or a shot, or to move you. Tonight I thought I would just stop in and say 'hello' and talk a bit.")

Our special entree as clergymen is subject to the charge: "Oh, but I don't have time." Maybe, but I don't think the pressures of time should allow us to become responders only, like all other professionals. Initiating-decisions are of a different order than response-decisions. I would obviously opt for keeping these areas of our work open.

Notes

1. Seward Hiltner. *Pastoral Counseling.* New York: Abingdon, 1949.
2. ———. *Preface to Pastoral Counseling.* New York: Abingdon, 1958.
3. Erik Erikson. *Childhood and Society.* New York: Norton, 1963.
4. Ibid., p. 257.
5. Ibid., p. 274.

Suggestions for Further Reading

Paul R. Clifford. *The Pastoral Calling.* Great Neck, New York: Channel Press, 1961.
Paul Mickey, et al. *Pastoral Assertiveness: A Model for Pastoral Care.* Nashville: Abingdon, 1978.
James B. Nelson. *Rediscovering the Person in Medical Care.* Minneapolis: Augsburg, 1976.

3

Ministering to the Woman Patient

Dorothy Faust, B.D.
(Retired) Former Chaplain
Grant Hospital
Columbus, Ohio

Unfortunately the complexity of human life today tends to belittle the importance of the individual. Without a clearly defined sense of identity, purpose, and dignity, life becomes flat and flavorless and soon disease grows to such proportions that hospitalization becomes a necessity for an increasing number of persons, especially for women.

Today the tempo of life makes communion with God seem less and less important. As a result, there develops a tendency to overlook or completely ignore the spiritual renewal which enables one to gain dominion over one's environment rather than to be submissive to it.

This paper will examine recent quantitative and qualitative changes in life patterns of women from this point of view. Methods will be suggested to help women enjoy being women.

Observation and research point out that the emotional reactions of all women have certain similarities. Even where differences may be of kind as well as degree, all begin with anxiety.[1] Women are not the same as men. They menstruate. They get pregnant. They have babies. They breast-feed. They have a different tie with children than men do, a unique physical relationship. All these factors are related to their anxieties, their emotions, their feelings, and particularly their well-being, health, and happiness. For some

women, illness is normal and good health is abnormal because they
have never experienced harmony, wholeness, or a day without
pain.

Sigmund Freud believed that much of the woman's psychological development was due to her emotional reactions to her own
female body. He emphasized the deep feelings of inadequacy and
envy he believed women felt because of their lack of a penis. He
wrote:

> Her whole development may be said to take place under the influence
> of her envy for the penis. She begins by making vain attempts to do the
> same as boys. Later with greater success, she makes efforts to compen-
> sate for the defect, efforts which may lead in the end to a normal
> attitude.[2]

Margaret Mead pointed out that although middle-class neurotic women frequently feel wounded by lack of male sexual equipment, this need not be true of all women. She said that such
feelings of envy develop against a general background of over-
rewards for the male position.[3]

Karen Horney, in views on women's emotional experiences,
wrote,

> What about Motherhood? And the blissful consciousness of bearing a
> new life within oneself? And the ineffable happiness of increasing
> expectations of the appearance of this new being? And the joy when it
> finally makes its appearance and one holds it for the first time in one's
> arms? And the deeply pleasurable feeling of satisfaction in suckling it,
> and the happiness of the whole period when the infant needs her care?[4]

My own mother had no time for conjuring up disease, cod-
dling it, engaging in sickly after-dinner talk, or running to a clinic
to get a tranquilizer. Her free moments were centered on healthy
recreational activities for the entire family or in enjoying the culti-
vation of roses.

Several years ago I was asked to write an article for *The
Journal of Pastoral Care* on the advantages of the woman chaplain. From that time to the present, I have gathered and filed
information which might be basic and of value to those women
who are interested in pastoral care in helping women in general to
have better health and more satisfying lives.

Grant Hospital in Columbus, Ohio has, at all times, approximately fifty more female patients than male and this does not include the obstetrical unit. I might add also that 50 percent of our patients have no church affiliation. The surgery schedule regularly shows one-third more female than male patients. Women live five to six years longer than men and their survival advantage is increasing.

In our modern society income is an important factor in life. Since success, achievement, and personal worth are generally measured by the financial yardstick, let us look at the American woman's situation in this regard. Only 39 million American women are employed outside the home. The remainder are dependent on other people for every cent they receive and spend and for all the social values that come with money. Such dependence cannot but cause all kind and degrees of anxiety. On the other hand, 55 million American men have joined the work force.[5]

Recently I was called to our emergency room to talk with a beautiful young girl who had taken an overdose of her mother's nerve pills. The girl was sixteen, white, dirty, and poorly dressed. She told me her mother was on welfare and had three younger children at home. The girl had left school because the particular school district in which she lived offered nothing for the slower learner. She did not have enough education to get a job. Next best, as she saw it, was getting a little money from "body services." She had lived with many boys, the longest time being six weeks. The night she came to the hospital she had taken her mother's nerve pills, "because he told me to get out since he had found an older woman who would give him no worries about pregnancy." Then she added, "I tried to move on to find out if there really is a God, and now I've failed even at that."

In one week I was called by the Medical Supervisor of our emergency room to consult five other similar cases. In each I did just three things; (1) listened to the story of the patient; (2) sought cooperation of the patient and her family to be sent to the Suicide Prevention Center and (3) made appointments and gave a brief summary of what I knew about the situation to the social worker at the Suicide Prevention Center. There has been no opportunity to date for any kind of follow-up.

Women's work, whether in the home or outside, is character-istically monotonous, repetitive, and confining. In the January issue of *McCalls,* 1969, one author wrote, "Nobody, neither men nor women, really want to do about 99 percent of what constitutes 'women's work.' Not only is it boring, but it is not valued by society. Physicians give orders; nurses do the unpleasant, repeti-tive, and maintenance jobs."[6]

The great decrease in birth rate is well known. This decreased desire for children automatically gives more importance to wom-en's unique biological role. Breast-feeding and tender loving care of babies are again becoming fashionable. These changes may do much to help women enjoy being women.

Since all disease begins with anxiety which is the mainspring of all psychosomatic disorders and is the motivating force in all nervous and mental illness, management of the anxious patient becomes a major contribution to general health and happiness. Anxieties that become prolonged lead into organic illness and finally into chronic conditions. A very prominent surgeon recently told me that ten years ago he would have said that 50 percent of his operations were brought about by mental stress. Today, however, he would say this might well have mounted to 90 percent. So often I hear patients say, "Well, I finally convinced my doctor I need surgery, and he is calling in a specialist."

In 1935, I finally had a hysterectomy after two years of con-stant testing to eliminate an infection-causing, low-grade tempera-ture. First came a tonsillectomy, bed rest for possible tuberculosis, bed rest for rheumatic heart, and finally in 1935 several specialists decided that an ovarian cyst was probably causing the trouble. I was an oddity. Nuns, nurses, and medical interns came to question and look. The surgeon was a God-centered man with much con-cern for patients. He spent much of the time both before and after the operation explaining that I need not develop male mannerisms or a masculine vocal tone. He assured me that much of this would depend on my attitude and my need for personal attention. I cite this because, looking at any recent surgery schedule in our hospital, I see at least four to eight hysterectomies listed. Only once in the last month did a nurse call me to talk with a patient who was crying, "I am no longer a woman." At the time I had surgery the schedule for operations showed approximately one-half page for tonsillectomies and the other half for goiters. In our hospital during the last month we have scheduled only one goiter operation and one or two tonsillectomies. We do have many cataracts, breast biopsies, radical mastectomies, and hysterectomies. I find today the first query on the lips of the woman suddenly told she must have surgery is, "WHO WILL LOOK AFTER THE CHILDREN?"

"The Times They are a' Changing," sang Bob Dylan, and the indications surely are everywhere around us. Most of our magazine stands today are full of publications about the crumbling of traditional values. Much is written about the anxiety, frustration, and fear of the once happy middle-aged woman of the middle class. Has the turbulence from the young side of the generation gap loosened traditional regard for hearth and home? Have anxiety, alienation, apathy, and an anarchic repudiation of once precious values made apple pie and Mother's Day obsolete?

Any illness is a threat to us in a number of different areas and in a number of different ways. Illness is psychologically a threat of death. But, "We in America live in a death-denying society where age seems the great concern instead of the quality and meaning of life. Perhaps from the revolution in religion today we will learn to build deeper roots."[7]

Sometime ago a minister called and stated that a woman ninety-four years old, a member of his congregation with no living relatives, was coming in for a breast biopsy. His concern seemed to be about her age and possible death. I saw no evidence of either on the part of the patient. The biopsy showed need for a radical mastectomy at once, with a follow-up of nineteen radium treatments. The day before she was to be released she called me and confided that she wanted to be fitted with artificial breasts before either her pastor or the men at the retirement home where she lived saw her. She showed more anxiety in that conversation than in any other during her stay in the hospital. She said, "What have I done to deserve this?" Her need was for biological support, while her minister's concern was regarding her age and possible death.

Women are different from men. Changes have taken place in modes of living which cause greater anxiety and lead to breakdowns in the contemporary woman's body, mind, and spirit. Let us quickly look at a few methods which I hope will be helpful in ministering more effectively to the woman patient. Women like to know that your concern is for them, so take care that you never leave the impression of being in a hurry.

LISTEN

The true pastor is one who has learned in the pastoral setting to give up preaching and grant the patient the privilege of selecting her own subject. Listening takes time but the patient will lead you to her need if you give her your time. She will discover redemption and salvation if you are sufficiently active-passive to permit her the opportunity for exploration and discovery.

OFFER REASSURANCE

To reassure a patient one does not hesitate or apologize but one offers a positive statement. This is possible only after one has listened carefully, demonstrated emotional maturity, shown genuine concern and is spiritually healthy.

Environmental setting can be a potent force in encouraging and discouraging a woman patient to express feelings and reveal anxieties. For example, in the labor room, delivery room, or maternity ward, a woman will sometimes freely discuss feelings that she would not reveal to her closest friends at home.

If the pastor approaches each woman with the feeling, "here is a unique personality with whom I am willing to share my best," then each will have a better chance of becoming healthier, happier, and holier for having experienced the togetherness. An unhurried, calm, spiritually healthy attitude allows the anxious woman patient to become calmer herself and to discover her own spiritual resources, which is surely one of the finest services that can be rendered to her.

Notes

1. Ainslie Meares. *Management of the Anxious Patient*. Philadelphia: Saunders, 1963.

2. Sigmund Freud. *An Outline of Psychoanalysis.* New York: Norton, 1949.
3. Margaret Mead. *Male and Female.* New York: Mentor, 1949.
4. Karen Horney. The flight from womanhood. *International Journal of Psychoanalysis.* 12:360–374, 1926.
5. *World Almanac and Book of Facts, 1980.* New York: Newspaper Enterprises Associates Incorporated, 1979. p. 92.
6. J. Richie. "Church, casts and women. *Christian Century,* January 21, 1970.
7. Dr. Elizabeth Kübler-Ross. Phil Donahue Show, January 21, 1970.

Suggestions for Further Reading

Boston Women's Health Collective. *Our Bodies, Ourselves.* Simon and Schuster, 1976.

Phyllis Chesler. *Women and Madness.* New York: Doubleday, 1972.

Mary Daly. *The Church and the Second Sex.* New York: Harper and Row, 1968.

Nancy Friday. *My Mother Myself.* New York: Delacorte, 1977.

Betty Friedan. *The Feminine Mystique.* New York: Norton, 1963.

Germaine Greer. *The Female Eunuch.* New York: McGraw-Hill, 1971.

Kay I. and Kermit T. Hoyenga. *The Question of Sex Differences.* Boston: Little, Brown, 1979.

Emma J. Justes. Theological reflections on the role of women in church society. *Journal of Pastoral Care.* 32 (1): 42–54, 1978.

M. T. Notman, Changing roles for women at mid-life. In W. H. Norman and T. J. Scaramella, eds. *Mid-Life: Developmental and Clinical Issues.* New York: Brunner/Mazel, 1980 (pp. 85–109).

Joseph C. Rheingold. *The Fear of Being a Woman.* New York: Grune and Stratton, 1964.

Betty and Theodore Roszok. *Masculine/Feminine.* New York: Harper and Row, 1970.

Ann Belford Ulanov. The feminine and the world of CPE. *Journal of Pastoral Care,* 29 (1975:) 11–12.

4

Depressive Reactions and Pastoral Care

Joe Boone Abbott, B.D.
Director
Department of Pastoral Care and Counseling
Baptist Medical Center
Birmingham, Alabama

I read the following words from an interview with J. B. Phillips (noted Biblical translator):

> I found that I could usually struggle on pretty well during the day. But at night it was as if I were the picked target of the enemy. Irrational fears gripped my spirit, unreal guilt swept over me. Even my sense of God disappeared, though it never reached nihilism nor utter despair. Still, when I reached to God for help, He seemed remote and unapproachable.

J. B. Phillips was describing the devastating experience of depression. One of the most common complaints among people who frequent minister's offices, physicians' offices, hospitals and clinics is the pain of depression. It can be a very minor problem, just a "blue day" when one's spirits are low; or it can be a serious critical state of mind that, if left untended, results in death.

Depression affects a sizeable number of patients admitted to the general hospitals. I have interviewed several physicians in the Baptist Medical Center in Birmingham who concur in the estimated figures that "three or four persons per 1000 suffer from affective disorders requiring treatment."[1] There is a growing awareness that depression causes many complaints that relate to physical illness. The depressed person has the whole physical system on emergency standby, with no outlet except the person himself.

"Depressive states are also encountered as affective equivalents—periodic, spontaneously remitting physical illness, such as rheumatism, asthma, peptic ulcer, and dermatitis."[2] With suicide the twelfth most common cause of death in the United States, we ministers who deal with ultimates must be skillful in our dealing with such human states.

One of the patients with whom I have worked almost lost her life when, in the grip of depression, she placed a rifle against her heart and pulled the trigger. She came to me upon referral from her physician and her minister. The body was healed, but the wound was merely the symptom. The true pathology was locked deep inside and she was far from being well or whole.

The patient felt that no one loved her and that she was spiritually alone. God seemed remote at best. People, though close by physically, seemed very distant. She found strange thoughts racing through her mind. She could not do the elementary tasks of housework. Feelings of worthlessness shouted at her, and her conscience screamed at her failure to do her work. She lost interest in her appearance, and at one point she stopped going to all meetings outside the home. She felt acutely guilty for not going to church and would resolve to attend regularly, but she could not face people. She soon found that sleep was no longer an escape and for her, "hell" had come to earth. After months of this inner pain and little or no sleep, she felt that God had abandoned her. It was in this period of utter despair that she pulled the trigger on her rifle.

The hospital chaplain may be of special help to the healing team, because he may represent both authority and forgiveness. His identification, in the minds of many people, with ultimate authority affords the patient a target for hostility. The chaplain's identity as one that represents forgiveness and salvation aids the patient and provides hope of release from guilt as the patient searches for meaning in life.

In order to better understand issues concerning depression, I have divided this paper into four parts: 1) modern psychiatric interpretations of depression; 2) symptomatology and frequency of occurrence; 3) pastoral care of depressed patients and 4) theological dimensions of depression. I must confess that this subject is beyond one paper, but I hope that I may stimulate the reader to pursue the subject further.

Modern Psychiatric Interpretations of Depression

Modern dynamic psychology and psychiatry have added new dimensions to the understanding of depressive reactions. Depressive reactions are divided into physiological and functional. It is difficult to separate these two because the basic etiology remains unknown. Depressions of the greatest frequency are seen in the psychotic form (manic-depressive reaction), neurotic form (reactive depression, affective disorder), and a typical depression, or a secondary factor of other emotional conflicts.

The most difficult of all is the manic-depressive reaction. There seems to be a high correlation between incidence and family history of depressive-prone persons. The most significant factor is the basic personality. Usually depressed individuals have cycloid temperaments. There are three types of these: 1) depressive—the person who is shy, serious, moody, anxious; 2) hypomanic—the person who is euphoric, agitated, excessively optimistic; and 3) cyclothymic—the person whose mood swings between the depressed state and the hypomanic state.

Obsessive-compulsive behavior is usually classified as a neurotic reaction. Patients are generally obsessional persons before the onset of a depressive reaction. They are avid perfectionists with a compulsive need for approval. They cannot say "no" to a request which plays to their dependency needs, because they cannot tolerate hostility. Obsessional people lack self-confidence and are hypercritical of themselves. They display passive-aggressive patterns, and the real feelings are directed in toward the self. Emotion, rather than a balance with rational reality testing, dominates these people. The antidepressant compounds have benefited the manic-depressives but have limited therapeutic value for persons who are reactive depressives or obsessionals.

The behavior-modification theorists view depressive reactions as an inappropriate learned behavioral pattern in dealing with hostility and guilt. The reality-oriented therapists see depressive reactions as the direct consequence of guilt. Analytically oriented therapists view this as symptomatic of deeper personality disturbances residing in the unconscious. Almost all of these would make the distinction between the unreal guilt (neurotic) and real guilt. The reality therapists see these as clues to the "real" guilt. Analytical therapists see the conflict residing in the frozen past of the person. Infantile conflicts long repressed create pressure on the ego, with superego rejection causing depression.

Symptomatology and Frequency of Occurrence

The most common level of dysfunction, the neurotic form, is frequently seen in the general hospital. The reactive-depressive persons are anxiety dominated. They are egocentric, intolerant, aggressive, and exhibitionistic. They tend to capitalize on their symptoms and direct blame towards others. Karl Menninger, in *The Vital Balance,* describes these as the second level of dysfunction. He states that the neurotic patterns are characterized by: "1) Blocking the aggressive and other dangerous impulses out of consciousness by extreme repression and disassociation; 2) Diverting aggressive energies from target to the self as a whole or parts of the body; 3) Altering aggressive discharge, not so much in aim as in quality; symbolic and magical maneuvers of various kinds carry the aggressive force and at great expense to the ego."[3]

Symptomatically, neurotic-depressive reaction is expressed by lowered spirits, loss of self-esteem, loss of appetite and sleep, and feelings of self-depreciation. Guilt takes a very prominent place in the mood disturbance, fatigue, restriction of interests, and concentration. Generally the patient looks dejected, tired, apathetic. The voice is usually flat and lacks color. Though the neurotically depressed patient has only limited impairment of reality testing and interpersonal relations, he will present himself as empty, lonely, inferior, inadequate, and deprived of emotional support. These feelings are extremely painful to the person.

Suicidal threats must be taken seriously no matter how lightly they appear to be given. Suicide among hospitalized patients has been the subject of articles in recent hospital journals. Suicide hints are given in subtle forms, such as, "I can't go on; it seems no use to try to get well, I just guess I'll throw in the towel."

> Depressions occur most often after age thirty, have peak incidence between forty and sixty, and taper off shortly thereafter. In practice, most manic-depressives are between thirty and fifty years old when first seen for an affective reaction. Average age of all in one study was 40.3. For men, the average age was 41.6, and for women the average age was 38.2 years.[4]

The reactive depressive can be seen at any age and sex. Grief is a common cause of depression which is reactive, and only becomes pathological when the symptoms persist after about one year. The duration will depend on the situation and, more importantly, on the basic personality of the individual.

Depressions after adolescence and prior to age thirty average six to twelve months; between thirty and fifty years, average nine to eighteen months. The cyclothymic person is usually depressed twice to three times as long as he is elated. One interesting study reveals that depressive cycloids who exhibit religious delusions, with strong feelings of unworthiness and inferiority, often are melancholic for long periods of time and have slow recovery.

The symptoms of the depressed are obvious to persons other than close family members only after the depressive reaction is well on its way. It may begin with chronic fatigue coupled with restless sleep and loss of appetite. The effort needed to get started in the morning and the difficulty in controlling morbid thoughts adds to the growing distress. The person may then begin to awaken at 2 to 3 AM with disturbing dreams. Physical symptoms such as crying, weight loss, sleep disturbance, fatigue, constipation, irritability, and psychomotor slowdown are frequent with growing depression. Sexual interest decreases. As the depression grows, thoughts of a compulsive nature may present themselves, with crying spells, suicidal ideas, and wishes to be free of the "black feeling." The person, then, is almost unable to function without great difficulty and effort. The isolation from others only adds to the acute pain, and a sudden lag in normal interests may be an attempt to cope with depression.

Pastoral Care of Depressed Patient

Pastoral care of the depressed patient must be entered into with complete cooperation and close communication with the healing team. The chaplain may be mainly a supportive person in the total care of the patient. This is an essential service in the care. "Since a depressive reaction is essentially an affective state characterized by a loss of self-esteem, the therapeutic task is to examine the circumstances of this loss and the factors that predisposed the patient to it."[5] The chaplain may be the key support through which his role and through his use of religious resources which have been meaningful to the patient in the past. It is important to keep the healing team informed of what he is doing and why, because the role need may change abruptly. This can happen when guilt becomes a key factor. The harsh superego, the damning Parent, or the conscience may be cathected toward the chaplain. The patient may feel acute guilt. Guilt has to do with punishment and he may use suicidal acts as fulfillment of the guilt feelings. The hostility directed inward may be outer-directed to the chaplain as God's representative. A nonjudgmental but firm relationship will give the patient a proper object for his hostility.

The key at this level of involvement is the relationship with the patient. If the chaplain can establish a relationship of trust, he may become the target of hostility. Occasionally the authority role of the chaplain aids in precipitating the outward projection of the anger of the patient. One basic job as therapist is to become involved with the patient and then get him to face reality. When confronted by the therapist with reality, the patient is forced again and again to decide whether or not he wishes to take the responsible path.[6] The shift of the patient's feeling is critical for recovery. The chaplain may be the key person to aid the patient at this point because he is not one upon whom the patient is physically dependent. "The most important task of the pastoral counselor is to help the counselee shift his concern from guilt feelings to what he is genuinely guilty of and help the person explore and find ways of making value decisions about his life and acting on these."[7] The exploration of new behavior patterns may be better done by someone who stands adjacent to but outside of the "routine" people in direct patient care; hence the chaplain.

The goals of pastoral care of the depressed person are to aid him or her uncovering the issues that prevent him or her from securing the type of object relationships necessary for self-esteem, to modify the harsh attacks of the Parent (extropsyche) and the unrealistic guilt feelings, and to find a more appropriate self-image and ego ideal.

Theological Dimensions of Depression

It is the whole clinical picture that gives rise to some theological concerns. These people are in distress and they need help, not only with the physical problems, but with the meaning of life. Life has either dealt them a blow that they cannot cope with or has given them a temperament prone to pessimism, either of which states can make existence a frightful experience.

Paul Tillich coupled depression with the word *despair*. He stated that the word means without hope and expresses the feeling of a situation from which there is no exit. Soren Kierkegaard, in *Sickness Unto Death,* described the sickness of despair as the point where death means beyond possible healing. In the second volume of his *Systematic Theology,* Tillich further stated,

> Despair is the state of inescapable conflict. It is the conflict, on the one hand, between what one potentially is and, therefore, ought to be, and on the other hand, what one actually is in the combination of freedom and destiny. The pain of despair is the agony of being responsible for the loss of meaning of one's existence and of being able to recover it. One is shut up in one's self and in conflict with one's self.[8]

Depression reveals the struggle of the person with his self-identity. It seems that Jesus experienced a difficult bout with depression in the wilderness temptations. He had no food and little

sleep. He was tempted to leap off the temple, if only in a hallucina-
tion, and the struggle of His soul was the search for His own
identity at that moment in his life.

People cannot escape the fact of feeling responsible. This
makes the identity question more crucial. "What am I?" is immediately paralleled by "Why am I?" in the existential reality of being.
In depression, the person feels estranged but still responsible. It is
in the quest for meaning that people ask such questions; in the
crisis of depression man is forced to ask for the meaning of life.
Here, Tillich defines neurosis as "the way of avoiding nonbeing
by avoiding being."[9]

A person's limit as a finite being is a theological issue raised in
the depressed person. The boundaries of existence are birth and
death; over these people have little control. It is a leap of faith to
live, whereas, despair may be a leap to death. The death is not
merely biological: it is personal.

> He (the despondent) surrenders himself in order to save his spiritual
> life. He escapes from his freedom (Fromm) in order to escape the
> anxiety of meaninglessness. Now, he is no longer lonely, not in existen-
> tial doubt, not in despair. Meaning is saved, but the self is sacrificed.[10]

The question of freedom arises here. To what extent is man
"free" to choose his own way and at what point does God hold us
responsible? This also involves our concept of sin and the nature of
divine forgiveness. To wit: if you are faced with preaching at the
funeral of a suicide victim, what can you say, particularly about the
specific situation, that does not minimize or oversimplify the theological issues? Now the deceased, by his act, asks all present the
existential question, "what does it mean for *you* to live?"

The quest for identity, the existence of death, the value of being
or meaning, are all vital theological questions that become more
than academic in the depressed person. In feeling estranged, the
despondent touches his boundaries, which forces him to commitment, live or die. Regardless of the method of inducement, I
contend that in depression the person must raise those questions of
"ultimate concern" (Tillich's phrase) which are never fully answered but only approximated in being found by God in the

experience of forgiveness. Here, forgiveness reaches a deeper level of meaning. Forgiveness is to the religious dimension what the application of medicine is to the physical dimension.

Let us return to the patient mentioned earlier who attempted suicide with the rifle. Clinically, her anger was all turned inward. She was reacting to strong inner incriminations that convinced her that she was weak, ineffective, hopeless, and unloveable. She could admit emotionally her hatred toward her mother, upon whom she was most dependent. Her mother used guises, manipulation, and control over the patient as symbols of love. This set up in the patient a mistrust of the symbols of love and acceptance. She was so depleted of self-esteem that she could not distinguish emotionally between the early counterfeits which were given for genuine love and the later genuine love in which she dared not believe. In her desperate need for approval, which she could not feel toward herself, she allowed herself to be manipulated, and this produced hostility. Between the crushing weight of her anxiety (fear of abandonment) and the growing hostility, she found herself trapped and weighted down. In the panic of feeling trapped, she sought to punish her *self* (to reject herself) by total annihilation.

In the clinical situation, theologically she needed a relationship where she was free to explore her feelings. She needed a new corrective experience where she could experience the reality of freedom, love and forgiveness (not words, relationship).

Also, in the acceptance of herself (forgiveness), she grew to accept God's forgiveness (acceptance). She gained independence and the courage to be herself. She described her whole experience as a spiritual rebirth. At the root of the depression was the need for rebirth, not a theological concept, but a shared experience. For her, it was a new beginning: "Old things had passed away, and all things became new."

In conclusion, let me say that I have sought to explore the task of clinical theology with you by grappling with but one human situation, depression. I end this paper with the hope that you may feel that theological issues arise out of life more crucially than at first appears. I must now cope with my own existential situation, for my perfectionistic needs demand that I exhaust the subject, or I may leave you a bit depressed.

Notes

1. Maga Gross, Slate and Roth. Depression. *Clinical Psychiatry Journal* (1960).
2. *Current Issues in Psychiatry.* New York: Jason Aronson, 2 (1967): 39.
3. Karl Menninger. *The Vital Balance.* New York: Viking Press, 1963.
4. Frank Ayd, Jr. *Recognizing the Depressed Patient.* New York: Grune and Stratton, 1961.
5. Silvana Arieti, ed. *American Handbook of Psychiatry.* New York: Basic Books. 3 (1966).
6. William Glasser. *Reality Therapy.* New York: Harper and Row, 1965.
7. Edward Stein. *Guilt: Theory and Therapy.* Philadelphia: Westminster Press, 1967. p. 189.
8. Paul Tillich. *Systematic Theology,* vol. 2. Chicago: University of Chicago Press, 1951.
9. Paul Tillich. *The Courage to Be.* New Haven: Yale University Press, 1954.
10. *Ibid.* p. 49.

Suggestions for Further Reading

Silvano Arieti and Jules Bemporad. *Severe and Mild Depression.* New York: Basic Books, 1978.

Eric Berne. *Transactional Analysis in Psychotherapy.* New York: Grove, 1961.

George W. Brown and Tirril Harris. *Social Origins of Depression: A Study of Psychiatric Disorder in Women.* London: Tavistock, 1978.

Henry A. Davidson. Suicide in the hospital. *Hospitals, Journal of American Hospital Association* (November 16, 1969), p. 55.

Richard Dayringer. Holiday depression. *Pastoral Counselor's Bulletin,* 1 (2): 1–3, November, 1978.

Paul A. Hauck. *Overcoming Depression.* Philadelphia: Westminster Press, 1973.

Edith Jackson. *Depression: Comparative Studies of Normal, Neurotic and Psychiatric Conditions.* New York: International Universities Press, 1971.

Calistra Leonard. *Understanding and Preventing Suicide.* Springfield, Illinois: Charles C Thomas, 1967.

Henry Laughlin. *The Neuroses.* Washington: Butterworths, 1967.

Gene Usdin, ed. *Depression: Clinical, Biological and Psychological Perspectives.* New York: Brunner/Mazel, 1977.

5

A Dynamic Concept of Praying for the Sick

James T. Hall, B.D.
Pastoral Counselor
Pastoral Counseling and Consultation Centers
of Greater Washington
District of Columbia

My experience in the clinical training of seminary students and clergymen from various denominations has convinced me that most ministers have serious difficulty in thinking their way through to a meaningful concept of pastoral prayer for persons in crisis. "When do I pray?" a minister asks. "Do I pray for every member in the room, or just for the individual I am visiting? How should I pray?" Let us consider the two basic questions: (1) When should I pray? and (2) How should I pray?

When to Pray

Most seminary students feel uneasiness when deciding whether or not to initiate prayer. Many experienced clergypersons feel somewhat uncomfortable when they begin to examine their rationale for the philosophy of prayer which they have adopted. At least two traditional concepts are widely used to alleviate the anxiety of deciding when to pray. The first of them is to adopt the practice of praying during every visit. Many pastors adopt this practice and feel it is wise. Often church congregations become accustomed to a pastor's routine prayers and grow to expect a prayer with every visit. Individuals will remark with hostility to their friends if the pastor fails to pray: "Do you know that Rev. Jones visited me in the hospital (or home) and he didn't even pray with me?" Clergymen adopt the practice of praying during every visit in order to solve this dilemma. However, another motive for adopting the pray-every-visit concept is an unconscious need on the part of the pastor to maintain himself in his role. This is especially true if he has assumed the old "cheer 'em up" concept of pastoral visitation, which holds that the spiritual part of the visit comes at the end, when the pastor prays. In order to persuade himself (and perhaps his parishioners) that he is spiritual, he needs to pray at each visit.

One of the difficulties of the pray-every-visit concept of prayer is the motive. Whose need is being met? Does the pastor pray because he needs to, or because the sick one needs it? Another difficulty is that prayer with every visit inevitably becomes ritualized, generalized, and superficial. It may even become pious, self-righteous, and authoritarian. It may encourage a magical view of prayer. When praying becomes ritualized, generalized, and superficial, we must ask ourselves once again the question, whose needs are being met?

The second traditional concept of praying with persons in crisis is to pray only when asked. One seminary student adopted this philosophy as a result of his pastor's visit to him while he was hospitalized. He was in pain and felt bitter toward God and the world. Nevertheless, his well-meaning pastor forced a prayer upon him, making it embarrassing to refuse the prayer and appear "unreligious." This experience made him so angry that he resolved never to pray with his own church members unless they asked for prayer. When we examine the motive for adopting the pray-only-when-asked concept we often discover resistance feelings toward praying with others. Furthermore, many persons are open to prayer who do not ask for it verbally.

In both of these traditional concepts of when to pray with persons in crisis, we see that the criterion for decision is pastor-centered. The pastor's decision is self-protective and centered in the pastor's needs, at least to some extent. Furthermore, the concept is rigid and inflexible. There is no freedom to adopt a difficult philosophy of praying in a given situation.

A dynamic answer to the question of when to pray lies in the needs of the person who is in crisis. The pastor will then pray or not pray according to the need the person has for prayer. He must therefore, reject both of the traditional concepts stated above as being too restrictive. He must listen to the person in crisis for indications that a ministry of prayer will be appreciated. He will follow these by asking the person, "Would you like for me to have a prayer with you?" An effort is made to sense the person's need and to respond to it. If necessary, an effort is made not to pray if the motive of the pastor is to pray in order to "meet his own need." If the pastor is in doubt whether or not the person wishes prayer, he can make it easy for the person to refuse by saying, "Would you like for me to have prayer with you today, or would you rather I wait until some other time?" A "push" method of asking if the person wishes prayer such as "may I have prayer with you today?" or, "would you mind if I had a prayer with you today?" is not permissible. This approach makes it difficult for the person to refuse prayer.

What are the indications that persons wish prayer? The most common lead is religious conversation. Often religious literature such as the Bible or devotional booklets near the patient indicate an openness for prayer. A rosary on the bed or a cross on a chain around an individual's neck may serve as a lead for prayer. The sharing of the anxiety of facing an operation or other serious concerns may indicate a desire for prayer. Information from family or hospital staff may reveal a need for prayer. Finally, that nebulous thing we speak of as the "spirit" of the person may serve as a lead for prayer. The "fruit of the spirit is love, joy, peace, patience, kindness, goodness, faithfulness, gentleness, and self-control" (Galatians 5:22). The experienced clergyperson may have learned to trust his intuition for openness to the prayer ministry. There are also rare occasions when emotional and spiritual oneness is so complete that the needs of both pastor and person call for prayer. This experience I call "the holy moment" for lack of a better phrase.

How to Pray

Our first guideline on how to pray is to be brief. How brief is determined by the objectives stated below. The hospital room is rarely a good place for long oratorical praying.

Second, the person's name should be mentioned in your prayer. It is important for clergymen working as chaplains in general hospitals to get the individual's name clear at the introductory portion of the visit in order that he can use that name in prayer if prayer is indicated.

Third, summarize the interview with the patient in the prayer offered to God. A good analogy is the summarizing which the pastoral counselor does at the conclusion of a counseling session. The prayer, however, should not include a great deal of interpretation on the part of the pastor. The emphasis should rather be on the individual's condition as he has shared it. The estrangement which the person has experienced during his hospitalization can often be alleviated by the courage of a pastor who will bring the "gut" concerns of persons and the understanding love of God together in prayer. Perhaps the phrase "incarnation praying" describes the effort of the pastor to identify with the anxiety and estrangement of the individual and to use prayer to help him discover the "acceptance-love" of God for his most earthy concerns.

Fourth, interrelated with the necessity of summarizing in prayer what the person has shared is the need to be *specific in prayer.* The vast majority of persons who come to our hospitals are victims of a kind of religious dualism in which God is associated with the ideal, the "ought"; and the emotions of anger, sex, anxiety, and so forth are evil and unacceptable to God. Individuals are not able to pray for themselves in terms of these concepts. Their prayers become defensive intellectualizing. In fact, it is very difficult for some pastors in clinical pastoral education to learn to pray specifically for hospitalized persons, lifting their real concerns to God. It is so much easier to "pray" generally using well-worn religious phrases. The hypothesis being developed here is that most persons are incapable of overcoming their estrangement from their own strength. They are dependent upon someone functioning as their pastor first to listen creatively to their anxieties and then to bring a sense of the compassion of God to them as they are in crisis, through prayer.

To be specific, in summarizing what the person has been saying in the interview means that the individual's "hot spot" must be mentioned in the prayer. The "hot spot" is that material which the person spoke of which contained the greatest emotion. Very often pastors in training will mention several things in prayer which the person has been discussing, but omit the subject material which was most important to him (contained the greatest feeling). It may be easy for us to pray for the person's relatives, his ten years of service in the church, his children, but difficult to mention to God the pain he experiences when he has a bowel movement following his hemorrhoidectomy. Somehow it seems very difficult for us to really believe that God is relevant to the most earthy of human concerns. It is no wonder that God is dead to us because we keep him for the superficial matter of our existence and are unable to pray to Him about our deepest feeling concerns. If God is to become alive to modern man, it must be in part because we will have learned to bring God and our "gut concerns" together in a dialogue of prayer.

In the case above, a pastor might have prayed, "Oh God we thank thee that Thou dost understand the pain which Mr. Jones experiences when he has a bowel movement since his hemorrhoid operation several days ago." This, at minimum, is what the phrase "incarnation praying" involves. God through Jesus Christ enters human life not only at the sophisticated teas in our church parlors, but he enters our lives (perhaps more profoundly) in our crises if we have individuals who can serve as pastors to us.

The following is an illustration of a visit followed by a dynamic prayer:

Chaplain: Good morning, Mr. Smith. It is good to see you sitting up this morning.

Mr. Smith: Good morning, Chaplain. Oh, I feel much better this morning.

Chaplain: Are you catching up on your reading?

Mr. Smith: Yes, a little. I just get so tired looking at these four walls and ceiling. I can tell you every spot in this room that needs painting.

Chaplain: You have had a long stay, haven't you?

Mr. Smith: I sure have, and it has been rough.

Chaplain: You have had it pretty rough.

Mr. Smith: They tell me I have come a long way. I sure hope so. By the way, Rev. W. was in to see me last night. I have had several preachers visit me since I have been in here, and I sure appreciated it. But you have been my standby. You have been awfully faithful and your prayers have meant a great deal to me. I have never called on God as much as I have since I have been here. I have lain here and prayed, "God, help me." But (pause) I don't know. I have just thought several times that God would hear better if I prayed through you.

Chaplain: You have thought that God wouldn't hear you?

Mr. Smith: (Pause) Well, yes. I have thought that, but I know I shouldn't say that. But that is just the way I have felt.

Chaplain: Mr. Smith, God understands our feelings and I think he expects us to be honest about them.

Mr. Smith: We can't hide them from Him like hiding something in a closet. There have been times when it seemed like I had just run into a brick wall. I just wanted some help. Everybody has been praying for me—my wife, you, two or three more preachers, my sister, and my two children. I really appreciate it, too. You can just bet I have. I hope God understands how I feel. I have just felt desperate. I want to just grab onto anything I can get my hands on and hold to it.

Chaplain: I imagine you have felt pretty desperate.

Mr. Smith: You bet I have. I just want to get out of here. (Patient began to cry.) There I go, crying like a baby. I'm sorry, Chaplain.

Chaplain: That's all right, Mr. Smith. Sometimes it helps to cry.

Mr. Smith: Sometimes I seem to upset myself too much. At times my emotions seem to be out of proportion, if you know what I mean. I get too upset for no reason and I am afraid it isn't good for me medically speaking. But it isn't easy not to get upset. (Pause). I just want to get out of here as soon as I can. I have some things to do. (Crying).

Chaplain: What do you mean?

Mr. Smith: I have some things to take care of. (Pause). I've got to get my church membership straightened out. Chaplain, I used to be active in the church. I was head usher, trustee, financial secretary, and almost anything else you can think of. I did all the heating and plumbing work for the church, and I was once a lay leader. But I drifted away. I was a member of the . . . church before they sold it to the blacks. After that, I stopped going to church. We went occasionally to the church near our house. (He gave the name of the church and described its location.) We just drifted away and I have been thinking, "Here I am asking God to do all of this for me when I haven't done anything for him." I want to change all of that. So I want to get out and get started. My wife and I are going to join the church near our house and I am going to do all I can for it.

Chaplain: You feel that you haven't done as much as you should?

Mr. Smith: That's right. Right now I don't have any church membership. I guess my name is still on the roll at . . . church but for all practical purposes I'm not a member anywhere. I have done a lot of thinking since I have been here. I always thought I was a pretty good fellow. I always treated everybody right and led a decent life. But since I have been staring at the ceiling, I have questioned all of that. I have just thought that maybe I haven't been as good as I thought I was.

Chaplain: You have thought that your illness is due to your not being good enough?

Mr. Smith: Yes, Chaplain. That is what I have thought. I don't know what else to think right now. I had never been sick before until this happened. I just don't know any other answers. I have tried and tried to understand it, but I just can't.

Chaplain: There are some things that seem to be beyond our understanding.

Mr. Smith: You said it. I suppose we just have to make the most out of what happens, but it doesn't keep you from questioning.

Chaplain: It certainly doesn't.

Mr. Smith: But the questioning can get pretty uncomfortable when you begin to look at your own life. I try to have faith, but it isn't always that easy.

Chaplain: Faith isn't something we get by merely wishing for it.

Mr. Smith: How right you are. But I'm not giving up. I am going to keep on trying and praying. You'll never know how much it has meant that you come by and talk with me. (Crying) Everybody has been so good to me. (Here the patient began talking about the nurses. I felt that he had talked on the deeper level as much as he wanted to today.)

Chaplain: Mr. Smith, I will be going now. Would you like for us to have a prayer now?

Mr. Smith: (Grasping my hand) You bet I would.

Chaplain: Gracious God, Thou are our refuge and strength, a very present help in time of trouble. We thank Thee that Thou dost love us as we are. We thank Thee for Mr. Smith and for the progress he is making. We know that Thou dost understand him in his moments of doubt and desperation. (Here the patient squeezed my hand tightly.) Thou dost understand us in our suffering, and we are thankful that suffering can be redemptive. We ask Thy blessings upon Mr. Smith and his plans to become active in the Church. Continue to bless his wife, who has been so faithful to him during this illness, his son and daughter and his sister. In Christ's name we pray. Amen. (Patient gripped my hand tightly.)

Mr. Smith: Thank you so much, Chaplain (crying). Come in again soon.

Chaplain: Thank you, Mr. Smith. Have a good day.

In this verbatim interview, the chaplain summarized in a specific manner the needs which the person has been revealing. He referred to the person by name. He prayed for the person's doubts, his desperation, his church attendance decision, his wife, son, daughter, sister, and progress in his illness. That this prayer communicated meaningfully to the person is indicated by the material in the parenthesis. The tears at the conclusion of the interview indicate a need of the person to share more deeply. Nevertheless, the purpose of dynamic praying is not to probe into the person's problems in order to force premature exposure. It is to summarize in an accepting and supportive manner the needs which he has felt free to share. In this way at-one-ment between man and God is attempted.

Fifth, pray with reassurance and hope for healing. This is an immensely complicated matter which involves our understanding of God's will. A dynamic concept of prayer emphasizes the ministry to individuals rather than groups. The focus of the praying is to the person in crisis, mentioning to God what he/she has shared with his pastor. His/her family and friends, doctors and nurses may be included. However, this concept of prayer makes one reluctant to pray for other patients in the hospital room whom the pastor does not know (even if the person asks the pastor to pray for a roommate). The pastor is more concerned to visit each patient in the room, discern his/her needs, and pray specifically, than to pray a general prayer for all the persons in a room or ward and risk the antagonism of those individuals who do not want to be prayed for and have not asked for it.

Suggestions for Further Reading

William A. Barry. Prayer in pastoral care: A contribution from the tradition of spiritual direction. *Journal of Pastoral Care*, 31 (2): 91–96, 1977.

George A. Buttrick. *Prayer.* (reprint of 1942 edition) Nashville: Abingdon, 1977.

Jacques Ellul. *Prayer and Modern Man.* New York: Seabury Press, 1970.

Heije Faber and Ebel van der School Faber. *The Art of Pastoral Conversation.* Nashville: Abingdon Press, 1965.

Harry Emerson Fosdick. *The Meaning of Prayer* (reprint of 1946 edition) Felcroft, PA: Felcroft, 1976.

Edgar N. Jackson. *Understanding Prayer.* Cleveland: World Publishing Company, 1968.

Matthias: Confessional Prayers of a Pastoral Counselor. Lima, Ohio: CSS, 1976.

Walter Riess. *Prayers for a Time of Crisis.* St. Louis: Concordia Publishing House, 1966.

6

Justification by Faith as a Concept in Pastoral Care

Murray S. Thompson, Th.M.

Chaplain
Pastoral Institute of British Columbia
Burnaby, British Columbia, Canada

As a student in Clinical Pastoral Education I had the good fortune to be in a clinical setting which made possible a long-term relationship with one patient, extending over an eight-month period. It was also my good fortune to be enrolled in a program in which the student was required to draw upon his theological understanding and his clinical experience in the development of the thesis requirements of his graduate program. I kept verbatim accounts of all my sessions with this patient. The combination of these circumstances was of profound significance to me personally, and will be the basis of what I now share.

The patient was a thirty-eight-year-old white female, divorced and childless, diagnosed as a chronic schizophrenic and hospitalized for most of the previous five years, much of this time in a nationally known institution. On this admission, she was self-referred, but on the previous one she had been admitted in an extremely emaciated condition, "because God was telling me not to eat."

On the ward, Mrs. J. was known to the other patients as isolated and withdrawn. "She might speak to you, but she won't speak to us." These were the words of a patient who first pointed her out to me. Enquiry established that she was receiving large doses of medication. Her doctor was a resident soon to move on to the neurological service. It was his intention to continue his care of this patient in psychotherapy, but the daily supervision was in the hands of the ward physician.

Much to my amazement, Mrs. J. was very ready to speak with me. Since I was a Canadian a long way from home, she plied me with questions about myself, especially about the beliefs and practices of my denomination. She professed allegiance to the five fundamentals and said that it was important to her to be convinced that her beliefs were right. I must have been able, even at that stage, to mobilize enough acceptance of her to maintain fellowship in spite of theological differences. She was soon speaking frequently to me in these terms: "I think I need a minister more than a doctor. I think I'm through with doctors. You are helping me more." Not all of these conversations were reported to the ward physician! It was obvious to him, however, that some change was taking place as, in confessional vein, she "peeled the layers off the onion." For all intents and purposes I had become her therapist. She showed physical and other signs of responding to the medication where she had not done so before. When I asked one day why she thought I was helping her more than the doctors, she replied, "Well, doctors don't believe in sin, and you do."

After a Christmas leave from the hospital, she returned and began pressing for discharge. She also had a heavy cold. The doctor insisted that she was not ready for discharge, and all her plans, or lack of them, which she shared with me, showed how unrealistic her own judgment was at that time. She continued to meet willingly with me, insisted that I was helping her, but I couldn't feel much of significance was happening. In fact, the external evidence, eating, sleeping, and socializing for instance, clearly indicated deterioration. The ward physician's comments suggested that this was not a known pattern characteristic of the illness, and not understood.

Then came a memorable day, though its significance was not realized at this time. Because of its critical issues, I report it to you as I put it down in verbatim form at this time:

Patient: (with a bit of a grin) I wish people wouldn't always expect me to be different than I am.

Chaplain: This is what you experience?

Patient: Yes, they want me to talk more, to be more outgoing, to be like Mrs. K. (a vocal and aggressive patient).

Chaplain: You feel they don't accept you as you are?

Patient: That's right. I don't see why I should have to be like Mrs. K. I just want to be myself.

Chaplain: You say you don't see why you should be like her?

Patient: No. I don't see why I should.

Chaplain: Frankly, I don't either. Tell me, do you feel that I have been pushing you to be different than you are, to be more talkative and outgoing?

Patient: (Timidly) Yes.

Chaplain: I guess you are right. I have been wanting you to reach out, and I guess this means that I have been unwilling to accept you just as you are. That is not the way I want you to feel about me.

Patient: I think that you haven't really rejected me. What you have wanted is what you think is in my best interests.[1]

Not long thereafter it was evident that another change was taking place. Again she was on the mend. A combination of circumstances pointed to her possible discharge at the same time my program was completed. She had no need to return to the hospital for some fifteen months, and then only for a few days while a social worker unraveled some domestic tangle.

As in so many instances of psychotherapy and counseling, there are a number of variables which make it difficult, if not impossible, to prove the therapeutic effectiveness of the chaplain's intervention or to demonstrate that the history of the illness was in any way affected by him. However, in the absence of any other explanation it seemed justifiable to look closely at that relationship.

The intriguing question for me surrounded the "why" and "wherefore" of the long weeks of gradual change for the better, followed by long weeks of decline and then the further about-face leading to discharge.

It was after a course on St. Paul's letter to the Romans with particular attention to the meaning of righteousness that a possible parallel emerged, which offered a theological interpretation of the clinical experience and, possibly, pointed to a dimension of spiritual therapy not characteristic of other forms of psychotherapy.

The concept of righteousness, basic in Paul's letter to the Romans, is commonly articulated by Christians as the doctrine of justification by faith. However, it is the theme of much of the Old Testament as well. It has to do with the establishment of right relations between persons, specifically of right relations between man and God. In this aspect, the Biblical view is that righteousness is not achieved through man's efforts, but comes through the nature and activity of God. I refer to N. H. Snaith's discussion of this concept in Alan Richardson's *A Theological Wordbook of the Bible*.[2] The popular view that Judaism was based on a works righteousness, he maintains, obscures the fact that the Old Testament, as firmly as the New, affirms man's dependence upon God for a right relationship with Him. Rabbinic interpretations and popular beliefs distorted the Biblical message in much the same way as many contemporary Christian practices seem to contradict the gospel of salvation through grace by faith.

Yet, that is what the Reformation centered upon—justification by faith—a right relationship with God was possible because of who He is and what He has done in Jesus Christ. Nothing, not even the response of faith on man's part, deserves or earns or establishes a claim upon God. Even faith is God's gift. Man knows himself to be forgiven and receives a new life with promise—all this through Jesus Christ.

The parallels between the clinical and the theological data are striking. There is the common view of man as accountable, subject to God's judgment. This is the meaning, I think, of Mrs. J.'s statement that the significant difference between the doctor and the minister, in her experience, was this, "Doctors don't believe in sin and you do." She was saying, "I know myself to be a responsible person who has acted irresponsibly. I am under God's judgment. I deserve to be condemned."

There is the common experience, despite the judgment, of forgiveness, of being accepted in the very moment of conviction. During the early phase of the clinical relationship, at least, there was no external demand that she be different, and that was characteristic of the later period as well.

There is, dare I say it, a common methodology. Neither the judgment nor the acceptance came in the form of an external pronoucement, but through a sharing in the experience of being human, and this, not from any position of strength, but by a mutuality which included the full impact of sin and its consequences.

There is the common evidence of new life stirring, the same evidence of satisfaction, if you will, and the same promise of ultimate triumph through the power of God.

Some of you may have anticipated the direction from which I now wish to challenge your thinking. There are trends in counseling and psychotherapy which are quite contrary to earlier traditions in the field. Almost a decade ago, Hobart Mowrer called for treatment of people with guilty feelings as persons who, in a very real sense, are guilty.[3] His edited volume entitled *Morality and Mental Health*[4] shows how widespread is the search for new modes of treatment and new theories to support them. Thomas Szasz, the psychiatrist, writes of *The Myth of Mental Illness.*[5] William Glasser speaks of psychoanalytic theory and practice as "subtly subversive."[6] And Glasser so popularized his theories and his methods, perhaps at the price of gross oversimplification, that he has won many disciples for what he calls "reality therapy."

Reality therapy has had a widespread appeal for clergy, I think, for a number of reasons, among which the following are prominent:

1. There is a frank acknowledgment of a place for standards (cf. the law).
2. There is a central place for the acknowledgment of responsibility and accountability (cf. judgment).
3. There is an understanding of the basic human needs as the need for relatedness and for self-respect, the frustration of which Christians may identify with sin, and the fulfillment as salvation.
4. Responsibility in Glasser's approach has an individual dimension which lives in tension with the social dimension, i.e., "the ability to meet one's own needs and to do so in a way that does not deprive others of the ability to fulfill their needs"[7] (cf. the family of God).

5. Health is seen as a derivative of commitment rather than of insight, understanding, and freedom (cf. repentance and faith).
6. Reality is seen as involving more than the "now." It includes the remote consequences of actions, the ability to strive and to endure privation for the sake of long-term gain (cf. eternity).
7. Treatment is essentially educative rather than corrective, a method in which parents, teachers, and the public may, indeed must, play a significant part.
8. The foundation is a positive regard for man's worth and potential.

Rejecting is an inappropriate motivation for being attracted to reality therapy, the opportunity it might afford to the pastor to tell someone "how it is," I maintain that the foregoing statements warrant the close attention of pastors to Dr. Glasser's work.

However, I am convinced that the doctrine of justification provides a necessary corrective. While Dr. Glasser stresses the necessity for involvement which encourages the functioning of conscience (his phrase), and while he stresses that the method involves honesty, concern, personal authenticity, and confrontation of a particular kind, his illustrations lack the depth and clarity evident in other aspects of his work. The characteristic quality of confrontation is not spelled out, nor the principles operative in "involvement." The model seems to be that of the wise leader, the teacher, the Shepherd, who from a position of strength and knowledge, if not superiority, directs the troubled person to the solution of his problem. The doctrine of justification by faith suggests that God's action for man's salvation was accomplished not through remaining outside the human condition, but through entering into it to the extent of death on a cross. The clinical material also suggests that help came, not in response to an external demand for responsible behavior, but through a sharing of the patient's life even to the point of acknowledging that there might be no answer, and, more than that, that I, too, had sinned in the aggressiveness of my desire to help her.

In attempting to provide more substance to the concepts of involvement and of a particular kind of confrontation, I am not casting any reflection on Dr. Glasser's ability to become involved or to provide the required kind of confrontation. I am simply underlining the usefulness of the kind of model which enables the therapist, counselor or pastor, to stand beside the troubled person, not over against him, in the experience of a judgment to which both are subject, and the experience of humanness which is the opposite of omnipotence, omniscience, and innocence. Such is not possible without acknowledgment of external standards which are not the property of the one or the other.

Perry London writes of *The Modes and Morals of Psychotherapy.*[8] With Glasser, he challenges the traditional theories and practices of psychotherapy. He insists that effective psychotherapy incorporates both a science and a morality but that many therapists refuse to acknowledge the latter. He insists on the necessity of a moral standard and expresses the hope that sometime in the future, rather distant he feels, there may be a science of morality, a day when man's scientific study of man will identify the standards by which man must live if he is to fulfill himself.

I must say that I wonder about that possibility—and, if it is achieved, I wonder what the outcome will be. It sounds very much like a new law, more identifiable, more consistent, perhaps, than the Law of the Jews and the Christians, but with the same limitations as the Law we have known.

Perry London, others whom I have mentioned, and many more, have become disenchanted with the medical model for coping with man's ills. Glasser turns toward an educative model which includes the affective as well as the cognitive. Yet another innovator is Charles Curran, S.J.,[9] who is critical of psychological and pastoral counseling treatment methods as too much oriented to the pathological. He prefers the educational model, then utilizes a methodology in which the "student" experiences growth through a reversal of roles by which he helps the teacher to fulfill his (the teacher's) needs. I ask why the pastor needs another model, be it medical, educative, or scientific, when there is the theological model of the Suffering Servant, the man for others, Jesus, the Christ.

That brings me to the conclusion of my reflections. I'm sure that I have argued as if the doctrine of justification by faith provided a most effective theory for the practice of therapy and/or pastoral care. And I believe that to be so—especially on those occasions when I can appear as a teacher, consultant, or as a trained chaplain or counselor!

However, the conclusion to my initial study, which came as a surprise to me and perhaps to you, is this—that the doctrine of justification by faith provides not so much a theory or a method for pastoral care, as an undergirding for the pastor or counselor. If it is part of this faith, it frees him to enter adequately into the world of another without the necessity, through need to produce results, to "lay a trip" on anyone or impose a judgment, an expectation, an interpretation, or a timetable, the net result of which might serve mainly to obstruct or impede. "For it is by His grace you are saved, through trusting Him; it is not your doing. It is God's gift, not a reward for work done. There is nothing for anyone to boast of. For we are God's handwork, created in Christ Jesus to devote ourselves to the good deeds for which God has designed us." (Ephesians 2:8-10, N.E.B.)

Notes

1. Verbatim material from my unpublished thesis: The relevance of the doctrine of justification by faith for pastoral care: an idiographic study. Perkins School of Theology.
2. Alan Richardson. *A Theological Wordbook of the Bible*. London: S.C.M. Press, 1950.
3. O. Hobart Mowrer. *The Crisis in Psychiatry and Religion*. Princeton, New Jersey: Van Nostrand, 1961.
4. O. Hobart Mowrer, ed. *Morality and Mental Health*. Chicago: Rand McNally, 1967.
5. Thomas Szasz. *The Myth of Mental Illness*. New York: Paul B. Hoeber, 1961.
6. William Glasser. *Reality Therapy*. New York: Harper and Row, 1965.
7. *Ibid.,* p. 13.
8. Perry London. *The Modes and Morals of Psychotherapy*. New York: Holt, Rinehart and Winston, 1964.
9. Charles Curran. *Counseling and Psychotherapy: The Pursuit of Values*. New York: Sheed and Ward, 1968.

Suggestions for Further Reading

Don Browning. *The Moral Context of Pastoral Care.* Philadelphia: Westminster, 1976.

———. *Atonement and Psychotherapy.* Philadelphia: Westminster, 1961.

Douglas Daher. Defining sin and its place in the counseling relationship. *Journal of Pastoral Care,* 32 (3): 200–212, 1978.

Frederick Greeves. *Theology and the Cure of Souls.* Manhasset, New York: Channel Press, 1962.

James H. Lapsley. *Salvation and Health.* Philadelphia: Westminster Press, 1972.

Henri J. Nouwen. *The Wounded Healer.* Garden City, New York: Doubleday, 1972.

Wayne E. Oates. *Anxiety in Christian Experience.* Philadelphia: Westminster Press, 1955.

7

Some Theological Implications of Illness

Richard Dayringer, Th.D.,
Eugene Mendenhall, Th.D.

Associate Professors
Departments of Medical Humanities and Family Practice
Southern Illinois University School of Medicine
Springfield, Illinois
Director, Five County Pastoral Counseling Centers, Inc.
Chillicothe, Ohio

Nobody really plans to get sick. Yet, counting common colds and stomach and intestinal upsets, the average person may have as many as ten or twelve illnesses yearly. There are four broad types of causal factors in illness: (1) defective organs; (2) invasions of bacteria, viruses, or poisons; (3) distortions caused by a life style of too much of this (calories or work) or too little of that (vitamins or sleep); and (4) accidents. When a person is overtaken by any of these, he is forced to take time to recover, adjust, or succumb.

During the period of enforced inactivity, a number of questions may crowd into his mind demanding attention and they may begin to spark his theological thinking. Many patients ask, "*Why* did I get sick?" Another type of question was raised by a young mother in a talk with the hospital chaplain: "I just don't know why this had to happen to *me*. I don't understand it. It doesn't make sense." Still another kind of question patients ask is, "Why did this happen *now* when I'm so busy?" They also wonder why it was this particular *thing* and not something else.

Some of their questions they may direct to their physician, as well as to God. Such a question is, "How long will I be sick?" Their fear of the unknown may prompt the questions, "What will be the *outcome* of my illness?" "Will I be crippled?" "Will I die?" To contemplate such questions as these can lead to a religious experience.

The ancient Jews considered God the author of good and evil. They believed that suffering and poverty were the direct results of sin. The three Hebrew attitudes toward sin can be classified under national, paternal, and individual retribution. The Hebrews thought in terms of a convenantal relationship with God. If they kept it, they prospered; if they broke it, they suffered. Jesus' vicarious view of suffering and Paul's "in Christ's stead" idea are presented in the New Testament.

On the contemporary scene the views range as widely as those presented by the various authors whose viewpoints are summarized in Table 7-1.

For the purposes of this study, theological implications will be defined as divinely oriented thinking and reactions motivated by the desire to find reasons for illness. The best way to discover the theological implications of illness is to listen to those who are sick. Of course, this subject can be approached scripturally or logically, but sick people don't necessarily think scripturally or logically.

TABLE 7-1.   Viewpoints of Suffering

Freud	Symptoms of disease have meanings.[1]
Weatherhead	Suffering shows that we are helping God in world suffering.[2]
Tillich	The main cause of meaningless suffering is "aloneness."[3]
Oates	Suffering produces transformations.[4]
Young and Meiberg	Spiritual unhappiness often expresses itself in illness. Symptoms are used as controls.[5]
Frankl	There is meaning in suffering. Love is the goal.[6]
Belgum	Pains show us our limitations.[7]
Williams	The solution for a lot of suffering is found in a union of the secular and sacred.[8]
Siirala	Illness is an indication of negativity in the personality.[9]
Bonhoeffer	Only God is the answer to our problems of suffering.[10]

So, to study the Biblical implications of illness is one approach and to examine the theological inferences that patients actually draw concerning their illness is a somewhat different one. An obvious difference is that in the former you begin with the scripture and apply your findings to modern life; in the latter, you begin with a problem in life and may find yourself driven to the Bible for help.

We felt that a survey of verbatim write-ups of patient visits would reveal the various theological implications expressed by these patients. We selected sixty-two write-ups containing theological implications in the conversations themselves or in the students' evaluations.

On the basis of our analysis of these sixty-two verbatim interviews, we identified six faulty and six feasible theological implications of illness.

Faulty Theological Implications

There are a number of popular interpretations of the fact of illness which have faulty theological implications. They infer things about God's involvement or lack of it which do not correlate with Biblical teachings. Six of these concepts are discussed in the following paragraphs.

GOD DOESN'T KNOW ABOUT ME

Many people, especially early in their illness, interpret it by saying, "It's just one of those things that happen." The patient seems to be simply aware that something has happened to him or her which interfered with normal work and play. He/she disassociates himself/herself from any involvement. The theological implication of this attitude appears to be, "God doesn't know about me, or care about me." Many of the professionals who surround his/her bed add to this interpretation. They think of disease as an invading enemy that they can stamp out without becoming involved with the patient as a person.

GOD IS DISCIPLINING ME

When ailments come, some people feel that God is testing them. "Maybe God has been testing us to see if we would remain faithful in a time of trouble," surmised one patient typical of this philosophy. Those who hold to the "testing" theory of suffering usually see present testing as preparation for some future opportunity.

Some people look upon physical ailments as chastisement or discipline. Hebrews 12:7–11 is often cited to support this position. True, the passage does discuss chastisement, but it never refers to illness as a means. The New Testament seems to teach that God characteristically uses a person's conscience to inflict chastisement.

Others go even further and consider sickness and death as divine punishment. One grieving mother said, "Oh, why did God punish me by taking her? I can't live without her!" This question is based on the same moralistic misconception that the Jews held in Jesus' day. "Rabbi, who sinned, this man or his parents, that he was born blind?" (John 9:2,3). Jesus' answer broke the causal relationship between suffering and sin.

GOD LET ME DOWN

Some patients can't understand why God let an ailment come on them. They point out their reasons for failing to understand: "I have lived a good life and I've never been a bother to anyone." Their statements indict God with not holding up his side of a bargain. The patient has lived an almost sinless life, but God has let him/her down. Of course, God is never presented in the Scripture as entering into agreements like this, but these people presume that such a situation holds true nevertheless.

GOD IS MAD AT ME

The patient who says this may be a person who is wrestling with guilt. He knows why God ought to be mad at him because he knows what he has been doing. Thus he blames God for his sickness. Blaming God is often a kind of rearguard action against yielding to an insistent sense of guilt.

MY FAITH IS GONE

A patient who loses faith is usually a person who is angry because God hasn't taken care of him. The Christian life is perceived as a kind of "protection racket." By church attendance, Bible reading, prayer, and so forth, you buy protection from illness, poverty, and notoriety. Such a patient is angry at God for not providing good protection. Just as we all tend to lash out at or withdraw from a person who angers us, the patient has an urge to "bad mouth" God and withdraw from Him. He doesn't want to talk to Him (pray) or listen to what He has to say (read Scripture). Faith in protection is gone.

IF GOD WILL HEAL ME, I WILL SERVE HIM

The patient who says this sort of thing seems to have learned his lesson and to be asking only for another chance. Is this really the case? Or, is he still trying to make a deal with God? He still sees the Divine as one who can be bargained with and who has a price. He may even see himself as a very unusual person who has every right to ask for and expect to get a special deal. However, God is no respector of persons and His grace is so sufficient that our works need not be punished.

Feasible Theological Implications

There are many attitudes toward illness which do seem to correlate with Biblical teachings and the health sciences. Six of these found in our study of the verbatims will be mentioned.

GOD KNOWS AND CARES ABOUT MY SICKNESS

One patient remarked, "Chaplain, it's good to have someone to talk to who understands what you're talking about." The chaplain replied, "I'm glad we can talk, but remember that the one I represent also understands and cares."

GOD WILL HELP ME THROUGH THIS

Another patient said, "I don't understand everything that happens to me, but I just try to accept it and go along with it whether I agree or not. And, as I trust the Lord more, I am able to understand more." This is the kind of faith that is most helpful in illness, not faith in recovery, but faith in God's love and presence regardless of the prognosis. We Christians are plagued with disease, disability, deformity, and death just like everyone else. The difference should be our recognition that God-in-Christ is with us, strengthening and sustaining us come what may.

I HAD SOMETHING TO DO WITH GETTING SICK

This is what a patient is acknowledging when he says, "I worry (or eat, drink, smoke, work, etc.) too much." Or, "I don't rest (or eat, sleep, play, talk, etc.) enough." The person recovering from a "heart attack" contemplates how he can "change his way of life." Our various ailments emphasize to us our humanity. The reality of our human frailty sometimes escapes us between illnesses. But during a time of sickness, we recognize our finitude and our need for faith in "The Great Physician."

I CAN LEARN SOMETHING IMPORTANT
THROUGH SICKNESS

Sickness usually shocks us out of our shallowness. It is a kind of crisis in selfhood. It can help a person to decide what is really valuable to him in life and to discover himself anew. Such growth is often painful, yet satisfying. Thus, an illness may challenge us both to try to put more into life and to get more out of it. With God's help, a person can usually find meaning in his sickness. Then, we can either adjust to it (as in chronic or terminal illnesses) or redefine our lives (as in psychosomatic or psychiatric ailments) so that we no longer need to be sick.

GOD ENABLED ME TO ENDURE MORE PAIN
THAN I THOUGHT I COULD

Many patients come to this conclusion as they move toward recovery. Most of us don't really know our capacity to endure pain. We don't know the strength of our spiritual resources until we experience serious illness or surgery. Such intense pain motivates us to move toward health. With God's help, we unify our inner health-giving resources and thus try to cooperate to the fullest with the physician's treatment. God seems to supply us with more "grit" than we thought we had and this surprises us. Upon reflection, our surprise convinces us that it was actually God who strengthened us.

I WILL NEVER GIVE UP HOPE

The person who believes in God always has reason to hope for the best. Nothing happens outside the jurisdiction of His natural laws. God's characteristic way of healing is through physicians, nurses, and medical treatment. He cures people or relieves their pain through the knowledge He has given those in the health field. Yet, many of us know of rare instances where healing occurred, or at least death was postponed, when even the physicians could not account for it. Medicine is a growing, burgeoning field of endeavor. New cures are discovered quite often. The patient who maintains hope, even in the face of a frightening diagnosis or a poor prognosis, is a patient who has a better chance for recovery.

Our attempt to classify these theological implications forced us to recognize two recurring themes. The phrase *will of God* was often spoken but almost never defined; the emotion of anger was often obvious though almost never admitted. These things seemed so recurrent we wondered how they had escaped our list. Yet, there seemed no way to confine either of them to a single place within our categories. We concluded that anger is the emotion that generally underlies all of the faulty theological concepts, while belief in the will of God shines through the feasible ones. Theoretically, an expression of the emotion of anger could lead to intellectual insights into the will of God in illness.

The Crisis of Illness

Many writers have called illness a crisis experience and for many reasons. For one thing, illness involves dependency. The patient cannot take care of himself. It is as though he were a child again and the doctor and nurse were his parents. It may also foster a greater dependency on God.

Sickness is usually a time of loneliness. Pain causes the patient to tunnel back into his own world where things happening outside his room become less and less important to him. Yet, God's love can break through that loneliness in the person of a visitor who really cares.

Illness has to do with spiritual tangibles as well as physical medicine. It is important to treat the whole man.

Illness is a learning experience. Problems that can be avoided during busy, healthy times march into the mind of the patient and demand to be given thoughtful consideration. Thinking runs as deep or deeper than it does in a university and the sick often come to realize the need for a relationship with God.

Sickness requires us to reexamine our values. We must face ourselves with the kind of life we have been living. Perhaps our style of life has added to our difficulty; if so, our pattern of living will have to be changed.

Thus, illness often involves a reordering of our lives. Our personal limitations become quite real to us, maybe for the first time. We begin to realize that we are "only human," that we must accept the fact of our illness and adjust our lives accordingly. Recognizing our humanness, we begin to trust, pray, and hope, and the crisis of illness takes on the dimensions of religious experience.

Notes

1. Sigmund Freud. *A General Introduction to Psychoanalysis.* New York: Permabooks, 1958.
2. Leslie Weatherhead. *Why Do Men Suffer?* Nashville: Abingdon Press, 1936.
3. Paul Tillich. *Systematic Theology,* vol 2. London: James Nisbet, 1957.

4. Wayne E. Oates. *The Revelation of God in Human Suffering*. Philadelphia: Westminster Press, 1959.
5. Richard K. Young and Albert L. Meiburg. *Spiritual Therapy*. New York: Harper and Brothers, 1960.
6. Victor Frankl. *Man's Search for Meaning*. New York: Washington Square Press, 1967.
7. David Belgum. *His Death and Ours*. Minneapolis: Augsburg Publishing House, 1958.
8. Daniel Day Williams. *God's Grace and Man's Hope*. New York: Harper and Brothers, 1949.
9. Aarne Siirala. *The Voice of Illness*. Philadelphia: Fortress Press, 1964.
10. Dietrick Bonhoeffer. *Prisoner for God*. New York: Macmillan, 1960.

Suggestions for Further Reading

William E. Baldridge and John J. Gleason, Jr. A theological framework for pastoral care. *Journal of Pastoral Care*, 32 (4): 232–238, 1978.
Charles V. Gerkin. *Crisis Experience in Modern Life: Theory and Theology for Pastoral Care*. Nashville: Abingdon, 1979.
Theodore W. Jennings. Theological perspectives on sexuality. *Journal of Pastoral Care*, 33 (1): 3–16, 1979.
C. Roy Woodruff. Toward a theology of maturity in pastoral care. *Pastoral Psychology*, 27 (1), 1979.

PART II

*Pastoral Care
for Patients*

8

Ministering to the Presurgical Patient

Dennis Saylor, Ph.D.

Chaplain
Presbyterian Hospital Center
Albuquerque, New Mexico

The uniqueness of the individual is never more apparent than in his reaction to the stress of surgery. Not only are there physical and anatomical differences which make each surgical procedure unique, but there are also psychological reactions to surgery which are idiosyncratic. But whatever the individual differences involved, the effects of presurgical anxiety are uniformly against the best interest of the patient. Perhaps at no other point do mind and body interact in such an obvious and deleterious fashion. This same evaluation is advanced by James Williams et al., who contends: "Excessive preoperative anxiety appears to affect a patient's physiological status markedly at the time of operation."[1] So for these reasons an examination of how to minister to the presurgical patient seems more than warranted.

The organization of this paper will consist of four basic divisions: 1) The Etiology of Presurgical Anxiety, 2) Relevant Research, 3) A Possible Model, and 4) The Minister's Role.

These ideas were presented in a modified form by Mr. Saylor in an article entitled "Understanding Presurgical Anxiety," *Association of Operating Room Nurses Journal*, 22 (4): 624–636, October, 1975.

The Etiology of Presurgical Anxiety

As with most behavioral phenomena, the etiology of presurgical anxiety is not directly attributable to a single factor operating independently of all others. It is not possible to isolate any one variable always present in patients. However, a number of variables can be examined which seem to be logically interrelated. Also, it is a reasonable assumption that the stress of surgery will not be greatly unlike that discerned in other stress-producing situations. As Irving Janis puts it:

> From a psychological standpoint, a major surgical operation constitutes a stress situation which resembles many other types of catastrophes and disasters in that the "victim" faces a combination of three major forms of imminent danger—the possibility of suffering acute pain, of undergoing serious body damage, and of dying.[2]

This being the case, the main causes of stress per se can be suspected of playing a role in presurgical anxiety. Moreover, to the extent to which environment may contribute to stress, the unique environmental milieu of the hospital can be viewed as a contributory cause. Therefore, a hospital patient has to deal with two aspects of anxiety: (1) those which arise from within the individual, and (2) those which arise from without and aggravate the inner stress.

Admittedly it is difficult to differentiate between the endogenous and exogenous factors involved in the etiology of presurgical anxiety. The discussion is divided in this way for organizational purposes only and no sharp line of demarcation is usually discernable at the clinical level.

FEAR OF THE UNKNOWN

One thesis often advanced is that presurgical anxiety is rooted in the fear of the unknown; therefore, the alleviation of the symptoms will be in proportion to the information and support given. M. A. Johnson says:

> Patients always experience a certain amount of apprehension before surgery, even when the operation is a minor one. Basically this is an

expression of fear of the unknown which may be exaggerated by fear of the anesthetic, the actual operation, or its outcome.[3]

Even though a patient has experienced relatively recent hospitalization, there is no guarantee that a present surgery will be greeted calmly. Lois Graham and Elizabeth Conley, using empirical methods, examined this variable and concluded: "There was no significant difference (X^2 = .01), therefore previous hospitalization cannot be said to be associated with either low or higher levels of anxiety."[4]

However, a past surgery (not hospitalization) may itself be a complicating force in handling the present anxiety. This is because the patient usually conceives of his/her present and future circumstances to be more threatening than the past. Thus, the temporal proximity of present minor surgery can create more anxiety than the memory of a successful major surgery can allay. Further, this is particularly true if the anxiety of the previous surgery was not dealt with adequately. The suppressed anxiety may surface again as a subconscious "flashback." It follows then that although a patient has experienced a successful surgery, his/her present needs should not be discounted or ignored.

FEAR OF OUTCOME

Especially when the surgical procedure is exploratory in nature, the fear of what might be discovered contributes to the patient's anxiety. Even in a so-called routine operation the fear of what might be encountered is a strong negative force. In our society the dread of cancer is very real and present, and visions of malignancy dance before the imagination of many surgical patients. For example, Dr. M. A. Ramsay found that 100 percent of the patients undergoing breast lump surgery are afraid of cancer.[5]

For those who undergo surgery knowing that a previous biopsy indicated a malignancy, there is also the fear that it might be impossible to remove the cancerous tissue or organ completely, or that it is in an advanced stage and spread throughout the body. Even with the physician's assurances to the contrary, some patients will maintain their high anxiety level, believing at the "gut level" that their doctor is deliberately misleading them.

FEAR OF DEATH

For many patients the fear of death has a spiritual as well as a physical dimension, for in some persons death as such is not as feared as is the hereafter. Often one's religious beliefs include an uncertainty about the attainment of eternal bliss. The possibility of dying under the judgment and wrath of God is held out; and inasmuch as the surgery may not be successful, it becomes the agency or means by which one enters eternity. As the time of surgery approaches the anxiety heightens if the patient entertains uncertainty about his/her relationship to God. The punitive and judgmental aspects of religious teaching are interpreted in an unconstructive way, until the patient may be almost immobilized with fear and may hesitate to consent to the surgery.

On the other hand a patient whose religious faith is working for him or her can derive great inner strength which becomes an asset in the surgical procedure. M. A. Bruegel, using a sample of eighty-five surgical patients, gave them the Institute for Personality and Ability Testing Anxiety Scale Questionnaire the evening before surgery. Independent variables she included were age, sex, socioeconomic status, education, religion, race, type of surgery, and so on. The dependent variable was the number of analgesic medications requested the first forty-eight hours postoperatively. She found:

> The relationship between anxiety and religion was the only one with significance: persons with no stated religious preference were much more anxious than either Protestants or Catholics (F = 3.17, p < .05).[6]

DEPENDENCY NEEDS

Another factor besides fear of the unknown which seems to be involved in the etiology of presurgical anxiety is what may be referred to as dependency needs. According to this line of thought, most people can be classified with respect to behavior which is labeled high or low dependency. Further, the extremes on the dependency continuum are to be avoided. Thus, those patients who find it difficult to allow themselves to be dependent on anyone (low dependency) also find it difficult to adopt a role of dependency such as is required by hospitalization and surgery. As Rosemary

Williams notes: "If such a person is forced into a dependent role through illness . . . he will experience a great anxiety and threat to self-esteem."[7] By the same token, patients who rate high on a dependency scale and are very dependent, also experience great anxiety. Williams further remarks:

> Illness and hospitalization can be extremely traumatic for such a person in that his psychological dependency, already excessively great, becomes completely blown out of proportion with the actual need to be physically cared for while ill.[8]

TYPE OF CONTROL

Closely related to the dependency factor in producing presurgical anxiety is the type of control to which an individual feels subject. Some feel that the control of events which influence them is entirely out of their hands. Fate, the will of God, and so on, exercise final control over their lives. These persons believe in external control. On the other hand, others feel that what happens to them is dependent on their own behavior. They believe that they "call the shots" and are responsible for their own destiny; they adhere to a belief in internal control.

Research which examines the relationship of this internal/external control variable on preoperative fear and postoperative recovery indicates that the length of postoperative stay is influenced both by internal/external control and birth order. Jean Johnson et al. found: "The data showed that firstborns stayed longer the higher their scores on internal control."[9]

In addition to these endogenous factors are the exogenous factors. The hospital, as the locus of the surgery, introduces a unique set of environmental stimuli which impinge upon the patient's perceptual field.

Although no suggestion is made that the factors discussed here are the only ones involved, they do seem to operate in the creation and maintenance of presurgical anxiety. Several exogenous factors will be suggested, but no significance is intimated by their order of presentation. Again it is emphasized that all of the elements indicated here may or may not be present in any one patient, but probably at least one is in evidence in most cases.

VISUAL PERSPECTIVE

Depending upon the degree of consciousness the patient has, his visual perspective may contribute to the aggravation of his anxiety. Normally the patient's visual field is perceived from a standing or vertical position. Except perhaps in the case of the chronically ill or bedfast patient, the surgical patient is placed in a horizontal position, often suddenly. His journey to the operating room is perceived from an entirely different perspective. Further, the movement of the cart, the loss of modesty involved in "prepping" procedures, and the effect of the sedative administered may make the patient feel uneasy and threatened. Feeling vulnerable, the patient may demonstrate the presurgical anxiety syndrome.

LOSS OF CONSCIOUSNESS

Unless the surgery can be performed utilizing a local anesthetic, the patient will be given a general anesthetic which involves loss of consciousness. For some patients, the fear of being "put under" is greater than the fear of the surgical procedure itself. At times this fear can be verbalized, brought out into the open and owned. In other cases it is submerged to a lower level of consciousness and can contribute to the general anxiety the patient experiences. It is possible that the fear of loss of consciousness is closely aligned with the fear of death and the two fears become confused and intertwined.

In a study reported by Ramsay 382 patients (183 male, 199 female), were interviewed twenty-four hours before surgery. According to a clinical assessment of anxiety, 73 percent of the patients had preoperative fears and of these 62 percent indicated that the anesthetic was their primary fear.[10]

PRESURGICAL PREPARATION

It is ironic that the fear of surgery may be increased by the very necessity of preparation for surgery. Because of the obvious need for sterility, various "prepping" procedures are carried out prior to surgery. The patient is often aware that something beyond ordinary hospital routine is occurring. It is possible that the patient may misinterpret the intention and efficiency with which the nurse carries out these duties and may become frightened. This is especially true when part of the procedure involves receiving an injection or limiting the patient's physical movements in any way. Their wearing of the surgical attire may make some patients feel self-conscious and ill-at-ease.

PREVAILING MYTHS

Possibly each surgical patient has his own personal repertoire of myths concerning surgery in general. This consists of a combination of the patient's own experience of surgery or that of a close family member or a friend, plus an accumulation of debris from popular magazines and TV shows. Misconceptions and distortions may have created a milieu in which the patient is steeped in old wives' tales. In pregnancy and childbirth, these myths may be more highly verbalized and obvious than in surgery, however, each patient likely maintains a highly personalized store of attitudes and emotions concerning surgery, most of which are anxiety producing.

The patient's family may compound his/her anxiety by hovering over him or her before surgery, uttering false assurances and inane clichés. These well-meaning gestures may be what triggers a whole barrage of unwholesome sentimentality.

Relevant Research on Presurgical Anxiety

ASSESSMENT

In addition to a consideration of the etiology of presurgical anxiety, a brief examination of the literature is indicated. Much of the empirical research conducted with hospital inpatients as subjects deals with an assessment of the anxiety the patient experiences. The reason for this emphasis is obvious, for no experimental data can be tested for significance unless and until a valid and reliable dependent variable is found. In order to assess accurately the effect of emotional and environmental variables, an accurate means of measuring anxiety is mandatory.

Several investigators have tackled this problem, each using different approaches. Some have used the existing psychological tests to measure the amount of anxiety encountered prior to surgery. For example, those using Cattell and Schiere's Anxiety Scale Questionnaire include Williams et al.[11] and Bruegel.[12] Others, such as Wolfer and Davis,[13] use observer ratings and self-reporting scales and inventories. Still others devised an adjective check list as did Johnson et al.[14] Graham et al.[15] used a printed guide composed of twenty-four characteristics. Winslow and Fuhs[16] also developed a check-list form to show baseline preoperative information. Shetler[17] developed her own "Operating Room Pre-Operative Interview Sheet" for use by the operating-room nurse.

In addition to using printed or published measures, some studies rely on the clinical, face-to-face interview. Among those utilizing this technique are Graham and Conley[18] and Ramsay.[19] Graham's study concluded: "The most useful and frequently occurring indicators of preoperative anxiety were the subjective responses of the patients during both the preoperative period and postoperative visit."[20]

A physiological approach to the measurement of presurgical anxiety was made by Williams et al.[21] Their instrument is called the Skin Conductance Anxiety Test which they feel has unique value in providing a reliable, valid, and quantitative index of patient anxiety. The technique involves the administration of an anesthetic to reduce and stabilize the galvanic skin responses (GSR). The quantity of the drug needed to accomplish this gives the measure of presurgical anxiety. Thus, the more drugs necessary to eliminate the spontaneous GSR, the higher the level of patient anxiety.

INDIVIDUAL DIFFERENCES

Several facets of individual differences have been the object of various studies. For instance, Ramsay[22] concluded that age was a factor in the amount of presurgical anxiety which a patient experiences. He found that patients at both ends of the age scale have less fear; that is, children and patients over sixty. Included in this study was the finding that sex differences are slight—70 percent of the males and 75 percent of the females showed anxiety according to clinical assessment. Graham and Conley[23] also found females to be slightly more anxious than men; but found no statistically significant differences in age. However, no patients below the age of twenty were included in their sampling. Wolfer and Davis[24] also found that female patients reported more fear than male patients.

Using a sample of eighty-five surgical patients (age range: eighteen to seventy years) and the number of postoperative analgesic and medication needed, Bruegel[25] examined age, sex, social-economic status, education, religion, race, and type of surgery. She found no significant differences except with respect to religion, as noted above.

These studies are unequivocal in the proposition that presurgical anxiety is an important aspect of patient behavior in the hospital setting, even though the methodology and hypotheses differ from study to study.

A Possible Model of Presurgical Anxiety

Another perspective on presurgical anxiety can be obtained by viewing the surgical procedure in terms of classical approach-avoidance conflict. It is herein advanced that some, probably not all, anxiety preceding surgery can be explained in these terms. Three brief case studies will be included to illustrate the possible application of these hypothetical constructs.

John S., twenty-six year old male patient was admitted as an inpatient via the emergency room with a diagnosis of possible appendicitis. He has never been in a hospital as a patient before and has been in apparently excellent health. His abdominal pain was severe, with nausea. Upon obtaining a lab report, the physician informed John that an immediate appendectomy was necessary.

What level of anxiety would be expected before surgery? Probably low. This is anticipated in that the patient faces a relatively simple approach-avoidance conflict. The positive valence of pain reduction is greater than the negative valence of the surgery to be performed. This situation can be viewed from the perspective of the hedonist—we avoid what causes pain and seek the gratification of comfort needs. Surgery is perceived as that which will give relief and so it produces no great amount of anxiety. No doubt this is an oversimplification, since many other variables may enter the picture. For example, the patient may have lost a near relative who had an appendectomy, etc. Generally, however, the basic expectation is for a low level of presurgical anxiety.

Consider another case:

Hazel J., thirty-one-year-old mother of two small children has been in the hospital several days. The lab report on a breast nodule biopsy definitely confirmed a malignancy. The patient was informed by the physician of the finding and of the need for a radical mastectomy.

What level of anxiety will be encountered before surgery? Probably high. This is anticipated in that the patient faces an avoidance-avoidance conflict. The fear of the pain of surgery and the threat to her female body image present a powerful negative valence; but a negative valence is also present if surgery is not performed, in that the malignancy would develop unchecked. Facing two undesirable alternatives will characteristically produce vacillation, tension, and a high level of presurgical anxiety. The patient will probably also verbalize concern for her husband's and children's welfare.

Consider yet a third instance:

Austin H., was an eighty-five-year-old widower in the Intensive Care Unit. His diagnosis was lower GI bleeding. The X-ray report showed a large tumor in the colon. Surgery was indicated and the patient was informed of this.

What level of anxiety will be manifest prior to surgery? Probably low. In this case the negative valence of fear of death due to surgery is minimized and the positive valence of the improvement of body function maximized, making for little indecision, less vacillation and anxiety. The patient verbalizes willingness and readiness to die.

These three cases are examples of a possible formulation for predicting the level of presurgical anxiety. Most simply put, to use this model only three questions need be determined.

1. What positive aspects of the surgical procedure are perceived by the patient?
2. What negative aspects of the surgical procedure are perceived by the patient?
3. Which valence dominates?

In determining negative valence it should be noted that for most patients, regardless of the scope of the surgery, surgery itself is a traumatic experience. Hospital chaplains Holst and Kurtz[26] make the observation that to the patient there is no such thing as "minor surgery." Nurses Bouchard and Owens[27] note:

> Every person will respond to this information (necessity of surgery) according to his own conception of what such surgery means. This will include (1) the physical, psychological, social, and financial sacrifices and discomforts involved and (2) anticipation of the outcome of the surgery—whether his condition will be improved or whether he will have a greater disability as a result of the surgery. Because of the threat that impending surgery represents to him, the patient may become withdrawn, exhibit signs of denial, "put up a brave front," or act positively.

Butler and Lewis further state: "People tend to become upset about any subtractive surgery, especially if it is a major subtraction like hysterectomy."[28] These negative aspects contribute greatly to the building up to a crescendo of the patient's anxiety. Often the positive aspects of a surgery are small or nonexistent. For this reason the minister needs to understand and empathize with the surgical patient. His role in helping will be considered next.

The Minister's Role

Whatever model one considers, there are many factors involved in any given instance of presurgical anxiety. However, the recognition and acknowledgment of the contributory agents and situations examined here may give some aids to the reduction of such anxiety. The minister is apt to encounter many surgical patients at various levels of anxiety. Generally speaking, the level of anxiety will increase as the time of surgery draws nearer.

Some patients have been scheduled for surgery weeks or months in advance; for others surgery is a sudden emergency decision. Depending upon the individual, it seems that the patient who is suddenly aware of the necessity of surgery is able to verbalize his fears more easily than the one who has known for some time that surgery was planned; however, his level of anxiety may actually be higher. Perhaps this is because the fears are nearer to the surface of consciousness and there is no time to indulge in the usual submersive processes.

In any event the pastor can be of great assistance to the patient, his or her family, and the surgical team. While he attempts no in-depth psychotherapy, he does listen acceptingly and helps the patient to verbalize and to own his fears. Often the patient only wants opportunity to acknowledge his fears to another caring human being. As Johnson put it: "It is important that the preoperative patient feel free to express his fears . . . for fear always seems to diminish once it is brought into the open."[29] Characteristically, the patient's family will not listen to or empathize with the patient's fears, but will try to deny them or to minimize the unpleasant realities of the situation.

It is important that the minister explore the depths of the patient's despair and anxiety fully. The patient does not want or need a superficial, Pollyanna-ish glossing over of his/her feelings. The minister should strive to create an atmosphere of acceptance and understanding of the patient's attitude. Even if it seems that the patient's fears are disproportionate to the circumstances, the minister should not minimize those fears. They are very real to the patient. On the other hand if the pastor has reason to believe that the patient does not react appropriately to the seriousness of the surgery, he should open the door to as full a discussion of it as is productive. Often the patient's denial is the best defense mechanism he can construct.

The pastor, however, not only listens attentively but communicates to the patient God's abiding love and continuing concern for all His creation. By using selected Scripture passages that emphasize the eternal good purposes of God, the pastor can help to assure the patient that God never fails or forsakes, but is as near as he will permit Him to be. In his prayers he emphasizes and underlines the sincere concern of one human being for another in a time of uncertainty and invokes the blessing of the transcendent God who formed man in His own image.

Another significant aspect of ministering to the presurgical patient is the administration of the sacraments. The minister should be alert to express his willingness to assist in the patient's desire.

A pastor's visit is also indicated for those patients who have been scheduled for surgery, but whose surgery is suddenly cancelled. Whether it is cancelled due to a change in the patient, such as an elevated temperature or electrolyte imbalance, or because of a change in the scheduling, the result may be the same. This type of presurgical patient may be either depressed or hostile or both.

While the minister should never attempt to "play doctor," he can offer routine explanations and give general information, especially to one facing surgery for the first time. At the same time the minister stands ready to listen to the patient's apprehensions, disappointment, or anger.

In summary, as the minister recognizes the various sources of presurgical anxiety he is in a better position to help the patient, his/her family, and the hospital staff by identifying himself with the needs of the patient and interpreting to the patient some of the reasons for his presurgical anxiety.

Notes

1. James Williams, John R. Jones, and Barbara Williams. A physiological measure of preoperative anxiety. *Psychosomatic Medicine,* 31, no. 6 (1969): 522–27.
2. Irving L. Janis. *Psychological Stress.* Psychoanalytic and behavioral studies of surgical patients. New York: John Wiley, 1958.
3. M. A. Johnson. *Developing the Art of Understanding.* New York: Springer, 1967.
4. Lois E. Graham and Elizabeth Conley. Evaluation of anxiety and fear in adult surgical patients. *Nursing Research,* 20, no. 2 (March–April 1971): 113–122.

5. M. A. E. Ramsay. Survey of preoperative fear. *Anaesthesia*, 27, no. 4 (October 1972): pp. 396–402.
6. M. A. Bruegel. Relationship of preoperative anxiety to perception of postoperative pain. *Nursing Research*, 20, no. 1 (January–February 1971): 26–31.
7. Rosemary Williams. Handling anxiety. *Nursing '73*, 3, no. 9 (September 1973): 25.
8. *Ibid.*
9. Jean E. Johnson, James M. Dabbs, and Howard Leventhal. Psychosocial factors in the welfare of surgical patients. *Nursing Research*, 19, no. 1 (January–February 1970): 18–29.
10. *Op. cit.*
11. *Op. cit.*
12. *Op. cit.*
13. John Wolfer and Carl E. Davis. Assessment of surgical patients' preoperative emotional condition and postoperative welfare. *Nursing Research*, 19, no. 5 (September–October 1970): 403–414.
14. *Op. cit.*
15. *Op. cit.*
16. Elizabeth H. Winslow and Margaret F. Fuhs. Preoperative assessment for postoperative evaluation. *American Journal of Nursing*, 73, no. 8 (August 1973): 1372–74.
17. Mary G. Shetler. Operating room nurses go visiting. *American Journal of Nursing*, 72, no. 7 (July 1972): 1266–69.
18. *Op. cit.*
19. *Op. cit.*
20. *Op. cit.*
21. *Op. cit.*
22. *Op. cit.*
23. *Op. cit.*
24. *Op. cit.*
25. *Op. cit.*
26. Lawrence E. Holst and Harold P. Kurtz, eds. *Toward a Creative Chaplaincy*. Springfield, Illinois: Charles C Thomas, 1973.
27. R. Bouchard and N. F. Owens. *Nursing Care of the Cancer Patient*. 2nd ed. St. Louis: C. V. Mosby, 1972.
28. Robert N. Butler and M. I. Lewis. *Aging and Mental Health*. St. Louis: C. V. Mosby, 1973.
29. *Op. cit.*

Suggestions for Further Reading

Don Damsteegt. Pastoral visits to presurgical patients. *Journal of Religion and Health,* 14 (January 1975): 43–69.
Kenneth R. Mitchell. *Hospital Chaplain.* Philadelphia: Westminster Press, 1972.
Dennis E. Saylor, *And You Visited Me.* Medford, Ore.: Morse Press, 1979 (cf. Chapter 12, Counseling the surgical patient).

9

Crisis Intervention in Orthopedic Surgery:
Empirical Evidence of the Effectiveness of a Chaplain Working with Surgery Patients

John L. Florell, Ph.D.

Director, Pastoral Counseling and Consultation Service

The Health Center

Bloomington, Illinois

In the past ten to twenty years there has been considerable growth in the establishment of departments of pastoral care, social work, psychiatry, and broader nursing services that have augmented the traditional medical procedure with spiritual and emotional support within the hospital setting.

Spokesmen for these helping professions say that they take some of the patient load off already overtaxed physicians and nurses. They claim they are accessible and that they make few demands of the patients. The problem has been that little of an empirical nature has been done to evaluate the impact of these professionals on the hospitalized patient.

For over twenty years studies have been reported that seemed to confirm that emotional preparation can aid healing. In the early 1950s pediatric patients were prepared for hospitalization and surgery by visits to the hospital, rehearsals of surgery, and having their family close throughout the hospitalization.[1] Janis's[2] research indicated psychological preparation could lower postoperative anxieties in such patients. In the early 1960s Egbert et al.[3] showed preparation of adults also seemed to have a positive effect on the healing process. Mason[4] found in certain types of surgery the speed of healing was dependent on the patient's faith in the healer, the healer's method, and the feeling that the method was relevant to the cause of the illness. Andrew[5] even found that with certain types of patients tape-recorded preparation could be helpful to the healing process.

In relation to the hospitalized patient, chaplains have long taken a supportive stance that seems consistent with the findings of the research cited above. The primary aim of the chaplain is to show the patient he is cared for and that any feelings the patient has are acceptable to deal with.

Crisis intervention theory, which refers to treating people around one of the crucial points in their lives, advocates an intense relation between the person in crisis and a professional who can help the person deal with his problem. The basic presupposition of crisis intervention work is that people are more open to help when they are under intense stress. Actual intervention seems to help because another person, who is more stable, is participating in the crisis with the person who is under stress, assuring him that his feelings and reactions are acceptable, and that the crisis can be resolved.

Development of Treatments

To find how the basic techniques of chaplain's support and crisis intervention could be applied to the hospitalized patient, forty-four orthopedic patients were interviewed, before any research was done, to find which patients felt helped or hindered in their recovery. Generally, these patients seemed to lack elemental information about the way that the hospital was operated and were in the dark as to whether their feelings about their operations were normal. Those patients who had a positive attitude about their operation emphasized their relationship with the staff or with their physician. Thirty-six out of forty-four felt that there had been an attempt by a member of the staff to deal with their feelings about surgery.

Two treatments were devised on the crisis intervention model to help patients deal with surgery. The first treatment, called support, was based on the primary stance of the chaplain. In the treatment the chaplain showed his concern for the patient through regular visits, when the patient's feelings and anxieties were talked about. The patient was assured his feelings were acceptable and that the chaplain would be with him if needed.

A second treatment, called support-information, was devised to augment the basic-supportive treatment with information that would help explain the hospital rhythm, role expectancies that hospital personnel had for patients, and practical knowledge of how to gain relief from pain, who to ask about recovery procedures, ordering food, etc. It was felt that this information would help prepare patients emotionally for surgery through anticipation and could reinforce the patient's confidence in the counselor and the entire hospital staff.

Method

Several different measures were used to evaluate the impact these treatments had on the healing process. These included identifying material such as age and sex; surgical-medical history, such as the number of previous hospitalizations, length of stay in the hospital, and the type of surgery being performed; basic psychological make-up, such as the Spielberger transitory anxiety scores[6] and treatment ratings; and physiological and nonreactive measures from medical records and calls for service, such as pulse and respiration rates, amount of pain medication used, lines of nursing notes written, and calls for the bedpan, medication, and other services.

Orthopedic surgery patients were studied before, during, and after hospitalization in the following areas: length of stay in the hospital, use of pain medication, state of anxiety, physiological measures, comparison of physician and patients' ratings of the patients' pain, stress, and satisfaction, the patients' own rating of their treatment, and the amount written about each patient in nursing notes.

Patients were divided by three different phases in the study. In all there were three groups: the control group N-50, a support group N-30, and a support-information group N-70. In the first phase, group number one, called the control group, received normal hospital care. During the second phase two groups were formed using random number selection. Group two, N-30, called support, received the support treatment, and group three, N-30 called support-information, received the support-information treatment. During the final phase group three with N-40 was continued from the second phase and received support-information treatment.

Groups were compared on the variables listed above, using a one-way analysis of variance. Patients were measured on certain variables before and after surgery and with the type of data gathered on these variables, sign tests were constructed and chi-square scores were calculated to compare the impact of the treatments on the healing process.

All groups were found to be relatively equivalent presurgically on all the following variables: age, sex, number of previous hospitalizations, type of surgery, manifest anxiety, pulse, respiration, temperature, amount of pain medication, lines of nursing notes written, and calls for bedpans, medication, and service. Therefore, it was postulated that any differences among the three groups postsurgically on these variables would be a function of the treatments given to them.

Both the support and support-information groups were found to have significant impact on healing when compared with the control group. Though less dramatic, the support-information group seemed to have a greater impact than the support treatment alone. All results reported were significant at the .05 level of significance.

As shown in Figure 9-1, the control group stayed almost a day longer in the hospital after their operation than the support group, and two days longer than the support-information group. Figure 9-2 shows that treatments given before surgery raised the transitory anxiety of both treatment groups almost four points higher than the control group. However, Figure 9-3 demonstrates that the transitory scores of the control group increased almost five points after surgery, while the support group decreased 1.8 points and the support-information group 3.3 points. Thus the control group had

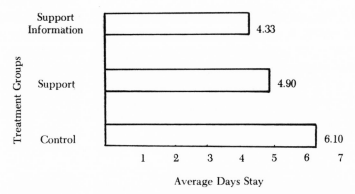

FIGURE 9–1.   Days of stay in the hospital from the day of surgery.

transitory anxiety scores over two points higher than the support group and four points higher than the support-information group. Figure 9-4 indicates that the control group made many more calls for service than either treatment group, and that the support group made more calls than the support-information group. The control group patients were more incongruent with their surgeon's assess-

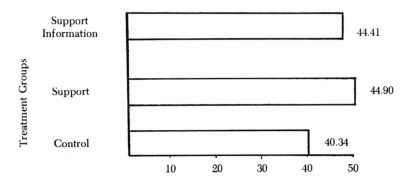

FIGURE 9–2.   Transitory anxiety scores after treatment and before surgery from the Spielberger[6] State-Trait Anxiety Inventory.

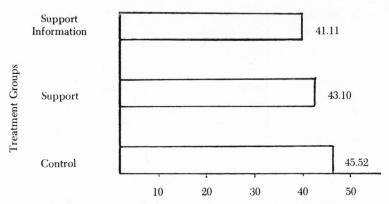

FIGURE 9-3. Transitory anxiety scores on the second day after surgery from the Spielberger State-Trait Anxiety Inventory.

ment in their own assessment of the pain and stress they endured during surgery than either treatment group as shown in Figure 9-5.

Table 9-1 provides additional evidence of the effect that the crisis intervention treatments had on the surgery patient. Treatment groups used less pain medication, had lower physiological responses, and had less written about them in nursing notes than did the control group.

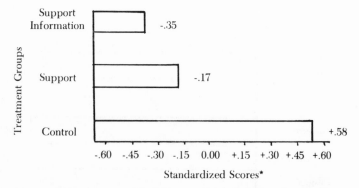

FIGURE 9-4. A comparison of monitored calls by group using standardized scores. Scores were standardized from a checklist kept on calls from pain medication, bedpan service, and physicians and nurses using OMNITS. Lower scores indicate fewer calls.

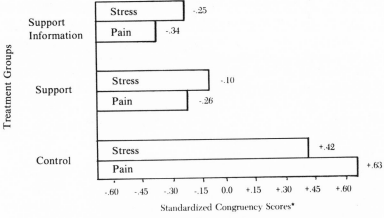

FIGURE 9-5. Standardized congruency scores comparing physician and patient ratings of pain and stress. Scores were standardized from physician and patient ratings of the patient's pain and stress using OMNITS. Lower scores indicate more agreement in ratings.

Discussion

The most pragmatically significant result of this study appears to be that patients were able to leave the hospital from one to two days sooner in the groups that received crisis intervention treatment. The implication of this for hospital administration is obvious in terms of bed availability, physician time, cost, and patient satisfaction.

Another significant finding could be seen in the change of the Spielberger transitory anxiety scores from before surgery to after surgery scores. These scores indicated that treatments raised patients' anxiety in anticipation of their surgery. Control patients, though their anxiety scores rose before surgery, were far below the treatment groups rises. It seems helping patients face their fears of surgery raised their anxiety initially, but helped them adapt to recovery and lowered their anxiety postsurgically. Patients who received support and information were significantly less anxious than the support group. (See Figures 9-2 and 9-3.) The present study indicates that the anxiety of the treatment groups presurgically was

TABLE 9-1. Measure Taken the First and Second Days after Surgery and the Third Day after Surgery till Release

	1st and 2nd Day	3rd Day till Release
A. The Quantity of Pain Medicine Used by Group		
SUPPORT—INFORMATION	3.76	1.76
SUPPORT	4.47	2.60
CONTROL	5.16	3.30
B. Respiration Rate by Group		
SUPPORT—INFORMATION	17.84	17.83
SUPPORT	17.93	17.78
CONTROL	19.18	18.42
C. Pulse Rate by Group		
SUPPORT—INFORMATION	81.36	76.87
SUPPORT	80.47	75.69
CONTROL	86.42	80.02
D. Lines of Nursing Notes Written for Each Group		
SUPPORT—INFORMATION	9.26	4.60
SUPPORT	9.93	5.17
CONTROL	13.30	7.50

helpful in that it was directly related to the realistic threat of surgery.

Recent research conducted by Spiegel has shown that the level of a patient's anxiety can influence his perception of pain. The correlation of the use of pain medication and the transitory anxiety of patients seems to support this thesis. In addition, it indicates intervention treatment can affect the use of pain-killing drugs.

The calls each patient made to the nursing station were noted on a prepared check list. The control group made many more requests for service from staff than either of the treatment groups. It appears that the treatment team, consisting of chaplains, social workers, and the nursing staff, was able to lower the demands patients made on the regular staff and their physicians. Use of auxiliary personnel already present in many hospitals may make a significant impact on patient healing, especially if such personnel can give information to orient the patient to his treatment and to the operations of the hospital.

Both the support and the support-information groups appeared to affect the physiological responses of the patients. These responses were seen in the lower respiration and pulse rates (Table 9-1), indicating less anxiety and physical tension. Thus, it appears that the treatments used aided the patients' physical recovery.

Patients in the support and support-information groups were more realistic in their attitudes about their operations than were the control group patients. Figure 9-4 shows their ratings of pain, stress, and satisfaction were closer to the more objective ratings of their physicians.

These same patients were also more satisfied with their treatment than were the control group patients. An important part of the attitude patients had was related to their feeling less pain, recovering more quickly, and being able to be released ahead of the control group. The positive attitude these patients had holds important potential for the hospital. It is good for the hospital image in the community, and it could be of benefit if the patient needs hospitalization in the future.

Summary

In conclusion, it appears that the crisis intervention technique used in this study had a significant impact on the healing process. Evidence seems to show that chaplains were effective in using these techniques.

This study indicates that giving the patients a reference point, helping them focus on the experience of surgery, aiding them in making sense out of the whole experience of surgery and recovery through information, and letting the patients know they were cared for has a significant impact on the healing process.

Notes

1. K. Jackson et al. Behavior changes indicating emotional trauma in tonsillectomy children. *Pediatrics*, 12 (1953): 23–28.
2. Irving Janis. *Psychological Stress*. New York: John Wiley, 1958.
3. L. Egbert et al. Reduction of postoperative pain by encouragement and instruction of patients. *New England Journal of Medicine*, 270 (1964): 825–827.
4. R. Mason, et al. Acceptance and healing. *Journal of Religion and Health*, 8, (1969): 123–142.
5. J. Andrew. Recovery from surgery, with and without preparatory instruction, for three coping styles. *Journal of Personality and Social Psychology*, 15 (1970): 223–226.
6. C. Spielberger, et al. *The S.T.A.I. Manual*. Tallahassee, Florida, 1969, Mimeograph Copy.

Suggestions for Further Reading

Ed Christian and Judy Vanderman. A study to determine if visitation of the hospital chaplain decreases anxiety. Copies available from Christian: Chaplain's Office, Porter Memorial Hospital, Denver, Colorado. 80210.
Stephen E. Skov. *The Role of the Pastor to the Surgical Patient*. Springfield, Illinois: Concordia Theological Seminary, 1968.

certain patients.[4] However, there is often a concomitant increase in anxiety as the patient begins to realize the situation he is in. As Beard has put it, he is caught between "the fear of death and the fear of life."[5] Tolstoi has written of one of his characters ". . . Ivan Illych knew that he was dying; but far from growing used to this idea, he simply did not grasp it—he was utterly unable to grasp it." Yet, with regularity, the dialysis patient is reminded—either by his lack of strength, or by his diet restriction, or by the dialysis periods themselves—that life will never be the same again and at the end there is death. The universal response is denial to a lesser or greater degree. Denial has been defined as "a mechanism of defense in which the facts or logical implications of external reality are refused recognition in favor of internally defined, wish-fulfilling fantasies."[6] For the dialysis patient, "external reality" is "the Machine," all that it represents and actually is. The "wish-fulfilling fantasy" is the wish not to be ill.

It must be recognized that for these people denial may not be bad—it is often a very useful defense, and when it is strong it is best left alone. While each situation must be evaluated individually, I believe that intervention should not be attempted unless the denial is moving toward psychotic proportions, or unless it is having a destructive effect on the patient's family. While denial may appear to make a difficult situation more acceptable, its unacknowledged operation may prove to be counterproductive if it is masking a reality that can be better handled in another way, one that is within the reach of the patient concerned. The objectivity of the chaplain in the renal team's discussions can be of great help when decisions about "good" and "bad" denial are taking place.

By the third or fourth week, an equilibrium has usually been reached, and it can be judged how well the person is going to tolerate being on chronic hemodialysis. In a recent paper, Fishman et al. presented important findings which verified clinically what we have long known—namely, that laboratory values can be quite independent of the patient's affective condition and his physical symptom.[7] Medical staff can be seduced by the values given them by the technicians who monitor BUN, creatinine 8, and other blood and urine values. A non-medical person is needed in the hemodialysis unit who will respond to what the patient is saying and feeling—not what the laboratory values are saying. That person can be the chaplain. At times I have been struck by the discrepancy between the way the patient will describe his condition to me, and the description recorded by the doctor in the patient's chart. On reflection it is easy to understand that if the doctor keeps telling the patient he is doing well—which is what the latest values show—when the patient feels badly, it must become easier as the days go by for him to tell the doctor nothing about what he is feeling, or what he is troubled about.

The patient should know that with his minister it is OK to talk about his aches and pains, that his weakness and breathlessness and rotten feelings are acceptable. If the patient does not know that from the minister, he must sometime begin to wonder if his struggle is worthwhile. The patient should also be given opportunity to talk about "the Machine" which looms large in his ambivalence. As one patient told me—"I hate it. It makes me a living cadaver." There are many feelings in the area of depersonalization and changes in body image, exploration of which will help the patient.

A second area of conflict lies in having to depend on the machine, a technician or family member to help with dialysis, a limited diet and a doctor on the one hand, while on the other hand he is expected to be "normal" in maintaining his family relations and his work schedule. The tension between being dependent and independent can be resolved in many ways. He may have the flexibility to adjust to the tension, but if his dependency needs are unresolved he will either wholeheartedly embrace the sick role, or he will rebel against the whole program. Excessive dependency is seen in the person who makes little or no attempt to learn the procedures taught in the home-training program, who becomes very demanding, especially on the family, saying he can do nothing for himself because he is sick. The counterdependent will take little or no care of his shunt or machine, and will abuse his diet. It usually takes three to six months on dialysis before this conflict is fully resolved and the patient can resume something similar to his former pattern of living. Contact with the pastor during dialysis can give the opportunity to the patient to share his thoughts and feelings about the bind he is in and the way his problems are working out. This is best done not in the presence of the spouse, especially if the spouse is the other person involved in the dialysis regimen.

A third area of conflict, as mentioned above, is the person's ambivalence about living or dying. For the dialysis patient, the question is simply, "Is it worth living?" Most patients consider suicide at some point. According to one study which considered data on 3,478 dialysis patients in the United States after "unexplained" and "accidental" deaths were excluded, it was shown that approximately one out of every twenty terminated their lives through direct or indirect suicidal behavior.[8] The usual indicators suggesting suicide, plus behavior that would lead to death, such as eating binges, drinking excessive amounts of liquids, and so on should be watched for by the minister.

A consistent relationship with the pastor in which the above three areas of conflict can be explored may mean the difference between life and death for the patient.

Ministry to the family will depend on the condition of the patient, and the kind of support that the immediate family can receive from the extended one and the local community at large. The future always has a question mark against it, and social, economic, and marital problems are always present to a greater or smaller extent. I have found that the children in the family are the forgotten ones in this situation. I encourage parents to bring their children to the hospital so that the family and I can sit down together, and the children be encouraged to share their fantasies, and to ask any questions that they have.

The Nephrectomy

The person who elects to receive a transplanted kidney will usually have both his kidneys removed before the transplant itself, the surgery being done at least three weeks prior to the transplant. The minister visiting a patient before his nephrectomy will experience a person like any other who faces major medical procedure, with a number of unique aspects added. In a way the patient is relieved. At last something is going to be done to "cure" him.

However, the surgery also intensifies any doubts about what he is committing himself to. He knows that medically he needs help because without it he will surely die, but many persons, even when their kidneys have produced no urine for an extended period, hope that the kidneys will magically begin to function again. The Christian may look for a "miracle." After nephrectomy, that hope is gone, and after surgery the patient may need help to mourn his kidney loss. He must also wait for his new kidney, which when it comes from outside the immediate family may mean a period of six to twelve months. Ministry should provide opportunity for ventilation of feelings of frustration, anger, and doubt. These feelings may be found in day-to-day matters, or within the context of religious questions the patient raises. The patient may say he has begun to lose his faith, or that God is no longer real to him, that he seems to have lost touch with God.

No matter how well the patient is tolerating his dialysis regimen, he will at times be subject to other than his normal mood swings, and a typical (for him) emotional response. The spouse and children must live with these, as with the constant apprehension about death, economic insecurity, the stress of role change, and sexual frustration. They too benefit from a situation in which they can ventilate and think about the future.

Finding a Kidney

When a person opts for transplant, the first problem is finding a kidney that is suitable. This involves sophisticated testing of blood and tissue from both the recipient and the potential donor. The greatest chance for a successful transplant is when the donor is related to the recipient, and so the choice may fall on the siblings or parents of the patient. For some families, the decision to give a kidney is made with little turmoil, but for many it is not an easy choice. The strain involved for the patient and his family is well documented in papers with such titles as "Family tension in the search for a kidney donor."[9] The pastor best ministers to the patient by helping him to clarify his own feelings about the person who may be the donor. He ministers to the family as a whole by attempting to ensure that the decision is made openly, without scapegoating or blackmail on the part of any family member.

The Transplant

After the surgery there is only one concern—is the kidney working? Ministry will depend on the answer to that question. When the answer is yes, and the kidney continues to function well, and there are no complications, the patient is surprised at his own progress. He may even be euphoric from the drugs he is receiving. But if the kidney functions poorly or not at all, the patient becomes depressed, occasionally sullen and hostile. He may also feel guilty, believing that he has let the donor down, a concern that masks feelings of disappointment and anger. If the person has to go back to the kidney machine, it is as if all has been for naught.

The impact of the drug regimen is significant. Two drugs, Prednisone and Azathioprine, are used to prevent rejection of the new kidney. The former produces widely varied responses in people, from nothing noteworthy to a toxic, "psychotic" state, the latter more often in older persons in my experience.[10] Relatively common responses include euphoria, insatiable appetite, intensified response to lights and colors. The minister can help the patient at this time by assuring him that what he is feeling is largely due to the drugs, and that the side effects will go away in time. If a patient does begin to slip into a psychotic episode, the minister can allay some of the patient's fears by simple and frequent reassurance that he is not "going crazy" or "losing his mind." Azathioprine is used to prevent rejection and one side effect of this drug is to lower the patient's white blood cell count, making him more vulnerable to infection.

As he is told more about these effects, and of other drugs after surgery, the patient may be learning for the first time that he will have to be on drugs for the rest of his life. A new awareness begins to impinge. Perhaps for the first time, the patient knows in a fuller sense that his surgery has not cured him, only extended his life. He can live a normal life, but with limitations. Most patients can accept these as the price they must pay for continued survival. The super-independent will go his own way; the anxious and fearful tend to restrict their lives unnecessarily, and need strong permission to begin to live again. After an extended period of sickness it is hard to believe that one might be well again!

Some patients who have received a cadaver kidney are interested in knowing where it came from. I attempt to know little and preferably nothing about the source of a cadaver kidney. There have been reports in the literature about situations where the recipient has learned the source with unfortunate consequences, and we have attempted to avoid such situations. Certainly the fantasies that surround the newly received organ, while not as dramatic as with a transplanted heart, are nevertheless important. A forty-two-year-old black man had received a new kidney five weeks previous and was still waiting for it to begin to work. He shared a fantasy related to his disappointment. He said the kidney was a "white Irish kidney—you know, very stubborn and prejudiced."

Convalescence

As patients recover from the surgery, and if the new kidney works well, they begin to return to their former selves to the astonishment of staff members who never knew them as they were. Their affect returns to normal and their dreams may revolve around food, and the preparing of elaborate meals. The emotional response of one patient can be gauged in her serious comment, "I had it (the first urine she made) in the measuring glass, and they went and threw it out. I wanted to keep it and take it home."

During this period, many people reflect on their recent experiences and often speak of their "new birth" or the "miracle" that God has worked. In my experience, the majority of patients speak of their transplant experience in religious terms. They often wish to reorder their lives. In a real sense the gift of the kidney they received is also a burden they must carry. Many younger patients begin to think of their life's vocation in terms of service to others. Older persons wish to give more of their time to the Church, or the local Kidney Foundation, or to some other community-minded group. The feeling seems to be one of indebtedness that must somehow be repaid.

With the recovery of urinary output and completion of the healing process, a new set of ambivalences must be resolved. The dependent person who has enjoyed the gratification of being sick must decide whether he wishes to continue in the sick role, or whether he wishes to be well again. Though it was more obvious several years ago, the transplant patient still enjoys something of a celebrity role—a status some persons reject, but which some play to the hilt. The clergy's ministry should include a close scrutiny of the way the patient sees his future, and what use he wishes to make of his experiences. If it is not accepted as simply one episode—albeit, an important one—in the person's life, it may become a god around which his life revolves.

From a chronic, debilitating illness, through a medical regimen involving considerable physical, emotional, and spiritual impact, to an almost normal life—that is the magnitude of the changes which must be met. For this reason we have not been surprised when patients have reported that when they first went home, for perhaps the first six to nine months, they found themselves irritable at times, and wishing to be left alone. The pastor can help in the area of interpersonal relations at this time. As stated above, the period of increasing renal failure has often created considerable tension in the family. Spouses may need help in clearing away some of the unresolved emotional baggage they are carrying. The spouse should know that in spite of the surgery the patient is not fully recovered, and will never be the same as he was before he became sick.

The patient may have fears for the safety of his kidney, now lying in the front of his body. There may be fear of physical damage, for instance that in playing with children he may be kicked in the stomach. There may be fantasies associated with intercourse. Though rarely verbalized, the patients are often apprehensive that their sexual organs will not function, or that if they have intercourse they may damage themselves in some way. One man asked me if his kidney could "fall out" if he had intercourse.

Doctors are usually reluctant to encourage their women patients to become pregnant, though several women are known to have had successful pregnancies following transplants.

In some patients, especially but not exclusively the younger and unmarried, changes in body image secondary to the drugs cause worry and anger. The patient needs support and should know that these changes will disappear when the daily dosage of Prednisone is less than 25 mgm. per day.

Summary

I have described the impact and cumulative effect that renal failure and its aftermath has upon a patient and his family. Pastoral care must be provided both within the hospital and outside, for the presence of severe renal failure in one family member leaves that family system in some degree of tension until that person dies. The pastor should be aware of the possible emotional responses at different stages in the treatment course, and respond appropriately. It is a demanding ministry, but one in which the courage and resilience of the human spirit can only evoke awe and wonder.

Notes

1. G. E. Schreiner. Mental and personality changes in the uremic syndrome. *Medical Annals of the D. of C.* 28, no. 6 (June 1959): 316–323.
2. G. Duea. Peritoneal dialysis and hemodialysis. *Medical Clinics of North America,* 55, no. 1 (January 1971): 155 ff.
3. *Ibid.* 159 ff.
4. The wide difference in the way persons tolerate dialysis is striking and has been carefully studied, but with no great consensus, c.f.
B. M. Glassman and A. Siegel. Personality correlates of survival in a long-term hemodialysis program. *Archives of General Psychiatry,* 22, no. 6 (June 1970): 566–574.

P. Sand, G. Livingstone, and R. Wright. Psychological assessment of candidates for a hemodialysis program. *Annals of Internal Medicine,* 64, no. 3 (March 1966): 602–609.

M. J. Short and R. J. Alexander. Psychological considerations for center and home dialysis. *Southern Medical Journal,* 62, (December 1969): 1476–1479.

5. B. H. Beard. Fear of death and fear of life—The dilemma . . . *Archives of General Psychiatry,* 21, no. 3 (September 1969): 373–380.

6. J. R. Nemiah. *Foundations of Psychopathology.* New York: Oxford University Press, 1960.

7. D. B. Fishman, A. A. Gottlieb and C. B. Pollock. Psychobiochemical case studies of 3 hemodialysis patients. *Psychosomatics,* 13, no. 5 (September 1972): 333–336.

8. H. S. Abram, G. L. Moore and F. B. Westervelt. Suicidal behavior in chronic dialysis patients. *American Journal of Psychiatry,* 127, no. 9 (March 1971): 1199–1203.

9. R. G. Simmons, K. Hickey, C. M. Kjellstrand, and R. L. Simmons. Family tension in the search for a kidney donor. *Journal of the American Medical Association,* 215, no. 6 (February 1971): 909–912.

10. H. P. Rome and F. J. Braceland. The psychological response to ACTH, or cortisone, hydrocortisone and related steriod substances. *American Journal of Psychiatry,* 108, (1952): 641–650.

Suggestions for Further Reading

H. S. Abram. Psychological dilemmas of medical progress. *Psychiatry in Medicine,* 3, no. 1 (January 1972): 51–58.

H. S. Abram. Psychiatric reflections on adaptation to repetitive dialysis. *Kidney International,* 6, no. 2 (August 1974): 67–71.

Barbara Brackney. The impact of home hemodialysis on the marital dyad. *Journal of Marital and Family Therapy,* 5, (1): 55–60, 1979.

R. C. Fox and J. Swazey. *The Courage to Fail: A social view of organ transplants and dialysis.* Chicago: University of Chicago Press, 1974.

M. T. Friedell. Organ transplantation and the quality of life. *International Surgery,* 59, no. 3 (March 1974): 135–136.

M. Lewis. Kidney donation by a 7-year-old identical twin child: psychological, legal, and ethical considerations. *Journal of Child Psychiatry,* 13, no. 2 (Spring 1973): 221–245.

M. E. Marty, and D. G. Peerman, eds. *New Theology Number 10*. Bios and theology. New York: Macmillan, 1973.

F. T. Rapaport, ed. *A Second Look at Life*. New York: Grune and Stratton, 1973.

J. E. Schowalter, J. B. Ferholt, and N. M. Mann. The adolescent patient's right to die. *Pediatrics*, 51, no. 1 (January 1973): 97–103.

M. Viederman. The search for meaning in renal transplantation. *Psychiatry*, 37, no. 3 (August 1974): 283–290.

11

Ministering to Persons with Drug Dependency Problems

E. W. Belter, D.D.
President and Executive Director
The Addiction Center
Racine, Wisconsin

One of my father's favorite jokes came out of Prohibition. Someone asked a man if he was for or against Prohibition. He answered: Yes!

When I ask some questions about persons with drug dependency problems, it may seem that the answers are equally ambiguous. They are not. But they illustrate some of the complexity and at the same time the simplicity of ministering to persons with drug problems.

Question: Are there greater numbers of persons with alcohol problems or with drug problems?
Answer: Yes.

Alcohol is the number one drug of abuse. Conservative estimates tell us that there are at least ten alcoholics for every addict or abuser of other drugs. We must consider alcohol and all other drugs in a chemical package.

If we wanted to enumerate the other drugs in order of abuse prevalence, I would say: the depressant and stimulant pills rank number two, the hallucinogens rank number three, and narcotics rank last, in frequency of abuse.

Question: Can we characterize the drug abuser or are they all different?
Answer: Yes.

There is indeed some commonality as we look at the various drugs of abuse. Alcohol is primarily abused by middle-aged men and women. We are rapidly approaching the point where there are almost equal numbers of male and female alcoholics. The pills are likewise primarily used by middle-aged people, especially women. Half of the woman alcoholics have a dual or triple addiction to alcohol, barbiturates, and/or amphetamines. There is a large proportion of youthful drug abusers who are on pills. Hallucinogens are primarily abused by youth and would-be (middle-aged) youth. Narcotics are primarily abused by youth and young adults. There are very few middle-aged or old narcotic addicts.

Question: Is addiction a moral problem or a disease?
Answer: Yes.

It is most probably a disease. By medical definition a disease is both progressive and predictable. So is addiction. There are charts of the progressive and predictable nature of addiction to alcohol. It would be quite similar for addiction to the barbiturates.

The workable definition of addiction is the "loss of control" factor. Anyone who is addicted, either psychologically or physically, loses control over his ingestion of the drugs. While there is a great deal of wrangling over what is and what is not addiction and what is abuse, I really fail to see the significance. From a working point of view, as a pastor and as a therapist, either psychological or physical addiction creates problems for the abuser or addict. Therefore therapy is needed.

One of the mistakes both for the general public and the abuser, is to dwell on the disease concept. Carried to an extreme, it permits the public to say there is nothing that can really be done because we cannot treat a disease where the sick person doesn't want treatment. It allows the diseased person to say that he can't help his condition. He is the victim of this progressive and predictable illness. Addiction has been equated with diabetes or other diseases. There is however some marked difference. Please, never let an addict "cop out" by saying he can't help his condition because it is a disease.

There is a responsibility that addicts bear for their disease. No one forced them to drink. No one forced them to shoot heroin. No one forced them to pop pills in their mouths. Most addicts did not intend to become addicts. They probably began as social drinkers or prescription-drug users or social hallucinogen users. Yet, through carelessness, peer pressure, social circumstances, and other excuses, their use turned to misuse and to abuse and to addiction.

Cancer can easily be detected by an inexpensive pap smear. Yet how many women come in with cancer that has progressed and is predictably terminal because they were careless about getting tests? How many people overwork and have a heart attack? The motivation may have been admirable, but the resultant neglect of self makes them responsible for their death. There is indeed a certain responsibility on the part of the addict for his condition.

Dr. Nelson Bradley, one of the most knowledgeable men in the field of addiction, defines it as a "spiritual cancer." This resolves a great many problems for pastors who are trying to wrestle with the disease concept versus the moral degeneration theory.

At the root of all addiction may be self-centeredness. This encompasses the entire alibi and denial process that will permit self-centeredness to prevail. It allows pride to predominate. This is morally indefensible. It finally brings a person to the point of addiction where they have lost all control and no longer have anything to say about their ingestion of drugs.

Question: Do we address the moral cause or ignore it when ministering to these persons?
Answer: Yes.

We do not initially go to a "root cause," be it moral or otherwise, when we begin to work with addicts. We focus on the present identifiable problem. They are abusing some chemical. They are harming themselves and their families. They are perhaps jeopardizing their jobs or their schooling. This is a "handle" that we can grab in trying to deal with these persons.

If you try to find some root cause, you will spend all your time wandering in the labyrinth of the past. The addict will have effectively blocked you from confronting him with the present problem. I know of no more ineffectual way to deal with addiction than to wander the pathway of the past.

Yet, we must deal with guilt. Here again there are some differences and some commonalities among addicts. The alcoholic feels guilt very deeply. The last thing an alcoholic needs is preaching. Whatever defense mechanisms that they may employ, almost all of them know and sense the guilt of their past immorality very much. The narcotic addict is much like the alcoholic. Given sufficient time on narcotics, the addict is well aware of the illegality and immorality of his or her life. This is part of narcotic addiction: professional thievery and prostitution are the only ways to support a habit that may run to $100 a day or more. They therefore reach a point where they can't bear this kind of guilt; they want a better life.

The youthful abuser also knows guilt but generally refuses to face it. The common technique is simply to change his base of morality. Deny any wrongdoing. Yet, time after time, youngsters, coming to the point of really trusting us, will admit that things are not right. Then, they begin to admit what is wrong. They wrestle with the problem more acutely than older addicts. Two young addicts finally admitted to our staff that someone in our office was trying to sell hash. Now, they didn't want to squeal on her, yet they knew that she couldn't do this in the A-Center. It would ruin the program because it would create mistrust of our motives and procedures. So even though they were reluctant, by youthful standards, to get the pusher in trouble, they finally realized they had to do it. They did it uneasily but they did it. They finally recognized that right may be painful, but it is right.

Never let an addict off the hook of responsibility for the immorality of his abusive chemicals or concomitantly immoral life. Alcoholics Anonymous zeroes in on guilt with two painfully marvelous steps from their Twelve Step program. Step 4 says: "We will take a searching, fearless moral inventory of ourselves." Step 5 says: "We will admit to God, to ourselves, and to another human being the exact nature of all of our shortcomings." I have samples of a guide that we use for patients to take the fourth step. These are questions that help them to examine themselves and to take their inventory. The inventory is not primarily concerned with the chemical abuse at all. It is concerned with self-centeredness, greed, lust, envy, prejudice, pride, and phoniness. It deals with the things that are the addiction of all of us. For we are indeed addicted to our sins. We are helpless of our own power to do anything about our wrongdoings. This same guide is then used as they articulate their shortcomings, in detail, to a clergyman. This process is devastating. It is like violent vomiting. It hurts and tastes horrible coming up, but it must come out. Only then can something nourishing be put in to take its place.

This fourth- and fifth-step process is useful for all persons who abuse chemicals. Indeed, it is useful for each one of us. I recommend that you take a fourth step and a fifth step. It could do wonders for you.

There are some differences in holding the addict accountable because of the process of denial of the basic morality that most of us would hold true. The youthful rebel is more difficult to bring to the point of confession and repentence. It takes a longer process, exposure to the discipline of love, exposure to the visual and verbal proof of drug-free peers. This seems to be the best approach to use with youngsters. It can also be done with older people who are completely honest, completely loving and gracious.

Usually the accountability is first admitted to the pastor or to another personal counselor. He is the personification of their accountability to God. Then, there seems to be another step regarding accountability to the law of the land and to society as a whole.

Question: Can a diagnosis and evaluation of a person's spiritual condition be known by the pastor or is it entirely a personal matter with the addict?
Answer: Yes.

The spiritual life certainly is a very personal and individual thing. It differs from person to person. At the same time, it can indeed be known by the pastor. Just as there can be a rather precise medical, psychological, and social diagnosis and evaluation, so it can also be with the spiritual life of a person.

You have been given a sample of a spiritual diagnosis we use at the A-Center. We measure the externals: Baptism, Confirmation, worship record, Communion record, membership, use of scripture and Church activities. We can also measure their concepts. These frequently do not measure up to a seemingly strong but obviously superficial membership and Christian education. At the same time, some indicate that their catechism took real root when they were youngsters, for they still hold concepts that are not only orthodox and sound but intensely personal convictions.

It takes some practice, but you can learn to diagnose the concepts. Do they really know God as a person or is He some abstract power? Do they really apply goodness and sin against the will of God, or only the will of society, or merely their own preference? Can they concretize love and mercy regarding their own relationship to God and other people or is it an abstract theory? Do they want a soft, "piddly" kind of love and mercy and goodness, or do they realize the discipline of love and grace? These are the kinds of questions you can began to ask. Following this with their ideas of how they can relate to God, the Church, and a pastor and how they do now relate gives you further indication of their progress and the commitment they have to their religion.

Yes, indeed it is highly individualistic, but it is also measurable. I encourage you to be as precise as you can in knowing the patient rather than going "by guess and by golly."

Finally, we come to this question, and here I will be as unambiguous as possible: Should you be primarily a pastor, a psychologist, or a social worker?

Answer: Be a pastor before you are anything else. Each of us is entranced with a medical model or the psychotherapeutic model. But we trained to be pastors. Be one, please.

The other day I was confronted by the wife of a man who was dying of a tumor on the brain. She asked: "Dr. Belter, would you please go and pray with my husband?" I inquired about her own pastor. She indicated that he came and talked and joked with her husband. He covered some personal financial problems where advice was needed. But he never prayed, never read Scripture, and administered Holy Communion only at the insistence of the wife. I phoned the pastor. He said: "I didn't want him to feel depressed. And when you start to pray with them and give Communion, they think they are dying." I said: "But the man is dying and nobody wants to tell him." Now I think the pastor had failed utterly. He may have been quite successful as a friend and jokester and financial advisor but he failed in his real role.

Each patient needs assurance of believable grace in Christ. The one thing that is unbearable in anyone's life is the feeling of rejection and unworthiness. Our Lord Jesus had himself killed to prove that the love of God exists for all people, no matter how rotten their lives may have been. If there is one truth in this world that is meaningful for everyone, it is the fact of the atonement, of love and forgiveness of God, despite our unworthiness.

Everyone needs relief from guilt. It does no good to detoxify them, to treat their liver damage or their gastro-intestinal problem or cardiac problem. It does no good to have psychotherapy or family counseling or marital counseling or vocational counseling or any other therapy if there is unresolved guilt. With guilt remaining there may be no self-image, no hope, no regeneration. There must be the grace of Christ to make the man feel clean. There must be the assurance of the power of the spirit of God to make a man new. We must remember that an addict has lost control and is helpless.

Then, let the medical man treat him medically, let the psychotherapist deal with that aspect, let the counselors deal with the social problems and family problems. But let us first and foremost deal with his relationship to Christ. As one member of a team that treats the whole person, we must bring him to face guilt; to hear the gospel, the good news of God's love and grace; to surrender to Christ's forgiveness; and to know the power of the Holy Spirit for rebirth each day. Then, with other help from other disciplines, we will see a new man raised to live a new day.

Suggestions for Further Reading

A. Y. Cohen. The journey beyond trips: Alternatives to trips. *Journal of Psychedelic Drugs,* 3 (Spring 1971): 16–21.

C. Nahal, ed. *Drugs and the Other Self.* New York: Harper and Row, 1971.

James O. Orcutt and Richard E. Caril. Social definitions of the alcoholic: Reassessing the importance of impartial responsibility. *Journal of Health and Social Behavior,* 20: 290–295, 1979.

John D. Spangler. *Pastoral Care of Young Drug Users and their Families.* New York: National Council of Churches, 1971.

John L. Young. Coping with student drug use. *Journal of Pastoral Care,* 28 (March 1974): 40–50.

12

Balm for Burned Patients

Claude V. Deal, Jr., B.D.
Chaplain Supervisor
The Williamsport Hospital
Williamsport, Pennsylvania

Is there no balm in Gilead? Is there no physician there? Why then has the health of the daughter of my people not been restored?

Jeremiah 8:22

The lamentations of the Old Testament prophet over the shortcomings of his fellow countrymen ring clearly in this passage. In his moment of despair and grief, he was reminded of the similarities between those who are sick in spirit and those who are sick in body. Even from Gilead, the source of the medicinal salve called balm, there seemed to be no available ointment or healing hand to supply the needed curatives. Jeremiah longed for delivery from the sicknesses afflicting his people and pled for their restoration to health.

At times I have felt some identification with the lamentations of this ancient sage. Few patients tax the physical facilities, the medical acumen, and the emotional resources of the hospital as much as the patient who has been burned. The effects of burns are particularly devastating upon those at either end of life's spectrum, the very young and the aged. Care for the burn patient is surely one of the more demanding activities in terms of total hospital confinement, medical costs, and continuing rehabilitative treatment. Its strain upon family life, financial resources, and the energies of all concerned is beyond question. A known fact is that few institutions are able to handle more than a few of such patients at one time. Of the more than 6,000 hospitals in the nation, only around 180 have established special units to treat those who are burned.

A review of morbidity and mortality studies reveals wide variants in the number of people involved in burn episodes each year. Some of the more reliable statistics suggest that approximately 75,000 people are hospitalized annually for treatment. Of that number, 12,000 die from burn injuries or related complications. Despite the ever-increasing population, the number of fatali-ties continue to remain fairly stable as medical techniques for treating these patients improve.

My initial interest in the burn patient came a few years ago when a training program assignment on the Burn Unit of the North Carolina Memorial Hospital led to a research study. Data was recorded on thirty patients whose stay in the hospital ranged from three days to eight months. Many of the conclusions drawn through this study have been incorporated in the body of this chapter. Continuing involvement with the unit, directly and indirectly, has brought about some additional thinking, concerns, and ideas on my part.

The "Aggressor" Strikes

When the badly burned patient is admitted to the hospital, he is often in a state of severe physical pain and shock. He may be only minutes or hours removed from the traumatic moment when he was transformed into a "human torch." More than likely, the incident is blurred with mental pictures of himself in flames and the excited efforts of helpers who pommeled his body until the fire was reduced to invisible internal "burnings." Many of the mechanisms which were then set in motion will seem to him more like a nightmare than reality. Amidst the constant pain and discomfort, a continuous series of treatments began which included Hubbard tank baths, debridement, skin graftings, intravenous feedings, pills and needles in rapid succession, and many other frightening new medical adventures.

During the acute phase, almost every burned patient shows extreme concern over the injury. The immediate problem is, "Will I survive?" This question can persist for six to eight weeks and occasionally even longer. One nine-year-old girl continued to express fear of death through her four and one-half months of confinement in the hospital. The youthful mind seems especially prone to misinterpret and magnify the nature of bodily injuries. The danger of death is real, however, and many who enter the hospital never return home.

The presence of intense pain and prolonged discomfort is a persistent reality and practically every therapeutic procedure attempted adds to this pain. Even the more routine nursing activities such as changes of linen and bed baths contribute to the discomfort. What intact skin areas remain are used for graft donor sites or for injections. The Burn Unit is quite often, therefore, a place where much crying, moaning, screaming, and shouts for relief can be heard.

As a patient begins to realize that death is not imminent, he also becomes increasingly aware of the endless days and weeks he has spent in the hospital. Anxiety often gives way to depression during this stage. A man who had served a term in prison described his convalescence after later being burned as something akin to "being on the chain gang." Another said it seemed as though he was "going to be here forever." Family and friends do not visit as often at this stage and the initial flood of cards trickles down to almost zero. He is alone and the whole experience is seen for the most part as an unwelcome and disheartening one.

Patient A was a sixty-year-old female of Greek background, born in Cyprus and a resident of this country for about forty years. She had 23 percent burns sustained from a fire in her home. Her husband was slightly injured in the same fire. At the time of admission, she was making plans to visit her ninety-year-old mother in Cyprus. She often cried during our visits and questioned why this had happened to her. It was difficult for her to accept the slowness with which her wounds healed. She vividly expressed on several occasions how her room seemed to be a "prison" for her and the walls were getting smaller and smaller. She would complain to the staff that, "I've been in the hospital too long." Her feelings of impatience were complicated by the intense desire to return to Cyprus. Hospitalization lasted for eleven weeks.

The patient is typical of many who find the recovery process extending far beyond their imagined estimates. Even the physician's projected deadlines often prove inaccurate. The length of confinement is, in itself, a depressing factor and the long days take on qualities of sameness and boredom. The staff may not appear to be as concerned as before. The stimulations of normal daily living seem far removed.

When the patient finds his doubts about survival subsiding, a new set of anxieties comes into play. He now asks "What handicaps will I have and what things will I be able to do?" "How long will it be before I can return home to those I love?"

The degree of fear related to disfigurement may be closely associated with the location of burn scars. Facial scars intensify these fears. These feelings are often generated as the burned individual anticipates going home where he must test out his "acceptibility" among old friends he has not seen since the accident. He already knows that strangers stare at those who have physical abnormalities and the disfigured patient wonders how he can handle such behavior. The black patient is especially concerned about his appearance when his face has undergone significant coloration changes.

The extent to which the patient harbors his fears about his future is of supreme importance. His vocational prospects and his ability to support a family may hinge on his coping with these fears. For a woman, it may involve her capacity to resume her role as a wife and mother. Of equal importance is the person's ability to accept permanent disfigurement and handicaps. Unless he can realistically face his limitations as well as develop his potentials, he may fail to return to his home and job and to function at an optimal level.

Other "Marks" That Show

The trauma of the experience of being burned creates within the patient an assorted series of crises, reactions, and demands. The burn accident inflicts not only physical insults to the body, but also places tremendous stress upon the emotional stability of the patient. These stresses are manifested in his feelings about himself as well as his feelings toward those who are involved in his total situation.

Patients struggle with the dilemma of being suddenly plunged into a state of helplessness and dependency. The burn patient may be unable to handle such normal activities as feeding himself and caring for bowel and bladder functions. In many ways, he finds himself back in the stage of infantilism. Knowing that he must look to the medical staff for fulfillment of his basic needs, the patient often becomes submissive and compliant. The fear of being viewed as a "bad" patient is very real. One person voiced the belief that if he were demanding or complaining, he would be punished by harsh medical care. Strong dependency behavior existed among twenty or thirty members of the study group. The greatest degree of dependency occurred during times of pain and anxiety and noticeably lessened just prior to discharge.

Guilt was most noticeable in adult patients who had to admit to excessive drinking or promiscuous sexual behavior. The accident was therefore interpreted as a form of punishment for past indiscretions. Parents of children who have been burned also experience a high incidence of guilt. Although a lack of adequate supervision prevailed in most situations, the parental self-reproach was usually stronger than reality would dictate.

Varying indications of depression were observable in 59 percent of the patients. The more overt expressions of this were as follows: frequency in crying, attempts to withdraw from the staff, preoccupation with concerns about pain, constipation, and medical procedures, lack of motivation in performing prescribed routines, feelings of hopelessness, and refusal to eat. Seven of the nine children were depressed during certain phases of the illness. They were more open in their demands for attention than adults and could more easily express their feelings of loneliness. The prolonged separations from home had great impact upon the child's sense of security and well-being. A frequently used adaptive mechanism was that of withdrawal and attempts to bring the child into more involved interaction often failed. Periods of depression were experienced by from 11 to 51 percent of the adult patients. Nine of them were observed having episodes of crying related either to their present illness or to some past events which had become a part of their current problem. Feelings of hopelessness and despair about the future were often verbalized.

The long-term separation from family and friends imposed hardships on these burned patients. Being sent to a referral hospital meant, for most, a separation from home of from one to two hundred miles. The need for close and positive contact with family members often went unfulfilled. The most frequent visitors came on weekends and their presence had seldom coincided with the crisis situations experienced by the patient. Children could express hostility at the absence of the parents, but adults more frequently blamed the absence of visitors on such things as job or family demands, lack of transportation, and financial limitations. It is worth noting that twelve of the twenty-one adults were experiencing marital difficulties or had at the time no spouse in the home.

Lingering memories of and preoccupation with the horrors of the accident proved upsetting for most patients. Frequently, they could give vivid accounts of their feelings of being choked, trapped in a burning room, fighting to extinguish flames, and assuming that death was imminent. It seemed necessary for some to recount their stories numerous times before finding some relief from the tormenting thoughts. Two patients were burned while having *grand mal* epileptic seizures. Their recoveries were unspectacular and smooth. The absence of any traumatic memory appeared to aid the treatment and rehabilitative process.

"Anointing" the Wounded

The minister has an opportunity for bringing healing agents into the medical programs for the burned patient. His knowledge as a theologian is of course unique among the several specialties on the team, although he is not alone in his humanitarian concern for the patient. Through the building of pastoral relationships he brings into play a specialized and spiritualized set of dynamics. The balm which the minister can apply must grow out of his own faith and life, and its application will depend upon the skills he has acquired in making these healing agents a positive and concrete reality.

One basic premise for ministering to the burned will be the minister's own ability to withstand what he visually perceives in the Burn Unit. Much of what is seen is distasteful. Patients with trunk or limb injuries will most likely be lying naked with only a suspended sheet above the body in tentlike fashion. One cannot avoid being deeply shaken.

A severe burn also tends to deface a person's ego and to damage his self-esteem. As one patient stated, "I feel so dirty." This feeling reflected a painful assumption that he was now unattractive to others as well as to himself. This loss of self-esteem made him feel more worthy of loathing than of love.

The minister must, therefore, guard against transmitting any feelings of revulsion that may be aroused by the sight of the burn. The reaction of horror by hospital personnel who visit in this unit has been strongly felt. For this reason, many nonprofessional workers, such as admissions officers, ward secretaries, and volunteer workers, avoid direct contact with patients who are burned. Family members have their own set of reactions and will certainly need assistance in dealing with these feelings.

Patient attempts to test their degree of acceptableness are so intense that their efforts at times verge on exhibitionism. I have found many of them anxious to show their wounds to the minister in order to receive reassuring support and help. The minister cannot deny the actual body before him, for much of the patient's inner suffering is inseparably linked with the pains of the flesh.

Time and repeated exposure to the burn patient environment does much to enable the minister to handle his own reactions. The initial shocks are soon dulled by familiarity with the visual aspect. And the minister begins, with time, to have his own successes in dealing with patients, which gives security to his work with new patients admitted for treatment. The knowledge that most of these people will not die and that life will most likely improve over its present state is vital. His theology of hope has important bearing on his attitude toward the present.

The minister has also an opportunity here for establishing continuity in the interpersonal experiences of the patient. The fragmentation of relating to so many different people within a teaching institution is disturbing and anxiety-producing for one who has been seriously burned. During the long months of hospitalization, there will likely be a continuous succession of interns and residents who begin and terminate contact with the patient. For this reason, I propose that Burn Units not be placed on rotation schedules for students in Clinical Pastoral Education.

Where the need to think of one individual as "my doctor" may go unfulfilled, the minister offers, by his continuous involvement, a framework for dependency upon "my chaplain." Especially is this so in the numbers of patients with few family contacts. There is little doubt in my mind that the patient is greatly comforted by the face of the familiar in the midst of changing staff and medical ministrations.

The minister must also be open to varieties of experiences within the relationship. His role is to be flexible and respond diversely to the many emotional and spiritual hungerings of the sick and dying. In moments of anxiety, he can offer the listening, attentive ear which has a sedative effect. As the patient struggles with his despair and sense of defeat, the minister portrays and conveys the elements of hope, expectancy, and determination which the patient himself is unable to sustain. When the world seems so narrow and life outside the walls of the institution so unreal, the minister can supply the stimulations of life in more normal circumstances and bring them into the realm of the believable. The fear that paralyzes is calmed by the voice that speaks of the closeness of man to man and God to man. A small triumph is celebrated with jubilation. The longings for the deeper revelations from another human being are answered by the words of a man who, too, has had his own crucifixion and resurrection.

The minister is, therefore, responsible to his patient and can share the fullness of his own person—projecting more than his role as a professional. He can be, in the course of a relationship, not only minister and counselor, but friend, father, advisor, pastor, brother, and a caring human being.

A third aspect of ministering which is believed to have especial significance for the burn patient is the use of body contact as a form of nonverbal communication and this I utilize with liberality. It may present some risk in the setting of the Burn Unit where surface infections are an ever-present medical concern. Special precautions must be exercised when moving from patient to patient.

The principal physical contacts used in the patient's regimen are often uncomfortable and pain-inflicting. Tactile stimulation ceases to have any positive rewards. A kind of "cringe" reaction to the advances of other people toward him results, as the consequences are so often hurtful. The patient's contact with flames was such a disastrous event, that his reflexes tell him to avoid external physical stimuli.

The minister does not carry with him the image of pain inflictor when entering the sickroom. The patient, most likely, will expect from him the more soothing of the administrations he is to receive. The opportunity for introducing body contact in the context of positive, reassuring, and pleasant experiences is extremely meaningful.

There are strong similarities between the person with a burn and one with a skin disease. In New Testament days, the individual with skin abnormalities was frequently isolated and considered unclean, and this reaction is not without some modern day parallels. The minister must therefore reassure the patient that his skin condition does not strike him with fear or revulsion. Reaching out and touching are part of the dynamics of human interplay. Walls of separation are removed and greater depths of sharing are often reached by the touching of the suffering one. The act of touching serves as a form of reassurance and identification with the patient in his state. The need for intimacy and warmth may be supplied in just this way. I am reminded of the young man just returned from painful plastic surgery whose first words to the chaplain were, "Touch me, Chaplain. Please touch me." His request arose out of fear and the craving for human concern.

Patient B was a five-year-old Negro girl admitted with 15 percent burns to the chest and legs. During our second visit, she began playing with my hands. From then on, she continued to express tactile forms of communication. We often talked about her family as she played with my rings, watch, and glasses. She enjoyed playing a game in which we pulled each other's noses. At times, she would take the "preacher's glasses" and wear them while imitating me. During the third visit, she asked that I kiss her, which I did. At times she referred to herself as "your little girl" and requested to go home with the chaplain. Such exchanges continued throughout the hospitalization and at the time of her discharge she was considered quite ready and pleased to be going home.

Though this child was more demonstrative in acting out her needs than most, I felt that her behavior was not inconsistent with the basic longings of many a burned patient.

Working with children is a particularly challenging, but rewarding ministry. Most of those in the study had little or no concept of the chaplain's role. Many approaches were attempted to stimulate interaction with these youngsters. There were periods when each child lost control of bladder and bowel functions. Many of the achieved skills of growing up deteriorated and physical and emotional regression became evident. Involvement in simple play and reading activities seemed helpful and a sense of trust grew in this "new man who doesn't hurt me." Some projects such as writing and painting will have already been initiated as occupational therapy exercises and the minister can offer supportive assistance in these. Because these children are isolated from normal pediatric playroom programs, these activities often get overlooked. It has been necessary to remind volunteer and pediatric workers of the special needs of these young patients. Parents should be encouraged to participate in the various therapeutic activities, and their involvement often helps to decrease the guilt feelings parents develop after their child has been burned.

Because of the isolated nature of a Burn Unit and the common character of the medical problems there, patients tend to become deeply concerned with the progress of their fellow patients. The death of one can create emotional reactions which will need the close attention of the minister. On the other hand, the progress of one will often give great encouragement to those farther down the rehabilitative ladder. Frequently, two or three patients will gather and begin to share some of their deeper fears and hopes. Such occasions can be therapeutically directed by the minister. Fellow patients can also be particularly tough, and in this way helpful, when they see someone "giving up."

The minister working with burned patients will find his use of religious resources and the sacraments very similar to those used with others who are sick. Among the twenty-one adults in the study, prayer was used during visits with 62 percent of them. Five of this number requested prayer during each visit and one asked that "you send up a prayer for me each time you come, even if I am asleep." Reading of scripture, discussion of religious experiences and subjects, and affirmations of faith were all part of the ministry. Patient A who had recorded two visions of God in her life was deeply disturbed that a further vision had not occurred during her time of special need. Another patient affirmed his belief that while awaiting transfer to Memorial Hospital, a "preacher prayed the fire out of me." He claimed his burns had, since that moment, caused him no further discomfort. The use of such religious resources varied with patients according to their previous practices and beliefs.

In this study five of the six Negro girls were burned when their clothing caught fire from an open heater or fireplace. The other child had her dress ignited by a candle with which she and her brother were playing. The little Caucasian girl, two years old, was burned by hot water she turned on in the bathtub while the mother was hanging up clothes outside. The Caucasian boy was attempting to start a fire in the kitchen stove when his clothing ignited. Both parents were at work. The Negro boy was injured while burning trash outdoors. His mother was in New York state making funeral arrangements for an older son. The total number of siblings in these nine families was sixty-three, an average of seven per child. Again and again, the story yields a picture of poor housing, unsafe heating facilities, large families, inadequate supervision of children, and children with responsibilities beyond their age or maturity. These facts are a part of a tragic, but much larger problem of socioeconomic poverty. In the Burn Unit, we find some of the untold manifestations of a national problem which most of us recognize. The child is unjustly a prime target.

The Burn Unit will also contain a sizeable number of the sick and unfortunate persons in our society. Alcoholics are among those who turn up in the wards, along with men who do public work under unsafe conditions. There are, needless to say, some "pure accidents," but many of the situations result from a combination of social, family, an emotional problems.

A significant attack is being made on one front. The Congress of 1967 passed a Flammable Fabrics Act which established standards for measuring the burning characteristics of fabrics and passed legislation to control the marketing of hazardous fabrics. Working to prevent needless tragedies is the purest form of balm we can administer.

The longing felt in ministering to the sick for their restoration to health is an ancient one. Jeremiah sought a figurative balm for Gilead. There is a balm for the burned patient. Under the conviction of God's grace, the minister can bring a healing force into the lives of these people of God. May God grant us the gifts we need.

Suggestions for Further Reading

Alexandria Adler. Neuropsychiatric complications in victims of Boston's Coconut Grove disaster. *Journal of the American Medical Association,* 123 (December 1943): 1098–1101.

N. J. Andreasen, R. Noyes, Jr., C. E. Hartford, et al. Emotional reactions in seriously burned adults. *New England Journal of Medicine,* 586 (1972): 65.

Curtis P. Artz. Burns in my lifetime. *Journal of Trauma,* (October 1969): 827–833.

Joseph C. Aub, et al. *Management of the Coconut Grove burns at the Massachusetts General Hospital.* Philadelphia: J. B. Lippincott, 1943.

Norman R. Bernstein, et al. The functions of the child psychiatrist in the management of severely burned children. *Journal of the American Academy of Child Psychiatry,* 8 (October 1969): 620–631.

E. E. Bleck. Causes of burns in children. *Journal of the American Medical Association,* 158 (May 1955): 100–106.

Gene Brodland and N. J. Andreasen. NJC: adjustment problems of the family of the burned patient. *Social Casework,* 55: 13–18, 1974.

Barbara Brodie and Susan Matern. Emotional aspects in the care of a severely burned child. *International Nursing Review,* 14 (December 1967): 19–24.

P. Caudle, R. Kaim, and J. Potter. Characteristics of burned children and the after affects of the injury. *British Journal of Plastic Surgery,* 23 (January 1970): 63–66.

Rawley E. Chambers, et al. Clinical importance of emotional problems in the care of patients with burns. *New England Journal of Medicine,* 248 (February 1953): 355–359.

Ruth Cowin. Social factors in treating burned children. *Children,* 2 (November–December 1964): 229–233.

Major P. William Curreri, and Lt. Basil A. Pruitt. Evaluation and treatment of the burned patient. *American Journal of Occupational Therapy,* 24 (October 1970): 475–477.

Shirlee Davidson. Nursing management of emotional reactions of severely burned patients during the acute phase. *Heart and Lung,* 2 (1973): 370–375.

Eleanor R. Feller. Getting under the skin: transactional analysis and burn patients, in Roger N. Blakeney, ed., *Current Issues in Transactional Analysis.* New York: Brunner/Mazel, 1977, pp. 163–170.

Irving Feller, ed. *International Bibliography on Burns.* Ann Arbor: Brown-Brumfield, 1969.

David A. Hamburg, et al. Adaptive problems and mechanisms in severely burned patients. *Psychiatry,* 16 (February 1953): 1–20.

Joan C. Holter and Stanford B. Friedman. Etiology and management of severely burned children: psychosocial considerations. *American Journal of Disabled Children,* 118 (November 1969): 680–686.

Information Council of Fabric Flammability, Proceedings of the Third Annual Meeting. New York: Information Council of Fabric Flammability, 1969.

R. H. Kampmeier. Symposium on burns. *Southern Medical Journal,* 56 (October 1963): 1063–1090.

S. R. Lewis, et al. Psychological studies in burn patients. *Plastic and Reconstructive Surgery,* 31 (April 1963): 323–332.

Robert T. Long and Oliver Cope. Emotional problems of burned children. *New England Journal of Medicine,* 264 (June 1961), 1121–1127.

John D. MacArthur and Francis D. Moore. Epidemiology of burns: the burn prone patient. *Journal of the American Medical Association,* 231 (3) 259–263, 1975.

E. I. Matteson. Psychological aspects of severe physical injury and its treatment. *Journal of Trauma,* 15 (3) 217–234, 1975.

Harry Estill Moore. Some emotional concomitants of disaster. *Mental Hygiene,* 42, (January 1958): 45–50.

Neurological and psychiatric complications of burns. *British Medical Journal,* 2 (November 1963): 1350–1351.

Eugene A. Quindlen and Harry S. Abram. Psychosis in the burned patient: a neglected area of research. *Southern Medical Journal,* 62 (December 1969): 1463–1466.

Maxine Rubin. Balm for burned children. *American Journal of Nursing,* 66 (February 1966): 296–302.

Berthold E. Schwartz. Ordeal by serpents, fire and strychnine: a study of some provocative psychosomatic phenomena. *Psychiatric Quarterly,* 34 (July 1960): 405–429.

Also Vigliano et al. Psychiatric sequelae of old burns on children and their parents. *American Journal of Orthopsychiatry,* 34 (July 1964): 753–761.

Alfred E. Weisz. Psychotherapeutic support of burned patients. *Modern Treatment,* 4 (November 1967): 1291–1303.

Barnes Woodhall. The situational pattern in childhood injury: data derived from North Carolina newspapers. *North Carolina Medical Journal,* 12 (March 1951): 89–93.

Joan Woodward. Emotional disturbance of burned children. *British Medical Journal,* 1 (April 1959): 1009–1013.

13

Implications of the Psychosomatic Approach of the Clergy

David Belgum, Ph.D.
Chaplain Supervisor
University of Iowa Hospitals and Clinics
Iowa City, Iowa

The adjective "psychosomatic" refers to the bodily consequences of emotional, social, and spiritual factors in an individual's experience, and, on the other hand, the psychological and spiritual changes wrought by organic factors. Some such reactions are not only normal but quite acceptable socially (as when a young bride blushes when the gushing hotel clerk asks if this is indeed her honeymoon). Increased output of adrenalin as a response to the emotion of fear is a safety measure and makes the whole organism alert to danger and better prepared for self-defense.

One could speak of a "psychosomatic condition" when a person's digestion and autonomic nervous system function well in part because, he is warmly supported by loved ones, trusts in God's providence, and is appreciated for his useful vocation of service. This man does not treat his neighbor so that he is in danger of revenge and retaliation. Covetousness and hatred do not gnaw away at his innards. His energies and attention are focused on constructive ends and his regard is for further contentment and well-being. He may even say, "I feel like a million," or "It's great to get up in the morning and go to work." This is a positive "psychosomatic condition," but this we take for granted just as we do health.

Since psychosomatic medicine is by definition the domain of
the physician and only comes to the pastor's attention because the
patient is already "sick" when admitted to the hospital, it is of
primary importance to consider what this all means to the physician in charge of the patient's care. This is even more important
when one considers the controversial nature of this aspect of
medicine. Hans Selye and other pioneers in this field are highly
esteemed by some and set down as unscientific by others. It is a
topic about which it is evidently not easy to be neutral. Let us
therefore first take a look at this question from the physician's
point of view.

The Physician's Perspective

If you are an inventor, it is not good news to discover that
your new invention is not needed. You would like to believe it
widely applicable and very likely the best available.

Now, let us assume that you are a very creative surgeon in a
great university teaching hospital. You have devoted your life to
perfecting subtotal gastric resection as a treatment for stomach
ulcers and have also discovered a method of freezing the lining of
the stomach as a way of cutting down on the ulcerative process.
You have developed a reputation and are now training surgical
residents from all over the world, some of whom may go on to
greater heights and make dramatic breakthroughs. Would it come
to you as good news that one patient, who has a mild ulcer for
which a small operation will suffice this time, may not have to
come back in three years for his subtotal gastric resection, because
he has been helped to avoid a recurrence by counseling, which dealt
with the life style that precipitated his ulcer in the first place?
Indeed not! What do you have this great surgical team standing by
for, if not to be used? It so happens that in just such a hospital there
was a fine medical psychology department with diagnostic testing
and psychotherapeutic resources available to help just such a patient, but it hardly ever received a referral from the surgical depart-

ment despite the great number of patients under its care. This
particular physician, dedicated as he was, obviously regarded other
services as competitive, not supportive. The moral is clear: any
clergyman who approached this surgeon with matter-of-fact suggestions about the psychosomatic aspects of one of his patient's
illnesses could expect very short shrift.

Another physician may have an entirely different approach.
Not only has she had many years of general practice and seen the
patient in his total social context, but she has had the time to
counsel some patients and has seen what the changed life style,
improved marital relationship, restored integrity, etc., have wrought
in the physical condition of the person. She may even have been the
beneficiary of some counseling in her own life as she dealt with
tensions and conflicts that plagued her own health. This latter
physician takes "psychosomatic medicine" for granted and makes
referrals to social workers, chaplains, psychiatrists, and, upon
occasion, extends some pastoral care on her own. Such a physician
is Dr. Paul Tournier, who believes in the priesthood of all believers.

The point worth making is that there is a great range of
attitudes among physicians concerning the psychosomatic approach
in medicine. One wonders if there is an equal range among patients.

The Patient's Perspective

Since it is the patient who generally presents himself for
treatment, he must have had some reason for selecting the source
of help. He may suffer from three pains at once: a physical pain, a
traumatic marriage, and a damaged self-image due to guilt, failure
or some other personal shortcoming. Is the physical pain a more
distressing one than the other two? Not necessarily. He may have
lost more sleep over his marriage, or had his life darkened by
thoughts of suicide because of existential anxiety over the meaninglessness of his life—and both are greater threats to him as a
person. Yet, it may be easier for him to go to a physician to check
out a specific illness with tangible symptoms, partly because it is

socially more acceptable to "come down with a sickness" than it is to come up with a moral problem or a failing marriage.

We have all known patients who have resisted any interpretation by their physician (or anyone else) that their recovery is being impaired by their attitude, style of life, values, motives, broken interpersonal relationships, etc. Such patients sometimes change physicians and seek someone who will give them the "right" medicine. They protect their ego against the ultimate insult that it is not just your body that is sick, but you.

We could go on to discuss the attitude of other significant persons; relatives, friends, employer, etc. The patient does not formulate his self-diagnosis in a vacuum. His health and his illness are important to others who need to have him either healthy or sick. There is the wife or mother who would become literally "unemployed" if her "patient" recovered from invalidism or alcoholism. Even from a religious point of view, she has built her life around the role of "suffering servant" or "martyr" and has been rewarded by society for her steadfastness amid tribulation.

But our chief concern is how the clergy fit into all of this.

The Clergy Perspective

The clergy can be as imperialistic as anyone else, for he, too, is a specialist who hopes his unique contribution will be appreciated. He may not be so different from the subtotal gastric resection surgeon cited above, toward whom we must have developed some negative feelings. For many of us clergy the concept of psychosomatic medicine has been a boon; it has "put us back in business" as it were. It is as though scientific medicine has undergirded our mission and sent us back to our pastoral task with renewed assurance of its value. Who of us has not felt encouraged to discover that a famous physiologist or professor of medicine has supported our work by "proving scientifically" that hatred, dishonesty, unresolved guilt, meaninglessness, and so on are bad for the health? If we have not said it, we have thought, "Ah ha!, just as it says in the Bible, 'The wages of sin is death.'" The list of physicians and scientists who have contributed to the psychosomatic approach in medicine is long: Alexis Carrel, Helen Flanders Dunbar, Sigmund Freud, Viktor Frankl, Paul Tournier, Hans Selye, Harold G. Wolff, O. Hobart Mowrer, to mention only a few.

It should be noted that psychosomatic disorders seem to parallel spiritual disorders, that is, they reflect negative and destructive spiritual factors. The case records of such patients are filled with accounts of hatred and repressed hostility, acted out or fantasized infidelity in marriage, covetousness covered by a veneer of well-wishing, unconfessed sins which a person hopes will not come to light (but which he fears may be exposed), and assorted basic irresponsibility. On the other hand, we do not find people developing psychosomatic symptoms as a result of honest confrontation with reality, dealing lovingly and responsibly with family and business associates, assurance of forgiveness and reconciliation for past failures, belief that life has a purpose and that he is accepted of God as worthy to have a place in the schedule of things. Would it be stretching theological language too far to label the former type as "sin" and the latter type as "being in a state of grace"? In fact, is it not the goal of pastoral care and counseling to transform a person in the former situation into the latter state of mind? I believe it is.

If the above is true, then it is little wonder that such a diagnosis may come as bad news to the patient. Once he sets his defenses aside and faces the implications of this information about himself honestly, he is likely to say something like, "Egad! What have I been doing to myself?" or "This is no way to live," or "Life is too short to waste time tearing myself apart this way." In Church language this is "repentance" or "change of heart." And it is the essential turning point (*metanoia*) at which he makes a crucial decision against his old life style which has been so wrong and destructive and toward a right ("righteous") way of acting, an honest way of thinking, and a salutary (*salus*—healthful) way of living.

How can the clergy facilitate this wholesome turn of events? It is really in the same way as in pastoral care and counseling generally: 1) Form a relationship of trust, concern, and respect, 2) Listen to how the patient wants to describe his situation and his distress, 3) Demonstrate in a loving but firm way that you are not taken in by rationalizations and other ploys, 4) Help the patient to see the various alternatives open to him, 5) Offer whatever religious resources the patient needs in order to return to his social setting and to reestablish relationships with significant others.

The other side of psychosomatic medicine should not be overlooked: the effect of physical and organic changes upon personality functioning. Brain tumors, chemical imbalance and endocrine malfunctioning, menopause, the aging process, mastectomy and amputation of limbs, severe burns, and numerous other bodily changes quite obviously affect the person's capacity to function. Indeed, in some instances, he may not be quite the same person. It is possible to have a marked personality change such as from extroversion to introversion, from a placid to an excitable nervous state, from optimism to depression. The implication for the clergyman's role is clear. He must accept, and help the patient accept, the things that cannot be changed. He must not naively assume that "mind over matter" is a simple answer for everything. For his guidelines he will be heavily dependent on the diagnosis and prognosis of physician, nurse, and others who can explain the facts of the case to him.

Meanwhile, let us not belittle the medical and surgical care given to our patient. No matter what caused the ulcer, the asthma, the arthritis, immediate steps are usually necessary to deal with the debilitating effects of the symptoms whether it be bleeding, shortness of breath, or painful joints. Nothing encourages a person more to break the vicious cycle than some tangible results. A case in point would be hypertension and anxiety combined, or anxiety and palpitation of the heart. The one continuously exacerbates the other. Even if the root cause should be primarily emotional, something must be done to slow down the spiraling cause-effect-cause-effect chain reaction and reverse the process. This may very well be drug intervention or some other organic and very direct treatment by the physician. The important point is that it not stop there, that we are not content to treat the symptom and be satisfied with temporary symptom relief. Here is where the clergy-person and physician need to have a good working relationship.

There is no place for rivalry and competition in the care of a patient, no place for the question, "Did you or I do the most good in healing him?" It is even futile to think that one has proved in a given case that the sickness was 80 percent emotional and only 20 percent organic, or vice versa. The important fact, and worthy of rejoicing in, is that the patient who was disabled is now enabled to live abundantly.

Suggestions for Further Reading

Franz Alexander. *Psychosomatic Medicine: Its Principles and Application.* New York: Norton, 1950.

Walter B. Cannon. *The Wisdom of the Body* rev. ed. New York: Norton, 1963.

Flanders Dunbar. *Mind and Body: Psychosomatic Medicine* rev. ed. New York: Random House, 1955.

George Engel. *Psychological Development in Health and Disease.* Philadelphia: Saunders, 1962.

Thomas H. Holmes and Minoru Masuda. Psychosomatic syndrome. *Psychology Today* (April 1972): 2, 71, 106.

Theodore Lidz. Personality development and physiological functions, in *The Person: His Development Throughout the Life Cycle.* New York: Basic Books, 1968.

Z. J. Lipowski, ed. *Advances in Psychomatic Medicine,* vol. 8, *Psychosocial Aspects of Physical Illness.* New York: S. Karger, 1972.

Hans Selye. *The Stress of Life.* New York: McGraw-Hill, 1956.

Eric D. Wittkower and Hector Warnes. *Psychosomatic Medicine: Its Clinical Applications.* New York: Harper and Row, 1977.

14

Pastoral Care of the Patient with Gastrointestinal Complaints

Robert B. Lantz, B.D.

Director
Maryland Institute of Pastoral Counseling
Annapolis, Maryland

It has been said that the stomach is the sounding board of the emotions. As people living in a modern day and age, we should know how true this is. We blame our troubles on nausea or heartburn when we know that many times losing our tempers or worrying over the events of the day has caused the attack on our digestive tracts—such things as "swallowing our anger" or "stewing in our own juice." These things we simply cannot stomach.

Most physicians agree that emotional factors play an important part in our bodily illnesses, especially in the case of ulcers. There is even scientific data to support this assumption. The walls of our stomachs are well supplied with autonomic nerve fibers, which provide lines of communication between our brain centers and vice versa. It is also thought that the reaction of our stomachs, having been conveyed to the brain and memory, is affected by certain patterns of the gastrointestinal tract which have been utilized in infancy.[1] Through our limbic system it is possible to associate not only oral and visceral sensations, but impressions of the sex organs as well. Combined with our brain, in which intellectual functions are carried on, the visceral brain which dominates our affective behavior is a relatively crude and primitive system.[2] This, then provides us with a clue to understanding the difference between what we feel and what we know, and gives us a foundation for further understanding of the connection between emotional problems and gastrointestinal illness.

Franz Alexander has categorized our bodily functions with three labels: taking in, retaining, and eliminating. These labels, he says, can prove very helpful in understanding the relationship between personality trends and the various symptoms of peptic ulcer and ulcerative colitis.[3] "Taking in" is the function of the upper end of the GI tract, where the peptic ulcer occurs. One outstanding symptom of a peptic ulcer is what the patient often calls "hunger pains." He/she strives to satisfy these pains by taking in, whether it be food or responsibility, attention or love. This, however, only heightens his/her frustration and his/her symptoms. "Retaining" and "eliminating" are the primary functions of the lower end of the GI tract, where ulcerative colitis occurs. Because of their dependency, these patients are oftentimes unable to return ("retain") affection and have a great deal of difficulty in expressing ("eliminating") their feelings. Diarrhea is usually one of the symptoms of their illness.

The Peptic Ulcer

A peptic ulcer is a small hole or several holes occurring either in the stomach or the duodenum. It starts with a crack or a fissure in the mucous lining which permits corrosive digestive acids to come in contact with the lower layers of the stomach or intestinal wall. In persons with duodenal ulcers, the glands which produce digestive acid are chronically overactive, and produce from five to fifteen times as much acid and gastric juice in the empty stomach as normal people do.[4]

Although the size of the peptic ulcer may vary, size is not necessarily significant. Small ulcers may bleed or rupture almost as easily as large ones. Generally however, the larger and deeper the ulcer, the more difficult it is to heal and the longer it will take.

As for the physical symptoms of the disease, they are pain and nausea, a sour taste in the mouth, belching and heartburn, often only relieved by the taking of antacids. In addition, symptoms often include vomiting, blood in the stool and in the vomitus. The pain may vary from a mild discomfort to a very sharp, severe, unbearable, and sometimes penetrating sensation. As we mentioned above, it is frequently described as a steady "hunger pain." This may radiate to other parts of the stomach or to the back, and is related to the digestive cycle. Physicians say it is usually absent before breakfast, appears from one to four hours after meals, and often is sufficiently severe at night to keep the patient awake.[5]

A peptic ulcer is considered a chronic disease and cannot be cured, but merely temporarily healed and controlled by diet and continuing medical care. Its cause is not known conclusively, but emotional factors are demonstrably involved. Certain stimulants such as hunger, alcohol, spicy foods, caffeine, and tobacco can produce acid secretion in the stomach, but research has shown that emotional factors such as anxiety, guilt, resentment, hostility, anger, worry, frustration, fear, and shock can also do so. Dr. Walter Alvarez has said: "Commonly the biggest factor in the production of an ulcer is a psychic one. A hundred times, after a patient has been operated on, I have seen him get a new and terrible ulcer as soon as he ran into a new emotional jam. And a hundred times I have seen a man lose his ulcer symptoms the day he got mental peace."[6] Because of this high probability of recurrence, surgical treatment is avoided if possible. As Dr. Angel Garma states, this is because surgical treatment removes only the symptoms of the disease. The psychic factors, against which a patient's ulcer was a defense, are still present and are likely to express themselves again in similar or other psychosomatic disorders.[7]

In the light of this evidence, investigators have attempted to characterize the nature of an ulcer personality. They have come up with patients who are sensitive, tense, hard-working, aggressive, and ambitious, usually with a heavy load of responsibility and often quite successful. These people flare up inside with anger and aggravation toward anyone who does not appreciate them or over anything that blocks their way, but they are outwardly passive and somewhat effeminate. They are not able to express their feelings but keep them bottled up inside.[8]

Alexander has said that these characteristics are often accompanied by a regression to the early stages of emotional life. Unconsciously, they have a strong desire for dependence, while consciously they are dominated by ideas of independence, activity and success. Richard Young and Albert Meiburg have supported this contention and have also noted that the peptic ulcer patient has often a domineering mother and a passive father.[9]

This, then, leads us to the question of treatment. Medical treatment will involve drugs, diet, and rest. However, social adjustment may also be a necessary part of treatment. This may involve changing jobs, getting a divorce, or simply taking a vacation to get away from a nagging wife, or the tension of the patient's day-to-day living. The aim is to remove or relieve the tension which may be aggravating the patient's condition. However, treatment aimed at doing this cannot be forced. Reassurance and support must be the key words for the pastor to keep in mind. He must assist the patient to come only to as much understanding of his own personality as he is willing to undertake. In short, therapy must be such that the patient will reveal himself.[10]

Ulcerative Colitis

Ulcerative colitis is an inflammation of all or part of the mucous membrane lining the colon. This is usually the result of sustained colonic hyperfunction.[11] The physical symptoms of the disease are diarrhea accompanied by blood, mucus, or pus, with abdominal discomfort and pain. There may be fever, loss of weight, and anemia during the time the patient has the ulcer.

Ulcerative colitis is thought to be brought about and aggravated by experiences which the patient feels threatened by. Like the peptic ulcer, the disease is usually chronic and intermittent. Emotion-laden situations such as sickness, death, bereavement, loss of money, as well as other precipitating factors, may bring about an aggravation of the illness. It has also been found that it breaks out after verbal humiliation in the presence of others, or the traumatic loss of a dependent person.[12]

Much has been written about the personality pattern of the patient with ulcerative colitis. He has been described as generally anxious, and eager to please, but difficult to establish a close relationship with. Because he prefers not to discuss his feelings and attitudes, he often says that he has no problems. Also, it has been generally noted that these patients repress their emotions, for instance several writers have remarked that it is almost impossible to get them to express feelings of hostility.[13] Patients are reluctant to assume responsibility and are dependent on others for their decision making. Because of this, they usually have only a small number of friends and acquaintances. Conflict arising between the desire to communicate emotions of hostility and, at the same time, to please and be accepted creates anxiety and tension within the patient. This tension is most often directed toward parents or spouses. Excessive routine is also characteristic of those with ulcerative colitis. For example, a housewife will go to great lengths to keep her home meticulously clean, often following a strict schedule in doing so.

As with the peptic ulcer patient, the parent-child relationship is an outstanding factor in the child's personality development. The mother is usually possessive and overprotective, and the father is often, but not always, domineering and aggressive.[14] As a total picture, family life is restrictive. Oftentimes family members hold each other in check by placating, nullifying, and subduing each other. Voice tone is often quiet and expressionless, and arguments, emotional anger, and affective responses are in most instances avoided. The patient learns to be submissive and passive. He is aware of pain and disharmony, even unhappiness, and yet there is an outward agreement that this will not be mentioned in front of the other family members.

Treatment for the ulcerative colitis patient varies, and includes regulation of diet and various drugs. A number of patients may eventually have their condition alleviated by surgery. The mortality rate is high in regard to surgery, though it has been suggested that this is more a result of the personality of the patient than of the hazards of the operation. Almost all literature on the treatment of ulcerative colitis emphasizes that the main factor in alleviating a patient's symptoms is a constructive relationship.

Included in the motivating interests of these writers is the concept that the "constructive relationship" can and perhaps should be offered by the pastor closest to the parishioner's need. In the situation of hospitalized patients in extreme conditions, this comes to the attention of the hospital chaplain or the department of pastoral care. The thorough pastoral treatment of the GI patient in the manner suggested may require some adjustments in the pastoral care model as it exists in some acute medical facilities, so that the chaplain engaging in the care of the ulcer patient will be assured of the time to consult with the patient both on an out-patient and in-patient basis, for it was outside of the hospital that the patient met the stresses which caused his hospitalization.

In our study it has been shown how difficult it is for patients to return to our offices following medical discharge from the hospital. Of those few who wish to continue to investigate their lives in search of the genesis of the disease a still smaller portion are willing to return for outpatient consultation. Those who do return, however, may well be the very individuals who were previously trapped in the self-destructive attitudes which allowed their disease to flourish and are therefore sensitive to the possibility that life could be less painful and more productive of personal satisfaction. This group will often have incurred painful periods of GI illness and possibly undergone surgery. The often repeated comments of sensitive physicians that the real problem is "up here rather than down there" may have raised at least a questioning posture which permits them to talk to the chaplain. And he is willing to become interested in them as human entities, entities that have a past as well as a present and future.

The concept of pastoral concern for the past of patients brings me to the most significant aspect of the pastoral care of the GI patient. Following the active, punctual, structured approaches advocated by some authors for the larger group of patients, there is the possibility of deeper interest for the smaller group who are motivated toward solution rather than maintenance. For this smaller group of GI patients who are willing to deal with their visceral reluctance to form substantial relationships of any kind, there is the possibility of a long-term pastoral relationship including daily visits while hospitalized and pastoral counseling of one to two hours a week for several months thereafter. The focus of the visits would tend toward relating the patient's past relationships and experiences to their current and expected equivalents. The goal of counseling would vary, however; some areas can be generally mentioned here. Since the GI patient has usually experienced cool, distant relationships with parental and authority figures, it is important that the minister offer a relationship which though authoritative by nature of the pastoral office, is nevertheless warm and symbolic of God's eternal understanding of man's soulful struggles.

In addition the minister will need to be acquainted with the socioeconomic background and aspirations of the patient. Since GI diseases are most prevalent in the more fluid upward-moving groups, it becomes therefore important to relate the socioeconomic struggles with the patient's concept of himself and his relationship to those persons significant in his life. The clinical material accumulated to date with this group of patients indicates that the individual feels a sense of entrapment in the culture, perhaps more felt than real. It is my impression that if our current findings continue we shall be able to establish that those patients who desire to break their patterns of distant, manipulative relationships will show a marked improvement in the painful symptoms which caused their hospitalization, which will make it worth the large investment of pastoral effort.

Notes

1. Weiss and English. *Psychosomatic Medicine, a Clinical Study of Psychophysiologic Reactions.* Philadelphia: W. B. Saunders Company, 1957, p. 254.
2. *Ibid.,* p. 255.
3. *Ibid.,* p. 256.
4. Richard K. Young and Albert L. Meilburg. *Spiritual Therapy.* New York: Harper and Brothers, 1960, p. 47.
5. I. W. Hel and Allen A. Goldbloom. *Peptic Ulcer, Its Diagnosis and Treatment.* Springfield, Illinois: Charles C Thomas, 1946, pp. 46–60.
6. William R. Vath. The month of the ulcer. *Today's Health,* (October 1964), pp. 56–70.
7. Angel Garma. *Peptic Ulcer and Psychoanalysis.* Baltimore: Williams and Wilkins, 1958, pp. 129–132.
8. Weiss, *op. cit.,* p. 295.
9. Young, *op. cit.,* p. 51.
10. Weiss, *op. cit.,* p. 302; and Young, *op. cit.,* p. 52.

11. William J. Grace, Stewart Wolf, and Harold G. Wolff. *The Human Colon*. New York: Paul B. Hoeber, 1951, p. 162.
12. Leon Marder. Symposium: psychiatric aspects of ulcerative colitis. *Southern Medical Journal,* 60, no. 12 (November 1967): 1281–1284.
13. *Ibid.,* and Grace, *op. cit.,* p. 165.
14. Young, *op. cit.,* p. 60.

Suggestions for Further Reading

C. Aitken, et al. Chemical psychosomatic research. *International Journal of Psychiatric Medicine.* 6 (1–2): 29–41, 1975.
Heije Faber. *Pastoral Care in the Modern Hospital.* Philadelphia: Westminster, 1971.

15

Pastoral Care in the Intensive Care Unit

David M. Hurst, Th.M.

Chaplain Supervisor
University of Michigan Hospitals
Ann Arbor, Michigan

What is unique about pastoral ministry in an intensive care unit (ICU)? What should a pastor know about the ICU philosophy and setting, and about the needs of those whom he encounters in this context? What does he/she have to offer toward the well-being of those he meets in the ICU?

These are among the principal questions that I sought to answer in my work as an ICU pastor-chaplain. The findings presented here are basically those discovered during a clinical internship in the medical-surgical ICU of the Crozer-Chester Medical Center, Chester, Pennsylvania, and in research on that subject for a Master of Theology thesis in pastoral care.

The ICU as a Setting for Ministry

A historical survey of intensive care concepts, and of the establishment of intensive care units in modern hospitals, very strongly suggests that this innovation in patient care is here to stay and will expand. This being the case, the potential and opportunity for pastoral ministry in ICU settings are also destined to increase. The intense psycho-spiritual stresses that acute or critical illness and emergency treatment procedures engender in patients, patient relatives, and treatment staff make the ICU an imperative setting for skilled pastoral ministry.

Importance of ICU Orientation for Pastor-Chaplain

To serve these persons adequately and meaningfully in ICU settings, the pastor-chaplain requires a fairly comprehensive understanding of the intensive care concept and setting. He/she requires this so that he/she may (1) be adequately sensitive to the needs and feelings of persons to whom he/she ministers; (2) serve as an informed, trusted lay interpreter of the unit, its purposes, and its procedures, to anxious patients, patient relatives and the wider public; (3) work complementarily, empathetically, and collaboratively with medical and nursing staffs for the optimum well-being of patients.

ICU Patient Characteristics, Feelings, and Needs

In this study, it was observed and concluded that not only do patients in a comprehensive ICU usually represent all walks of life and socioeconomic levels, all races and creeds, both male and female, young and old, they also present every psycho-spiritual need and emotion of patients in other hospital areas. Often the needs and emotions they feel are experienced with greater intensity and trauma than those of other patients because of the critical nature of their problems, made all the more apparent by the strange, anxiety-producing ICU. Death anxiety, generalized apprehension, boredom, loneliness, guilt, denial of the reality of their conditions, irritability, depression, despair, and resentment are all a part of the negativities which are experienced by ICU patients. In addition to the accumulation of negatives engendered by the setting, and by their physical condition, the patients bring all the negative baggage of their lives along from their communities and homes—concerns which then almost inevitably become magnified under the pressure of the unfamiliar new stresses.

Pastoral Role, Authority, and Function

In my research I assumed that the role, the authority, and general pastoral function of the ICU chaplain were identical with those of pastors in other settings. I concluded that the religious attitudes and perspectives purveyed by the chaplain might facilitate the confidence and the well-being of the ICU patient; or, on the other hand, if the chaplain communicated out of the unresolved inadequacies and lacks in his own life, they might reinforce neurotic defenses and have a disintegrative effect on the patient. It is therefore incumbent upon the chaplain (1) to seek out those attitudes and perspectives which make for optimum health in his or her own psycho-spiritual make-up and (2) to help the patient examine and reaffirm the attitudes and ideas that are most meaningful and wholesome in his or her experience, whatever his or her other religiocultural orientation.

Tasks and Approaches in Ministry
to ICU Patients

The tasks and approaches of ministry to ICU patients appear to be similar to those required in ministry to other general hospital patients, or even to persons in the general community. The essential differences are variations in the tempo and the emotional intensity, which call for unique adjustments of one's methodological models to the patient's condition and to the restrictions of the setting. Thus, those tasks, approaches, and models for ministry which have been found useful in other settings of pastoral care may—with adaptations—be applied to pastoral care in the ICU area.

Consistent, sensitive, sincere, friendly interest in the acutely ill patient can help him recover his ego strength and self-respect, both of which may have dwindled seriously under the severe blow illness or injury and forced dependency have dealt him. Pastoral care can help the patient realize and feel, once more, that it is good to be human and that he or she is a worthy and valued member of the human race. The treatment of his psycho-spiritual needs may be vital to his will to live.

Two Phases in Ministry to ICU Patients

In the clinical work of this study it was observed that there are two principal phases in ministry to ICU patients. From the perspective of the patient's condition these phases might be called the acute and the convalescent. From the perspective of the chaplain's ministry to persons in these two categories, they might be called the phases of "sacramental-role-representation" and of "friendship-relational-representation." The function and objective are pastoral in both styles of ministry. Sacramental-role-representation consists predominantly, in nonverbal communication, while friendship-relational-representation is heavily verbal in character. The former was found to be the more appropriate model to use with critically ill, sedated, very weak patients, as well as with patients who are in severe pain or who are somewhat disoriented. The latter model becomes more meaningful and appropriate when the patient is sufficiently improved to feel relatively comfortable, stronger, well-oriented, and alert; when he begins to feel loneliness and boredom bearing down upon him; when he craves companionship and conversation.

Other Persons in the ICU Setting Who Need Ministry

The ICU chaplain's pastoral opportunities and responsibilities do not end with the patients. The anxious relatives and friends who wait in uncertainty—often despair—in the ICU family waiting room, frequently need a skilled, sensitive, pastoral ministry more acutely than their sedated or unconscious loved ones do. The harassed nursing personnel and medical staff members, who endure the emotionally high-charged atmosphere of the ICU for hours at a time, need an understanding and strengthening ministry, too.

It was concluded that one of the more highly significant and important facets of the ICU pastor-chaplain's ministry is his attempt to meet the needs of patients, relatives and friends. My experience in ministry to such persons confirmed this conclusion. Empathic, supportive listening and relationships are generally appreciated and perceived to be strengthening to ICU patients, relatives, and friends.

A well-trained, staff pastor-chaplain may assume some leadership in increasing interdisciplinary understanding and collaboration among the various professional persons who bring services to the ICU patient, and thereby improve their efforts toward more effective patient care. Also, the chaplain may serve the need for improved patient care by offering and channeling constructive suggestions to nursing, medical, and administrative staffs; and these suggestions may bring about healthier, more humanized effects on the ICU environment.

The ICU pastor-chaplain performs a useful and important ministry to members of the medical and nursing staffs when he collaborates with them in attaining optimum patient care, helps to relieve the stress, and increases the sense of satisfaction of these staff members in their work. There is also a significant amount of opportunity for the chaplain to minister directly to the staff persons in their acute tension and concern, and in their personal problems.

Some of the more important objectives and tasks which the chaplain has to face, in relation to these professional persons, are these: (1) being an understanding and sensitive listener when frustrations, irritations, anxieties, guilt feelings, and discouragements mount in them; (2) encouraging them in their significant work of treating and caring for the sick, communicating a sense of regard and admiration for them as co-laborers with God in their healing, redeeming work with persons; (3) being a friend and confidant who is approachable and available when they need him; (4) making all possible psycho-spiritual resources available for their use in personal and professional growth.

Overall Objectives and Perspectives for ICU Ministry

On the basis of this study, it is affirmed that a primary concern of the ICU pastor-chaplain is (1) to help persons with an adequate theology or philosophy of life, objectify and reaffirm the focus of meaning and strength in that perspective, and (2) to make available such meanings to those who lack them. The chaplain, in performing this important task, must remember that the situations and concerns of those to whom he ministers defy all pat answers and academic hypotheses. The issues and processes of life and death confront these stress-ridden persons. It was out of such convictions that experimentation and evaluations were made in this study concerning the utility of theological-pastoral perspectives on the one hand, and psychotherapeutic-pastoral approaches on the other.

In my opinion, based on my research, the following perspectives are useful in ICU pastoral ministry:

I. Theological-Pastoral Perspectives
A. Concepts of God and of creation in universal, yet personal, relational, incarnational, growth-facilitating, fulfillment-seeking terms, which also take the problem of evil and imperfection seriously.
B. Ideas of judgment which view this aspect of divine activity as basically positive, reconciling and redeeming, while also confronting the individual with his guilt and responsibility.
C. Theological ideas which recognize the basic separation between the essential and the existential dimensions in the nature of man, as well as the constant inroads and threats of nonbeing and evil in his life.
D. Understandings of redemption which affirm both the suffering of God in the sufferings of his creatures and the triumph of God over suffering and evil, while also seeing the promise and the power of the New Being (Tillich) actualized and opened up for all men in Jesus, the Christ.

E. Views which provide a sacramental understanding of the universe and of human interactions, with applications of these understandings to the role and the ministrations of the pastor-chaplain.

II. Psychotherapeutic-Pastoral Perspectives

A. Adaptations of the Freudian concepts of "cathexis," "catharsis," and "abreaction" to provide the pastor-chaplain with tools for use in assisting persons to ventilate, externalize, or objectify traumatic experiences and unpleasant feelings which may be detrimental to their well-being if not so expressed and dealt with.

B. Rank's notion of strengthening the will of the person by affirming all that is positive about him and about his struggle, and providing him with additional opportunities for the exercise of his positive will.

C. Rank's idea of assisting the person toward the discovery and constructive use of all his emotions as a means of facilitating his health.

D. Carl Rogers' concept of "empathetic understanding" or of assuming the client's "internal frame of reference."

E. Viktor Frankl's view of man's "will to meaning" and of "spiritual values" as the essential resources in the satisfaction of man's universal "spiritual needs."

Suggestions and Warnings

A few practical suggestions and warnings, distilled out of this study, are offered for the use of those who expect to engage in an ICU pastoral ministry. These suggestions and cautions are summarized as follows:

1. The minister should first inform himself, as fully as possible, of the nature of the ICU and the kinds of situations he may reasonably expect to find there, so that he will experience a minimum of shock, anxiety, or revulsion over what he sees when he arrives at the unit.

2. The minister should always check with the ICU charge nurse to learn something of each patient's condition and needs before he attempts to visit.

3. He should approach each patient with an attitude of controlled confidence, hope, and expectancy.

4. His voice should be kept low and his manner unhurried if he is to communicate a soothing, strengthening influence—a sense of sincerely offering himself and the resources he represents to help make the patient's burden more bearable.

5. In his initial contact, the ICU pastor should immediately identify himself and the purpose of his visit to the patient, clearly indicating that it is his custom to visit all patients in this hospital area, to come to know them and to let them know of his interest and his wish to share a bit of the stress they feel. The reason for such an introduction is to avert the possibility of aggravating the patient's already considerable load of anxiety.

6. He should keep his visits brief and relatively frequent, unless or until the patient is improved enough so that longer visits will not be too tiring or otherwise injurious to his recovery.

7. He should use his informed intuition, and whatever principles and skills in pastoral care he has learned in other contexts, as the base from which he proceeds to develop more specialized skills and knowledge in the pastoral care of ICU patients, relatives, and staff persons in their highly stressful circumstances.

Suggestions for Further Reading

David Bakan. *Disease, Pain, Sacrifice.* Chicago: University of Chicago Press, 1968.

Lenette O. Burrell and Zeb. L. Burrell, Jr. *Intensive Nursing Care,* 2nd ed. St. Louis: C. V. Mosby, 1973.

Eric R. J. Emery, et al. *Principles of Intensive Care.* London: English University Press, 1973.

Joseph E. Gross. A study of pastoral care in a coronary care unit. Unpublished Th.D. dissertation. Southwestern Baptist Theological Seminary, Ft. Worth, Texas (1971).

Theodore Hodge. Pastoral care of families of selected critically ill persons. Unpublished Th.D. dissertation. Southern Baptist Theological Seminary (April 1975).

Carolyn M. Hudak, et al. *Critical Care Nursing.* Philadelphia: Lippincott, 1973.

Richard T. Hughes. Spiritual crises facing surgical patients. *Pastoral Psychology,* 22 (December 1971): 27–34.

David M. Hurst. Pastoral ministry in an intensive care area. Unpublished Th.M. thesis. Crozer Theological Seminary, Chester, Pennsylvania (July 1969). (Copy located with the library of The Rochester Center for Theological Studies and Crozer Theological Seminary, Rochester, New York.)

Mark B. Ravin and Jerome H. Modell, eds. *Introduction to Life Support,* 1st ed. Boston: Little Brown, 1973.

Edward Rubenstein. *Intensive Medical Care.* New York: McGraw-Hill, 1971.

Harmon L. Smith. The minister as consultant to the medical team. *The Journal of Religion and Health,* 14 (January 1975): 7–13.

16

Ministering to Cancer Patients

LeRoy G. Kerney, M. A.
Chief, Department of Spiritual Ministry
The Clinical Center
National Institutes of Health
Bethesda, Maryland

Ministry to cancer patients is both a threat and a challenge. It is a threat in that it exposes the inadequacies of our ministry, the tawdriness of our trivia, and tolls the bell of our own limited existence. It is also a challenge that calls forth our best insights, skills, and being, and helps us focus on the aspects of the Eternal that rise above techniques and scientific approaches.

It is well known that cancer is the number-one scourge of our people in the United States, second only to diseases of the heart and blood vessels. During our average lifetime of seventy years, it will affect one of every five of us and send one out of eight to the grave. Cancer is a major killer. But it must never be forgotten that in many instances cancer can be cured, arrested, and meaningful life added to the patient's shortened existence.

For this reason, I shall limit my discussion to a listing of ten focal questions that alert clergy raise in this ministry, and shall conclude with a much too short description of ministry to this type of patient.

Developmental Age of the Patient

In what developmental state of life is the patient? The chronological age of the patient given in his or her chart becomes the first clue to this question. This is readjusted by the appearance, attitudes, and experiences recounted by the patient. The important thing to consider is the accumulated effect of living through various ages of life and the concern for particular tasks and endeavors that come with each age.

There are a number of schemes that can be used to set forth the developmental ages of man. The following scale or "yardstick" has come out of my reading of Lewis Sherril's book *The Struggle of the Soul.*[1] These ages may be outlined as follows:

Age	Chronological Age	Task
Childhood	0–12	Becoming an individual
Adolescence	12–20	Becoming independent
Youth Adulthood	21–39	Developing an identity
Middle Age	40–64	Developing a philosophy of life
Older Adulthood	65–?	Simplification of life

It is obvious that a patient at the age of four with a cancer is different from a person of twenty-five or forty-five or eighty-five with a malignancy. I believe the normative patterns that are basic to a Christian point of view are implicit in the Gospel story of Jesus. The "gates" of his life can be listed as his birth, the experience at the temple, his beginning ministry with John the Baptist, his temptations, and his death on the cross. We see our lives in and through his career as a life of trust, and love, and hope.

Cancer as a Disease and Illness

What is known about the patient's diagnosis, therapies, and prognosis by staff, patient, and his family? The minister's main concern is not with the disease of cancer. That is the doctor's major concern. However, to know something, both in general and specifically, about the diagnosis, the therapies, and the prognosis is helpful to ascertain how well the patient and the family accept the reality of the situation and it also helps the pastor plan his day-by-day ministry.

I have found that medical material designed for nurses is usually written at a level of comprehension that fits my needs. I often turn to a book like *A Cancer Source Book for Nurses,* published by the American Cancer Society, as a source of medical background to this question.

If disease is primarily a concern of the doctor, a medical and scientific problem, illness may be seen as the response of the individual patient to his disease. The next question would then follow.

In what stage of illness is the patient? It needs to be remembered that despite the progress made in the treatment of cancer, the word itself is still a scare word. It is a disease that raises the anxiety of staff, friends, and family, as well as that of the patient. It is also a disease that cannot be controlled by the patient like some others, through diet, rest, exercise, and replacement therapies such as taking insulin.

From a medical point of view the progress of the disease may be outlined as:

1. *Initial stage*—the neoplastic disease has been verified by clinical evidence.
2. *Advancing stage*—when metastases or invasive cancer is confirmed.
3. *Terminal stage*—when the condition is considered irreversible.

Of course, the progress may result in arresting the disease or controlling it for long periods of time, or eventually in a "cure." Ruth Abrams, a social worker, has set forth the changes in patterns of communication of patients with cancer in a most revealing way. In the initial stage, the patient usually talks freely, honestly, and repeatedly about his diagnosis. In the advancing stage, "hope gives way to fear, truth to veiled and measured statements, and faith in physicians to fear of abandonment."[2] In the terminal stage, silence becomes the common language with a need for varying kinds of support from different persons.

In what phase of hospitalization is the patient? This question is somewhat similar to the one above. It is different in that it points up some of the sociological aspects of illness. A patient usually goes through three phases in the hospital—diagnosis, therapy, and convalescence. Sometimes the course is repeated so that some of the phases are shortened or bypassed. The final course may not be convalescence but may result in death.

If it is the first time the patient has been hospitalized, or hospitalized for this present disease, he is often apprehensive about the findings that come from the testing process. He is often lonely and frustrated with his dependent role and the change from his usual routine.

In the period of therapy there is usually an acceptance of the disease and a willingness to put himself in the hands of a doctor or doctors whom he trusts. Details of the therapies are on his mind.

During the stage of convalescence, he thinks more about home, his work, and his family, hoping to be able to leave the hospital but is often anxious about assuming his more normal patterns of living.

The Patient's Personal Situation

What is known about the patient's family, past and present? Being ill and in a hospital changes the role of a person in his family structure. He is often apprehensive about what the family will think and how they will accept this change. If he has had difficulty in the past in establishing meaningful and supportive relationships with members of the family, illness can threaten these even further. He may have to use a variety of coping devices to handle the problems. Many times the person for whom the minister becomes most concerned is a member of the family. This is true because the patient is not simply an individual atom in a lonely world. Rather he is like a molecule in a complex system with each part orbiting around the other.

What is the patient's occupation? This question can often lead to some projecting of the social status of the patient and his family. If the patient is under age or is a housewife at home, knowledge about what the father or husband does is the key. Occupation here means the use of time. It leads to questions about education, moving around the country, changes in working situations. For a child, the occupation may be play or school. This also includes questions about use of leisure and hobbies.

What is the patient's vocation? This question could also be formulated, "What do we know about the religious background of the patient?" I put it in the first form so as to broaden the question beyond the institutional aspects of religion. Who or what calls this person? Fame, success, being noticed, financial reward? The question includes attention to early childhood religious upbringing, changes in religious affiliations, roles of leadership, nature of involvement with value-giving groups. Clues are found in the patient's description of his religious practices, beliefs, values, that lead to ethical decisions.

Spiritual Dimensions of the Patient

What is the nature of the patient's faith? This question and the following two are closely related to the previous one. But to put the question in this general form sometimes helps to find attitudes that are not quickly revealed in material dealing with church membership, activity, and belief. To the patient who does not see himself as particularly "religious," consciousness of his own faith and articulation of the nature of that in which he trusts often come as a revelation to him.

What is the nature of the patient's love? This is very similar to the question above. What groups, what people, what institutions support and give meaning and significance to the patient? These may be obviously religious groups or members of his family. But often a club, a company, a way of life is the supporting reality or group or fellowship for a patient.

What is the nature of the patient's hope? Hope is an aspect of the spiritual nature of man that has been given too little attention. If there were more accurate ways of measuring a man's hope, we would know much more about him. To ascertain what a patient anticipates today, tomorrow, and in the future, determines in no small measure his attitude and outlook today. Hope must be measured both in concrete terms of medical progress and in the more eternal sense of meaning and religious relatedness.

The Clergy's Ministry

If the clergy's ministry begins in understanding, it must move beyond understanding to other forms of involvement. These include the following:

Being present with the patient. It is my experience that most patients are looking for community. Cancer patients often fear abandonment particularly during the terminal phase of their illness. This "silent sound of love" is most basic to an effective hospital ministry.

Giving opportunity for dialogue with the patient. There is a certain magic about words. When thought and feelings are put in words, and expressed to someone who can understand, there is healing. Much of the dialogue with a patient is between his conflicting parts. For example, he/she may both wish to live and wish to die. He/she may try to be strong but also knows he/she is weak and needs help.

Helping the patient celebrate life. It is no coincidence that the Christian Church has developed sacraments or rites to help the individual believer through the crisis times of life, birth, coming of age, vocational choices, marriage, sickness, and death. We need to develop more forms that will help patients individually and in groups to sustain and "concretize" religious meaning, trust, love, and hope in the hospital setting.

Notes

1. Lewis Sherril. *The Struggle of the Soul.* New York: Macmillan, 1951.
2. Ruth D. Abrams, M. S. *The New England Journal of Medicine,* 274, no. 6 (February 10, 1966): 317–322.

Suggestions for Further Reading

Ruth D. Abrams. *Not Alone with Cancer.* Springfield, Illinois: Charles C Thomas, 1974.
American Cancer Society, "The Psychological Impact of Cancer" (booklet), 94 pp., n.d.

American Cancer Society. *A Cancer Source Book for Nurses.* 1975.

American Cancer Society. The clergy and the cancer patient (pamphlet), 20 pp., 1975.

J. E. Englebert Dunphy. Annual discourse—on caring for the patient with cancer. *New England Journal of Medicine,* 295 (6): 313–319, 1976.

LeRoy G. Kerney. Pastoral use of "The Seven Last Words" in terminal care, in *Psychosocial Aspects of Terminal Care.* New York: Columbia University Press, 1972.

John R. Peteet. Depression in cancer patients. *Journal of the American Medical Association,* 241 (14): 1487–1489, 1979.

Carl Sachtleben. Pastoral care in breast cancer management. *Journal of Pastoral Care,* 33 (2): 104–109, 1979.

Elizabeth A. Smith. *Psychological Aspects of Cancer Patient Care: A Self-Instructional Text.* St. Louis: McGraw-Hill, 1975.

17

Pastoral Care of the Stroke Patient and His Family

Rudolph E. Grantham, M. Div.
Former Chaplain
Candler General Hospital
Savannah, Georgia

The Stroke Patient

A cerebral vascular accident (CVA) is a physical, intellectual, and emotional vortex. The illness involves delicate brain tissue which governs body functions. Many other problems are generated due to the length of the convalescence.

Strokes make a varied clinical picture. The effects range from immediate death or coma to no change in the state of consciousness. The physical damage may extend from mild numbness in a limb to extensive paralysis and dysfunction of extremities. Intellectual and emotional dysfunctions can range from mild confusion and amnesia to a radical change in personality and perception of the world. However in this varied clinical picture there are definite physical, emotional, and spiritual problems to which the pastor can direct his ministry.

COMMUNICATION

Communication difficulty is not only a physical problem in itself, but also generates emotional repercussions in the patient as well as in his family and in those who seek his rehabilitation.

If the patient is in a coma or some other "altered state of consciousness,"[1] verbal communication may not be effective. The conscious patient may be able to hear and comprehend and not to respond by speaking or writing. He/she may have one of several types of visual difficulties. He/she may recognize only his immediate family and childhood friends but not recent acquaintances. He/she may not respond to a clergyman's words of comfort yet respond warmly to a clerical collar, Bible, cross, or other symbols which have a personal meaning. Never assume the person in an "altered state of consciousness" is unable to receive communication! One common reaction to frustration in communicating is withdrawal from all effort to communicate.

PHYSICAL DISABILITY

The onset of a stroke frequently brings dramatic physical changes including changes in facial expression. The most common damage is hemiplegia (paralysis of one side) and speech difficulties. In spite of these extensive damages, almost all patients can make some physical progress.

In physical disability, as with communication difficulties, the vortex is at work. If the paralyzed limbs are not adequately treated, frozen joints, foot drop, and other distortions may result. Changes in physical appearance and functioning may generate difficulties in accepting the altered body image. Defense mechanisms may be expressed in denial of disability and uncooperative behavior. The repeatedly unsuccessful efforts to do for oneself contribute to emotional depression. Concern about permanent disability, vocational adjustments, and one's purpose in living may arise from preoccupation with the physical disability. Impatience over the slow rate of recovery is often seen. And embarrassment over inappropriate interpersonal relationships (such as crying or laughter at the wrong time) may lead to withdrawal from social contacts.

REGRESSION

A stroke is a dramatic example of physical, emotional, and possibly spiritual regression in the person affected. And if regression is not adequately met, it can become a part of the problem. Harry Olin writes:

> Neurology teaches a painful truism—the most recently acquired structures of the brain are the most liable to injury. The cortex is the area most susceptible to damage when subjected to insult.

> When brain structures are arranged in a hierarchy of age from the most phylogenetically and ontogenetically ancient to the most recent, the dictum that the last to appear is the first to succumb holds true. The higher brain (cortical) functions of the organism, such as abstract reasoning, disappear before older brain structures and their basic functions, such as respiratory control, are affected.[2]

This physical and emotional regression manifests itself in self-centeredness. The person concentrates on his body functions and loses interest in the wider world. He may become overdependent on others and impatient with their efforts to help him. Repetition of an idea and repeated verbalizations of a few words remind one of a child learning to talk. Mental functioning is affected, often manifesting itself as brief attention span and difficulty in abstract thinking. Memory of recent events may be impaired but early life experiences are easily recalled. Calling upon the security of mother (cf. Ps. 22:9) and other primitive means of security (touch, soothing sounds, etc.) express this regression.

With all these symptoms of regression evident, it is important to remember that it is only partial. The person is an adult and at one level aware of this, yet he is helpless to do for himself. This conflict between adulthood and enforced regression contributes to his emotional discomfort.

DEPRESSION AND ANGER

Depression and its related emotion, anger, is a dominant emotional state. Physical depression often accompanies emotional depression and both will provide the feeling that God is far away and "like a deceitful brook" (Jer. 15:18 RSV).

One factor in depression is the conflict between the fear of living and the fear of dying and a feeling of hopelessness about the future is related to this depression. Often the person will lash out violently both physically and verbally at family, staff, God—and his servant, the pastor. Uncooperative behavior may be a manifestation of the wish to be left alone to die, but suicide is seldom a strong possibility.

Breakdown in communication and physical ability in the form of paralysis, regression, depression, and anger stand out as central factors in our understanding strokes as "physical and intellectual impairment."

Goals of Pastoral Care

ESTABLISHING COMMUNICATION

The minister's first task is to reestablish communication. In acute cases with major brain damage, disordered functioning, and the patient in an altered state of consciousness, this can be quite difficult. And in some cases where we do manage to communicate, the patient may be unable to respond, thus leaving us unable to know if we have made contact.

Evidence of the need to establish communication is impressive. LeShan states: "There is a good deal of evidence that deep psychological isolation, the loss of ability to relate and to love, lowers the ability to fight for health."[3] This isolation in itself appears to weaken the capacity to deal with stress, to cope with pain, and to fight for life.[4] Establishing communication also counters the fear of abandonment. One writes: "In patients I saw, the greatest threat was not so much death (whatever dying is) but rather the danger of progressive isolation and the development of a sense of 'aloneness. . . .'"[5]

If the patient is in an "altered state of consciousness," we must be aware of this state if we are to communicate. Plum and Posner have described these levels between alertness and coma. "In the grading of impaired consciousness, lethargy means a state of drowsiness, inaction and indifference, in which responses to stimulation may be delayed or incomplete, and in which increased stimulation may be required to evoke a response. 'Obtundation' is a state of duller indifference that maintains wakefulness but little more.

'Stupor' describes that state from which the subject can only be aroused by vigorous and continuous external stimulation. 'Coma' designates a state in which psychological and motor response to stimulation are either completely lost (deep coma) or reduced to only rudimentary reflex motor responses (moderately deep coma)."[6]

Our approach to the patient should begin with the doctor or head nurse. After we have determined the patient's state of consciousness, we need to know his physical condition and emotional state. Conversation with the family about the patient and his religious life, especially childhood religious traditions, is also helpful. Next we need to ask ourselves the question: "Why do we want to communicate?" Also, we must always keep in mind, "Is it to the patient's advantage that we communicate with him at this particular time?"

Having learned these things about the person, we turn to the nature of the communication. Normally communication should be brief and simple. Words are spoken clearly and slowly. The message is one of comfort and help, and perhaps challenge. Oftentimes touching the person conveys the message of love and concern, and breaks the isolation better than words.[7]

Sometimes the unconscious patient will respond to hymns and to memorized Bible verses, such as the Twenty-third Psalm and Aaron's benediction (Num. 6:23–26). Where worship has been a meaningful part of the person's life, it may be the means whereby the will to live is strengthened.

Often the severely ill person who is unable to receive verbal communication will respond to personally meaningful religious symbols. With these patients a clerical collar, Bible, rosary, cross, or other symbol which has personal meaning may be the opening wedge whereby their isolation is broken, hope awakened, and faith strengthened.

The minister should also be aware of his own symbolic role. One patient said: "When you came into my room, you did not come alone. I felt God with you." A mentally retarded youth seeing a chaplain said, "Hello church!" The minister offers not only his love and services, he also symbolizes God's love for the patient. Whatever the form or symbol of faith used, the purpose is to make available the power it symbolizes.

At all times, but especially when dealing with acutely ill patients, the emotional state of the minister is important. The message that gets across will be emotional and spiritual in nature, and it is easy to be drawn into the patient's emotional vortex. At the emotional level, the minister should be able to communicate his own "warm regard for the patient as a person of unconditional self-worth."[8] And this is a very important message to communicate, for frequently the stroke patient feels he is now and always will be worthless, a problem to himself and his family.

Another element in the minister's relationship is faith—faith in the patient's own healing powers, faith in the doctor and healing team, faith in the goodness of God. Another element is understanding. He conveys that he is aware of the patient's inner chaotic world and accepts him as he is. The minister is a specialist in nonverbal communication, especially in conveying that which is spiritual—faith, hope, love—elements which Karl Menninger calls the "intangibles" of healing.

Even when auditory difficulties are present, the more common form of verbal communication is important. Frequently, though, the conversational initiative is with the minister. One disoriented patient responded with joy to the question, "When you were a little child, did you sing, 'Jesus Loves Me This I Know?'" To her look of joy the hospital chaplain added, "He still loves you and is helping you now in your illness." At this point to the surprise and delight of the family and chaplain, she talked lucidly about the revivals in her rural church when she was a child.

Another stroke patient was unable to speak. The minister asked, "Is it frustrating to have thoughts and not be able to put them into words?" He nodded yes. The minister continued, "It is not necessary for us to put our thoughts into words when we pray." Where the patient has an image of God as a personal being who desires to communicate, prayer can be a meaningful, nonverbal relationship.

If serious distortion in communication is not present, establishing a relationship can be done in a conventional verbal manner. The value of the "social call" should not be overlooked. Encouraging the patient to talk about himself, his favorite sports, foods, job, and family bears fruit. It induces relaxation, it widens his interest from preoccupation with his illness, it helps the minister discover the patient's strengths and weaknesses. Later, these topics may become occasions for in-depth pastoral counseling.

SUPPORTIVE COUNSELING

Howard Clinebell offers seven procedures for supportive counseling—gratifying dependency needs, emotional catharsis, objective review of the problem, aiding the ego's defenses, changing stressful circumstances, action therapy, and religious resources.[9]

A great deal of supportive counseling, as described by Clinebell, is needed by both the patient and family. Depression is a major problem. One patient said, "During physical therapy I could not see the opportunity for new life. All I could see was that dead arm." Another patient told a group of ministers, "Don't ask, 'How are you today?' ask 'How much better are you today?' or 'Where do you feel you have improved over yesterday?'" He explained that he was so filled with his disability and despair over the future that he could not see the positive. One patient described his depression as "massive but short-lived." Depression can also be handled indirectly through the counseling that strengthens the will to live as we shall see in our third goal of pastoral care.

Because of regression and the impairment of senses in perceiving external stimuli, the reception of an overabundance of internal stimuli may account for the severe depression we see in many stroke patients.

All small gains should be applauded, but never compare the patient with well people or encourage competition. Hopes should be raised but don't promise the moon! Admit the problems, but hold close to them the possibilities.

In supportive counseling the clergyman's basic ministry is one of being—being with the patient. In response to the patient's rejection of himself, the minister offers his acceptance. In response to his isolation, he says, "I am with you." To his despair about the fearful future, he says, "Live today." In response to anger and impatience, he says, "Together we will wait upon the Lord."

STRENGTHENING THE WILL TO LIVE

This phase of pastoral care can only begin when the aphasic patient has regained his ability to think abstractly.

The chief characteristic of this type of pastoral care is the search for personal resources. This is a welcome activity for those who are overly occupied with physical and intellectual disabilities. Life is a constant process of learning one's limits and strengths, and accepting and living with them. A stroke changes these strengths and limits and great personal searching is needed. Fortunately, we as ministers can help in this search.

Closely related to the search for personal resources is the reaching out for both spiritual and community resources. In Candler General Hospital's stroke unit, efforts are made to involve local church pastors and volunteers who represent the patient's faith community. A regular part of stroke rehabilitation is speech therapy, physical therapy, and vocational rehabilitation, and many companies manufacture equipment designed to help handicapped people.[10]

Much help is available—if the patient wants help, but motivating him to cooperate is sometimes a big task. It does no good to find strengths and resources if the search ends without purpose—"I don't know why God has left me here, but I've got to find out." Finding a valid new purpose for one's life is a concern for many patients, because what they lived for before their stroke no longer seems valid. LeShan comments that in the process of searching for and discovering goals, hope is reawakened and the person "appears to increase the ability to bear with pain and stress and to organismically fight for his life."[11]

Finding one's purpose or setting new goals have lofty implications which involve one's whole being; but the setting of humbler daily goals, such as "I'm going to try to cheer my roommate up today" are also important. (One patient, returning to the hospital for a visit, joked about having become his wife's automatic dishwasher.) Small tasks such as these help the person feel needed and help him to continue to want to live.

Acceptance of one's limitations and weaknesses is another characteristic which increases the will to live. Denial of one's true condition and pretense of being what one is not ties up life's resources in sham living. St. Paul offers help for this: "My grace is sufficient for you, for my power is made perfect in weakness" (2 Cor. 12:9). Sometimes we need to help a person let go, quit straining, and be merely a receptive vessel.

Another means of strengthening the will to live is the use of grief therapy—encouraging the person to talk about the significant persons and objects they have lost. This type therapy can be used with the stroke patient as with any other suffering person. In this case the lost object may be the person's body image, purpose in living, or vocational opportunity.

Having said this much about increasing the will to live, we must also remember that some patients will die from their stroke. In this event, our ministry as clergymen is not only to help people live, we also help them to die with dignity. However, one doctor has emphasized that most stroke patients who die are in a coma when death comes. In this case our ministry is quite limited, except, of course to the family.

THE FAMILY

We turn now to the family. Sometimes their shock and unfamiliarity with the characteristics of strokes create problems both for the patient and for themselves. The family experiences the usual emotions of any family with an acutely ill member: emotional and physical exhaustion, fear, pre-grief, financial problems, guilt, and disrupted work and life schedule. They are in some need of a supportive and educational ministry.

The family will often be aware that something in their relationship with the patient is hurting his recovery and that is when they will seek help. For example, they may find that yielding to the patient's dependence is harming him as well as themselves.

Some of the problems the family will raise come during the later phases of rehabilitation. Making referrals or helping with such concerns as finding wheelchairs or contacting Vocational Rehabilitation, social services, and so on, serve the double purpose of problem solving and reducing their anxiety.

In our stroke unit at Candler General Hospital, families of
the patients are invited to attend a weekly meeting. The purpose of
these meetings is educative and supportive. If the patient is physically able, he/she may attend the meeting in which a movie on
strokes is shown. After the movie the patients who are tired return
to their rooms and the families talk about their problems and share
their solutions with one another. They are urged to continue attending these group meetings after the patient is discharged from
the hospital. Our stroke program also provides "reunion" parties at
the hospital. Here they renew friendships, and progress and/or
problems are noted and help prescribed.

It is also through the family that the chaplain can have a
significant ministry to the patient. "When you have lived together
as long as we have, it gets to the point when one of us takes a
breath, the other finishes it." This woman was describing the intimate psychological unity of husband and wife. But this also illus-
trates the family's potential for helping or hurting the severely ill.

Freud wrote: "In the last analysis, we must love in order not to
fall ill and must fall ill when, in consequence of frustration, we
cannot love." Freeing the family of those factors which curb their
love, and encouraging their ability to express it, is a life-restoring
function of pastoral care.

Making contact, providing support, and increasing the will to
live—these are offered as general goals of the clergyman's spiritual
ministry to the stroke patient. To the family his ministry is one of
education and support.[12]

Notes

1. Charles T. Tart. *Altered States of Consciousness.* New York: Doubleday, 1972, pp. 1–2, "For any given individual, his normal state of consciousness is the one in which he spends the major part of his waking
   hours. . . . An altered state of consciousness . . . is one in which
   he clearly feels a qualitative shift in his pattern of mental functioning;
   that is, he feels not just a quantitative shift . . . (more or less alert,
   more or less visual imagery, sharper or duller, etc.), but also that
   some quality or qualities of his mental processes are different."
2. Harry S. Olin. Birth to death. *Psychiatry and Social Science Review,*
   3, no. 9: 4–5.

3. Lawrence L. LeShan. Mobilizing the life force: an approach to the problem of arousing the sick patient's will to live. *Pastoral Psychology* (October 1966), pp. 26–27.
4. *Ibid.,* p.25.
5. Samuel Feder. Dialogue on death: Physician and patient. Published in review form in *Geriatric Focus,* 5, no. 1 (Knoll Pharmaceutical company), p. 1.
6. Fred Plum and Jerome Posner. *Diagnosis of Stupor and Coma.* Philadelphia: F. A. Davis Co., 1966, p. 2.
7. James B. Ashbrook. The lost dimension of the physical: Some preliminary thoughts. *Pastoral Psychology,* 17, no. 161 (February 1966): 33–34.
8. Carl Rogers. *On Becoming a Person.* Boston: Houghton Mifflin, 1961, p. 34.
9. Howard Clinebell. *Basic Types of Pastoral Counseling.* Nashville: Abingdon, 1966, pp. 141–144.
10. *Do It Yourself Again: Self-Help Devices for the Stroke Patient.* American Heart Association.
11. LeShan. *op cit.,* p. 28.
12. William B. Daylong. Beyond the wall of silence: Pastoral Care of the stroke patient. *Journal of Pastoral Care,* 28 (June 1974): 122–3.

Suggestions for Further Reading

Books
William S. Fields and John Moossy. *Stroke: Diagnosis and Management.* St. Louis, MO.: Warren H. Green, 1973. (Proceedings of the Houston Neurological Symposium; written for doctors, quite technical.)
John E. and Martha T. Sarno. *Stroke,* 2nd printing. New York: McGraw-Hill, 1969. (For family and friends of stroke victims; in question-and-answer format.)
Journals
Stroke: A Journal of Cerebral Circulation. (American Heart Association; bi-monthly.)
Current Concepts of Cerebrovascular Disease, Stroke. (American Heart Association; bi-monthly.)
Pamphlets
Cerebral vascular disease and strokes. (U.S. Department of Health, Education and Welfare booklet #513.) Many pamphlets on stroke and rehabilitation are published by the American Heart Association. Obtain current publications by calling your local Heart Association.

18

Ministry to the Unconscious Patient

Alquinn L. Toews, B.D.
Chaplain Supervisor
and Director of Chaplain Services
Rochester Methodist Hospital
Rochester, Minnesota

In thinking about the unconscious patient we must consider the entire spectrum which consciousness and unconsciousness covers. Fred Plum and Jerome Posner, in their book *Diagnosis of Stupor and Coma,* have described unconsciousness in this way:

> It is not easy to be terse about the biological definition of consciousness because the term is an abstraction encompassing the total capacity of the brain to provide awareness, insight, thought and communications; indeed, it is the total complement of highest integrative functions adapting and relating man to his environment. Impaired or decreased consciousness reflects severe brain dysfunction, and coma means brain failure, just as uremia means renal failure.[1]

This suggests that consciousness or unconsciousness are not an either/or proposition, but that there are varying degrees between the two, to which one may be called to minister. Plum and Posner have suggested these levels:

> The term alert wakefulness means that the subject responds immediately, fully and appropriately to visual, auditory or tactile stimulation. In the grading of impaired consciousness, lethargy means a state of drowsiness, inaction and indifference, in which responses to stimulation may be delayed or incomplete, and in which increased stimulation

may be required to evoke a response. *Obtundation* is a state of even duller indifference that maintains wakefulness but little more. *Stupor* describes the state from which the subject can only be aroused by vigorous and continuous external stimulation. *Coma* designates states in which psychological and motor response to stimulation are either completely lost (deep coma) or reduced to only rudimentary reflex motor responses (moderately deep coma).[2]

Coinciding with the levels of consciousness and unconsciousness are the suggestions by Dr. Harrison McLaughlin in his book *Trauma* that there are stages of recovery from unconsciousness to consciousness:

> After the initial period of coma the patient becomes semiconscious. In this state he reacts to painful stimuli but does not speak. The next step in recovery is the state of confusion, in which the patient responds by carrying out simple commands, or speaks, but is not clear mentally. There are different degrees of confusion, and the patient may fluctuate between confusion and full consciousness. From the state of confusion he ultimately becomes fully conscious. The duration of each of these states varies with the severity of brain injury, and the stages of semi-consciousness and confusion may be so brief as to be unrecognized.[3]

Hence, the clergyperson may be dealing with a patient at any one of the levels of consciousness.

Clergy must remember that unconsciousness is not an independent state but is always a "symptomatic expression of disease . . ."[4] On the other hand, "Consciousness is not a single function but the combination of myriad factors of man's complex nervous system."[5]

When a pastor stands before an unconscious patient and his/her anxious family, the question he must first of all face is: "Who is the patient?" I like to think of this in these terms: I draw a small circle and label this the "patient primary." This is the person who is lying there in bed and exhibiting most dramatically the effects of illness. Then, I like to draw a larger circle around this smaller circle and label this the "patient secondary." In this larger circle is the wife, husband, sisters, brothers, sons, daughters, parents, etc. The most effective ministry must be directed to the entire patient, both primary and secondary. This then widens the scope of ministry, for the patient is part of the social context of the family. This is an important relationship for him as it helps him keep in touch with his life's fuller context wherein he may find his needed resources and security.

A rule so simple and mundane as to border on the unnecessary is to remember that the patient who is unconscious is still a person. In spite of his inability to initiate or respond, he is still a person whom God has created and he should be recognized and treated as such. Depending upon his level of consciousness, he may still be able to absorb his surroundings; his awareness and feelings may still be functioning at some level of efficiency. The problem is how to visit a seriously ill patient who may not be able to communicate either verbally or nonverbally, and yet who may be experiencing concerns, anxieties, and fears as do others.

The unconscious patient may be like the person who bottles up his feelings and does not express himself. The pastor should recognize this and try to provide some acceptable way to minister to his needs.

The primary support from the clergy needs to come from within through the symbols of his expression, manners, and words. This may convey positive or negative feelings or a mixture of the two. It is necessary that the minister come fundamentally to grips with his personal feelings and concerns so that they will not become an obstacle to his ministry, but rather through him, God's love and strength may be conveyed.

At this time of critical illness the patient primary may well be experiencing one of the feelings common at such a time—loss of self-worth. If he is not given the opportunity of experiencing, to the extent of his ability, fellowship with others, this feeling might be accelerated. When those persons about him no longer speak to him, but rather about him; when they ignore him and come in only minimally, he is driven deeper into this feeling. The pastor has the opportunity of combatting this feeling by regular visits with the patient, and by interpreting the experience to the patient secondary. The active support of the family might well provide the needed strength and hope to help the patient primary.

The attitude of the medical and nursing staff is also important. As they are able to handle their own feelings and relate to the patient primary in a normal manner, such as talking to him while giving care (even though he is unconscious), explaining procedures to be done, and encouraging him to greater awareness by turning on the television or radio, they can provide an environment of life and hope.

There is spectrum within the range of what is referred to as the "unconscious patient." While the patient may not be able to respond, he may be aware of his immediate environment. Therefore, a one-way communication may not only be possible but very meaningful.

One of the common ministrations the pastor may provide is prayer. Yet prayers are often neglected when the patient is unable to respond. This calls into question the whole concept of prayer. If prayers are effective only when the patient can hear them, God has been placed only within the confines of consciousness.

Ministry to the unconscious patient needs to be familiar and meaningful. This necessitates learning about the patient primary from all sources of information. Since the patient has impaired communication or none, the minister cannot always "read" how the patient is receiving and what he is saying. The most appropriate ministry does not require a response from the patient when he is unable to respond, nor continue beyond the patient's strength, nor require deep soul searching. It would rather be an attempt to help the patient draw on his own faith for the frustrating experience through which he is living.

The relatives are often nearby and their many concerns, fears, hopes, anxieties, guilt, and the moral dilemma of "prolonging life" need to be recognized, understood, and accepted by the minister. Verbalizing these feelings to the minister may enable the pressure to come out orderly and safely, and with time, patience, and love, the pastor may be able to help them work through and accept the reality life has presented them. Since hearing is considered to be the last sense to be retained by the so-called unconscious patient, it is most appropriate that conversations concerning him not be held in his room. Such conversations when overheard may be quite upsetting.

The pastor can have a ministry to the unconscious patient although he may not be quite as comfortable in carrying it out as with other patients. He can simply be present in the room for a few moments and perhaps let the patient know this, if possible by touching the patient appropriately. He can speak to the patient, stating the reasons for his visit, on the assumption that the patient might be able to hear. He can read a passage of scripture either silently or aloud. He may also want to pray audibly in the presence of the patient. There are many stories about pastors who have had the courage to carry out such a ministry and were later thanked when the patient regained consciousness and was able to explain that he had been able to hear for days.

The pastor needs to extend his sights to include the feelings of the staff who tend the patient. The doctors, nurses, and others have feelings concerning the patient, their inability to "help" him, moral dilemmas which may be involved, and their own personal concerns which become entangled with their relationship to their patients. These people dare not be overlooked for they also provide a meaningful ministry to the patient.

Notes

1. Fred Plum and Jerome B. Posner. *Diagnosis of Stupor and Coma.* Philadelphia: F. A. Davis, 1966, p. 2.
2. Harrison L. McLaughlin. *Trauma.* Philadelphia: W. B. Saunders, 1959, p. 656.
4. *Ibid.*
5. *Ibid.*

Suggestions for Further Reading

C. G. deGutienez-Mahone. *Neurological and Neurosurgical Nursing.* St. Louis: C. V. Mosby, 1965.

Joseph Fletcher. *Morals and Medicine.* Princeton, N.J.: Princeton University Press, 1954.

Barney G. Glaser and Anselm L. Strauss. *Awareness of Dying.* Chicago: Aldine, 1965.

Sidney M. Jourard. *The Transparent Self,* rev. ed. Cincinnati: Van Nostrand, 1971.

Merck Sharp and Dohme Research Laboratories. *The Merck Manual,* 10th ed. Rahway, New Jersey: 1961.

19

Ministering to the Dying

Carl A. Nighswonger
Former Director, Chaplaincy Department
University of Chicago Hospitals and Clinics
Chicago, Illinois

The purpose of this chapter is to present the basic assumptions implicit in an effective pastoral concern for the dying, and to examine the dimensions of the care which are essential to a responsible expression of that pastoral concern.

The comments which follow reflect the results of a four-year interdisciplinary research project on death and dying in which I participated with Dr. Elizabeth Kubler-Ross, Assistant Professor of Psychiatry at the University of Chicago.

The Basic Assumptions Concerning
the Dying Patient

First, we must reemphasize the holistic approach to man. He is a multidimensional being who can no longer be responded to in a fragmented, compartmentalized, or unilateral way. This may sound trite, or even clichéish, to those who have long been committed to a multidimensional understanding of man as physical, emotional, social, and spiritual; but, in the crisis of dying, it is amazing how

---

Carl Nighswonger died in 1972 while serving as the President of the College of Chaplains of the American Protestant Hospital Association.

frequently we continue to fragment and compartmentalize not only the patient but ourselves as well.

Not only is this evidenced in the unilateral care of the patient, but also in the manner in which the professional deals with his own feelings about the dying patient or person. Following a very intense interview with a thirty-five-year-old woman who was dying of a disease affecting both kidneys, and who had been rejected by three dialysis programs as well as diagnosed as an unacceptable candidate for a transplant, the observing group of professionals indicated their "gut" reaction was one of being "turned off." Further examination of the group revealed a great number of feelings including those of helplessness, frustration, anger, and guilt. Indeed, the patient and her situation had so threatened the group that they had repressed all feelings so that consciously they were able to say she "had turned them off."

To separate one's own feelings from one's response to dying is to compartmentalize and fragment the wholeness of the helping person and thereby to limit the possibilities for a meaningful interpersonal relationship. Our wholeness is as essential to effective pastoral care as the wholeness of the one whom we seek to help.

My second basic assumption is that the experience of dying reflects the twofold sting of death. Too often, we fail to recognize that this last chapter in the pilgrimage of life confronts us with both the threat of death and its meaning for life, and the grief which results from being separated from all that one has ever known in life, one's family, friends, work, and play. The sting of both is toxic and must be responded to with sensitivity and concern.

Freud understood the unconscious as being incapable of comprehending its own extinction, and of defending against death as a threat of annihilation. Philosophers and theologians have long emphasized the human being's capacity to transcend himself and to anticipate his own end. The anxiety produced by this awareness is a normal part of being human; it can enhance the meaning of one's life, or it can victimize one and cripple one's true personal fulfillment.

Although our society may create elaborate practices and procedures to deny the reality of death, the dying patient experiences the reality of the valley of the shadow, and, as the illness progresses, it becomes increasingly difficult to pretend that the "sting" is not, indeed, being felt.

Similarly, one's presence in the "valley" clearly reminds one that all that one has ever known and done in this life is passing away. It is human to grieve the loss of part of one's life; the experience of losing all that one has known is grief in its deepest sense! The loneliness and frustration of this experience may be far more painful and difficult to cope with than the actual malignancy causing the death.

Effective pastoral concern must reflect a sensitivity to both stings, and must concern itself with antidotes for the venom of both if it is to minister to the needs of the dying.

My third assumption is that the experience of passing through the valley of the shadow comes in a series of dynamic dramas, each of which may provide the state for growth in fulfillment, or may impede the fruition of one's pilgrimage. In each drama the dying must act out the specific issues and concerns of the conflict. Effective resolution enables him to move on in his pilgrimage; unresolved conflicts create further barriers against meaning and fulfillment.

From our patients, we have learned that there are five major dramas in dying:

1. Denial vs Panic
2. Catharsis vs Depression
3. Bargaining vs Selling out
4. Realistic hope vs Despair
5. Acceptance vs Resignation

Denial is the human shock absorber to tragedy. It is emotion's anesthetic to an otherwise unbearable reality. We need it to permit us time to muster our forces to cope with a situation which would otherwise overwhelm us. The "not me!" in response to the news of one's diagnosis may be both normal and healthy. Prolonged denial, however, indicates a person's inability to deal with the drama, and may well prevent him even from seeking further treatment for his condition. Partial denial, which is an intellectual acceptance without an emotional acknowledgment, may also be helpful, but it tends to compartmentalize the person's feelings so that they remain unexpressed and the conflicts unresolved.

Panic is the alternate response in this first drama. Rarely is it found to be constructive. All structure and reality checks become lost and the person resorts to impulsive, uncontrolled, and unrealistic behavior. The situation may become so fluid that he sees no way out except by escaping reality. Suicide may seem the only solution. In the case of one young mother of three children, the drama precipitated a psychotic break in which she was convinced that a faith healer had completely removed all disease from her body. She died six weeks later, still out of touch with all reality.

The dying need to be helped to move into the second drama of their pilgrimage in which they seek resolution either through catharsis or depression. If the panic can be averted, or the denial slowly gives way to reality, there is usually a flood of emotion, which either finds expression in catharsis, or is turned inward against the self in depression.

Two types of controls become active in conditioning the person's ability to ventilate. The external controls, which are imposed by family, friends, and staff, including the minister, may not sanction the anger expressed in his protest, "why me?" As one patient said, "When I get down in the dumps, people come in and try to cheer me up." She then quickly added, "and if there is anything that I do not need, it is cheering up when I am feeling blue!" Many of us are more comfortable if the patient is nice, pleasant, and cooperative, and we may unwittingly prevent them from letting their true emotions come out.

But, many persons also have strong internal controls against letting negative feelings out. It is wrong to be angry; it is un-Christian; or it is unloving, and therefore, they dare not express their anger at family, staff, or God. The feelings are swallowed, the anger is turned inward, realistic guilt and shame achieve neurotic proportions, and the drama stops!

The intensity of the guilt and shame in such depression may well force the person to resolve the conflict of the third drama by selling out instead of through the negotiations of bargaining. The badness and unworthiness he feels convinces him that he is getting what he deserves, or his alienation from others becomes so intense that he asks, "What's the use?" In either case, the drama ends in spiritual bankruptcy.

Hopefully, the person is helped to move from the "not me!" of denial, through the catharsis of "why me?" into the bargaining of "maybe not me!" The drama becomes one of attempting to negotiate a deal. Perhaps it is with the doctors: that if he cooperates fully, the staff will make an extra effort, and a new drug or a new treatment will be found that will get him out of the valley. Or, the negotiations may be with God, who can be persuaded to intervene on behalf of the person.

The danger in bargaining is that we ministers often get caught in the game and reinforce the bargaining. We should remain sensitive and understanding listeners, walking with the patient through this portion of the valley as he struggles to see if there is a way out. We need to remind ourselves that such negotiations are very human and normal, and may help the person to move through this period with a readiness for the next drama.

The fourth drama is a transitional period in which the person begins to come to a conclusion about his condition. The alternatives are realistic hope or despair. The spiritual bankruptcy resulting from selling out leaves him with little choice but despair. The awareness that he is dying simply confirms that there is no meaning and no hope. The despair may be expressed in a stoic bitterness, or it may manifest the symptoms of depression, but with a greater sense of doom and hopelessness. (I believe the minister has often failed to recognize the deeper theological dimensions of despair's emptiness and meaninglessness by equating it with the psychological dynamics of depression.)

On the other hand, the person may be helped to experience a realistic hope concerning the future of his pilgrimage. The tunneling process of his illness usually erodes his attempts to negotiate a deal, and he begins to accept the inevitable but with the type of hope that is often difficult for us to appreciate. We tend to associate hope with getting well and a cure, but for the person who has come to this point in his pilgrimage, hope becomes more realistic. It may simply be that his dying will not be prolonged, or without much pain or expense to his family. Or, as one patient said, "I hope that as my hand grows colder and colder, there will be a warm hand like yours to hold."

The final drama in the pilgrimage is concluded in acceptance or resignation. Resignation is the inevitable result of a pilgrimage that spiritually ended in the third drama: having sold out, and in despair, the patient resigns himself to the inevitable meaningless end of existence. He finds himself in the "sickness unto death."

But he may also say, "Yes, it is me," as an affirmation. The drama may lead him through the valley of the shadow to the place where he is able with the "courage to be" to affirm death as the natural fulfillment of life and the completion of its meaning and purpose. Though he may withdraw from those around him, one senses a spirit of peace and equanimity within.

The fourth basic assumption concerning the dying is the awareness of the uniqueness of each individual in his response to death and dying. Although we may generalize about the dramas of the valley, each one experiences them in his own way. It is our responsibility to remain sensitive to his focus of concern as it changes from moment to moment, and illuminates for us where the person is in his pilgrimage, and helps us to avoid identifying with him and assuming that his concerns are those we would have if we were in his place.

Likewise, we need to remain sensitive to the *circumstances* of the individual's pilgrimage. How often professionals fail to recognize the influence of particular circumstances in the patient's life; his personal and familiar history; the variables of age, social roles, and responsibilities as they affect his attitude as well as our own; the type, intensity, and duration of the illness; the family's ability to maintain an equilibrium; and the goals of life, fulfilled and unfulfilled, as he shares them in reflection and confession.

It also implies an awareness of the uniqueness of the individual's expectations concerning his illness and its consequences, and of the incongruence which so often exists in the expectations of patient, family, and staff. These variables reflect and illuminate the uniqueness of each person. The warp and woof of the fabric is always different; although the patterns may be similar, the color shades and the textures vary in a very human and a very personal way.

The fifth and final assumption suggests that the appropriateness which allows one to accept dying is only possible when meaning can be found through the dramas of dying. To be able to conclude one's pilgrimage with a sense that "it is finished" in peace and acceptance is to have found meaning and purpose in the adventure through the valley of the shadow, and that one's pilgrimage has not been in vain.

Reflection on the Pastoral Concern for the Dying

With these assumptions concerning death and dying clarified, let us now explore the dimensions of pastoral concern which shape a ministry to the dying.

The holistic approach to persons recognizes the spiritual dimensions of meaning and purpose. The "appropriateness" by which a person has been able to accept dying implies that such meaning has been found and that death offers a means of fulfillment.

However, meaning is found in two realms of reality. The question of "why me?" and "what is death?" are questions which illustrate the distinction between the realm of specificity and the realm of destiny. Specificity is that realm in which answers may be tested, verified, and validated in a specific and scientific manner. In contrast, answers to such questions in the realm of destiny cannot be tested, validated, or verified with specificity. Destiny is a realm in which one seeks the ultimate meaning of life and death. Answers emerge only out of hope and the assurance of their value only comes through faith which in turn can only be confirmed in love.

Thus, in the realm of specificity the question of what death is may be answered by explaining the factors which lead to the cessation of biological processes. These can be verified in a very specific manner. Similarly, the question of "why me?" can be answered in a most precise way by indicating the nature of the specific disease, the character of its program, and the particular susceptibility of the individual. Such answers can be through physical examination, clinical tests, and biopsy reports. (Further validation may be provided through post-mortem examination.)

But, although such answers may reassure the patient of the staff's medical competence, they do little to satisfy the pain and anguish of the two stings of death. For these penetrate to the depths of man's being which is the realm of destiny.

Ministry, must, first of all, concern itself with those cases which plumb the depths of the realm of destiny. The goal is to assist the dying person to find a relevant life perspective which will bring congruence to the two realms of reality, so that the pilgrimage through the valley of the shadow is experienced with meaning and purpose. Fulfillment in death can only come when one's life perspective adequately answers the question of meaning and purpose in the realm of destiny.

Basic to the Christian ministry is a life perspective which offers such an interpretation. The revelation of God in Jesus Christ discloses the reality of God's love for man, and reveals his concern for man's destiny. It proclaims the possibility of the reconciliation of man's being with the source of all being, God Himself. It calls for a radical obedience which centers life through a faith commitment which makes all other values and commitments, that are in the realm of specificity (work, family, play) relative to that total trust in the One who gives meaning to both life and death in the realm of destiny.

But a life perspective appears absolute only until activated through the responses of a faith commitment. The hymn which expresses, "Oh to Have Faith to Trust Him More," is particularly significant for the dying. The capacity for a mature faith commitment is conditioned by personality development.

It is important to recognize that religious faith may be measured on a continuum between extrinsic and intrinsic. Extrinsic faith functions as a defense mechanism within the personality. It is essentially what Paul Tillich meant by quasireligion which attempts to conceal, manipulate, or distort reality. It protects the person from reality.

In contrast, intrinsic faith is a basic internalized trust which allows one to affirm the reality of death and dying. One does not seek fulfillment along a narrow pathway of defenses, but rather explores the fullness of life and its meaning, centered in the confidence that life is good and that death has meaning.

Moreover, the Christian life perspective interprets the nature of that faith commitment as one which reconciles man, the creature, with the source of his creation, removing the deeper sting of separation. For while he grieves the losses in the realm of specificity, he finds consolation in the fulfillment of his destiny in his radical obedience which inseparably relates him to the Eternal which is victory over death.

Ministry, therefore, in its practical expression of pastoral concern for the dying, is threefold. First, it seeks to involve the person of the minister in the pilgrimage of the dying patient and enable the patient to explore the chapters of his life, past and present, and review the specifics with the illumination destiny.

Secondly, it becomes revelatory of a life perspective which leads to God's disclosure of His love for the very one who is living the drama of dying.

And finally, it becomes redemptive as the person is enabled to make a mature faith commitment which centers his personhood in the fullness of life itself!

Living is transformed into fulfillment. Dying is transformed into "Peace at last." The pilgrimage is "finished." The "Victory is won"!

Suggestions for Further Reading

Donald Bane and Austin H. Kutscher. *Death and Ministry: Pastoral Care of the Dying and Bereaved.* New York: Seabury, 1975.

Glen W. Davidson. *Living with Dying.* Minneapolis: Augsburg, 1975.

Richard Dayringer, Richard Pohl, and James Scobey. A study of grief ministry, in Irwin Gerber, et al., eds., *Perspectives on Bereavement.* Edison, N.J.: Arno, 1978.

Robert E. Kavanaugh. *Facing Death.* Baltimore: Penguin, 1974.

Elizabeth Kubler-Ross. *On Death and Dying.* New York: Macmillan, 1970.

———. *Questions and Answers on Death and Dying.* New York: Collier, 1974.

———. Issues on death and dying. *Journal of Pastoral Care,* (June 1972).

Robert E. Neale. *The Art of Dying.* New York: Harper and Row, 1973.
Robert Reeves, Jr., et al., eds. *Pastoral Care for the Dying and Bereaved.*
   New York: Health Sciences Publishing Corporation, 1973.
Bernard Schoenberg, et al. *Psychosocial Aspects of Terminal Care.* New
   York: Columbia University Press, 1972.

PART III

*Pastoral Care
for Children*

20

To Touch a Child

Robert B. Wedergren, B.D.
Chaplain, University of Texas
Medical Branch Hospitals
Galveston, Texas

I stood at the edge of the world and asked, what of life?

What of love?

What of pain?

What of feeling?

Who lives, who loves, who hurts, who feels?

I asked, but I heard no answer:

Only the emptiness of waves upon the shores, of wind in the trees, of sunshine and growing things in the land, the sea and air.

I turned my face to the sky, the sea, the mountains, the open spaces,

To the big things of the world about me,

Nothing came back that I could understand.

I turned my face to the cities and farms, to factories and schools and places of learning,

A babble of many voices and many people came to me in many tongues and many noises,

Some said words without meaning and others made sounds without words.

I said, It is because I do not understand their language for all are talking. The fault is mine because I have not learned to understand.

And I was angry at my ignorance.

A child took my hand and smiled:

I put my arms around her and felt the warmth of her small vibrant body against mine!

In her I felt love and I was not alone.

I said, I will learn their language and then I can understand.

I have time now for love, even the love of a small child gives me contentment and courage and meaning. Love gives me curiosity and patience and a tomorrow.[1]

It would be interesting sometime to put down in writing thoughts that can occur while reading a Scripture lesson to a congregation assembled for worship. Such an occasion arose for me right before the beginning of Lent. The lesson was the well-known love chapter of Paul I, Corinthians 13. And the particular verse was the eleventh: "When I was a child, my speech, feelings, and thinking were all those of a child; now that I am a man, I have no more use for childish ways."[2]

That reference to "childish ways" stirred a reaction of dismay. While not knowing Paul's mind here, I wondered if he was saying that childhood is a second-rate period of life. It does seem that few of the Lord's Apostles speak to and deal with children other than in a reference to giving respect and honor to parents. Parents are also to love their children, thus suggesting a mutually beneficial and healthy relationship. But was Paul meaning something to the effect: "Thank God I am not a child anymore! I've left that time of life and am now in a much better time . . . now I'm an adult"? Since the context of this verse is clearly love, it occurred to me that this verse must have the same flavor. But the wondering persisted.

Of greater significance is the Lord's contact with children in what might be viewed as a "touching ministry." A rather familiar text, employed in some baptismal ceremonies and certainly in many Sunday School plans, is the record of Mark 10:13ff: "Some people brought children to Jesus for him to touch them, but the disciples scolded those people. When Jesus noticed it he was angry and said to his disciples:

Let the children come to me! Do not stop them, because the Kingdom of God belongs to such as these. Remember this! Whoever does not receive the Kingdom of God like a child will never enter it. Then he took the children in his arms, placed his hands on each of them, and blessed them.[3]

To "touch a child" and to bless in this touching has compelling beauty in this account. Many of us have seen this scene portrayed by artists . . . and we may recall that the kids looked pretty healthy. Maybe they were . . . but perhaps some may not have been. Some might have been diseased, stricken, ill. At any rate, our Lord exhibits a definite fondness, appreciation, and love for children; a love that also came out in that brief but potent directive: "Take care of my lambs."[4] Evidently our Lord's world was also a world that included children, where childhood was its own time, a significant time, a time for needed understanding, a painful time on occasion, a time of all-embracing importance for the totality of the young life.

The tremendous impact of the whole of life upon children and the difficult road through childhood is currently receiving much attention. For instance, Transactional Analysis builds its case on the childhood years in a most creative way. And, too, some recent investigations reflect the critical importance of childhood experiences both on a relationship level and that of environment and situational exposure. In *Family Weekly* in an article entitled, "Experts Agree: Something is Terribly Wrong With America's Children," Alan D. Haas makes reference to a three-year study by prominent child psychologist, Dr. Olga R. Lurie. The particular study carried on in New York's affluent Westchester County reveals: "that one of every two children in homes with mid-range incomes is suffering from some degree of emotional impairment requiring mental health services."[5]

The same article indicates that studies done among the poor are even more disturbing. Here it is thought that four out of five children have some degree of emotional impairment." Emotional is a catchall term denoting "a malfunction in some important areas of the child's life—in school, with friends, or with his family. Common symptoms are antisocial or impulsive behavior, feelings of isolation, anxiety, and low self-esteem."[6]

It is interesting that in an effort to pinpoint causes, Lurie says something quite comforting: "Parents are on the whole quite intelligent and dedicated to doing a good job for their kids, but the strain of our stressful society is just too much for them to do it alone."[7]

In circumstances like this, "to touch a child" (and his parents) with a ministry of love and understanding, closeness and supportive appreciation, bestows a blessing. For as the 1970 White House Conference on Children established, "Children need people in order to become human."[8]

It is intriguing to think that all of us "touch a child" in a way that involves our own childhood. While we do acquire techniques and maturity and employ these, our own childhood background remains extremely influential. How much of our contact with children draws on the resources of our, "speaking, thinking, and feeling like children?" How much depth, dimension, and substance in our ministry flows from the well of those days back when?

A young woman came into the hospital some time back for treatment of a weight problem. She was a jovial person, exhibited a keen sense of humor, and was interested in a variety of things. Her weight problem had been with her from childhood, and she had tried on several occasions to lose, but success was only limited and temporary. During her hospitalization, which lasted well over a month, she completed her tests, and the rigid weight-loss regimen began. It was a tough, rugged experience. Incidentally, this woman was involved with children as a special-education teacher. She was creative, involved, dedicated to her class, and apparently quite successful.

On a second admission she was still losing, though slowly. And it was in this period that I learned how unhappy her childhood had been. Her father showed no attachment to her. She could recall no time when he told her he loved her or showed it with his touch. The relationship from his side was one of rejection so that she could never feel loved in his presence. So she grew up without the warmth and security of her father's love. While she craved it and longed for it, that love never came. Her mother, on the other hand, was very loving, and provided the caring and the security of a parent. However, as she pointed out, her mother would tend to offer food to replace the father's concern. So she grew up substituting food for her father's love. And her father died without ever having really "touched" his child. She still retains the wish that he could have loved her even though she realizes that door is now closed.

From what I have observed and felt in her presence, this young woman, in spite of that severe blow dealt in childhood, deals with her "children" with sensitivity, appreciation, and love. "I know how some of them feel in their home situation," she remarked. Was she not "touching" their lives out of her own childhood with all that this meant to her?

A nurse in Pediatrics for whom I have great respect exhibited a tender, warm relationship with children and parents alike. One day in conversation, I asked about her sensitive, caring attitude. Her childhood was relatively happy although she spoke of some communication problems with her parents. She did recall quite vividly a deep concern about animals. She felt that her compassion and interest in children were related in a way to this feeling for animals. She also recalled a serious involvement with her own feelings. She told of one example that occurred during her nurses' training. The group was asked to write an essay in which they discussed why each one wanted to enter nursing. "Everyone was shocked," she said. "I admitted that I was doing this not only for others but especially for myself."

Her honesty about herself and her feeling and involvement with children is the way she lives. I have seen her eyes register concern; I have heard her speak softly in love to those young, precious ones. She has supported many a child and parent with this "way" of hers. The good feeling on her floor is due in great part to her being there—"touching a child."

What both of these child-care specialists offer is a personal "touch." Surely their training and professional credentials are of value, but out of the context of their own vivid childhood. Out of the positive and negative influences of those days have come artists who have the "touch" for life.

At the start of a recent school year our son had some real difficulty and suffered from what I've heard termed as "school phobia." He would complain of upset stomach, headache, would visit the bathroom frequently, and would cry. My wife and I were quite upset as we tried to deal with it. Our frustration and anger did not help the situation. Some days we would get him to school only to have him call later to say that he was sick.

I talked to a psychologist who works in a nearby medical center and told him of our dilemma. He readily agreed to talk to our son, Jim, at his school. Well, Jim was quite impressed with this young man. He told me some of the things he suggested, but it was obvious that Jim just plain liked him. "Dad, you should see him, he looks just like Tim Conway!" (a favorite comedian in our house). This psychologist has continued to see Jim from time to time just to say hello and see how he is doing. My impression is that, while this man is capable and adept as a professional, he is also a man whom our son just likes. I mentioned this to the psychologist and he said, "So many of these kids feel like I did. I can honestly say to them, 'I know how you feel.'" He "touches" children so well. And he does this from his own personal experience.

By becoming aware of the continuing significance of his own childhood and by noticing the great importance that Jesus gave to children when he "took them up in His arms and blessed them, laying His hands upon them,"[9] the pastor can learn to "touch" a child in his ministry.

Notes

1. Russell L. Dicks. *Principles and Practices of Pastoral Care.* Englewood Cliffs, New Jersey: Prentice-Hall, 1963.
2. From the *Today's English Version of the New Testament.* Copyright American Bible Society, 1966, 1971.
3. *Ibid.*
4. *Ibid.*
5. Alan D. Haas. Something is terribly wrong with America's children. *Family Weekly Newspaper Magazine* (January 16, 1972).
6. *Ibid.*
7. *Ibid.*
8. *Ibid.*
9. *Ibid.*

Suggestions for Further Reading

Eric Berne. *What Do You Say After You Say Hello?* New York: Grove, 1972.
Audrey E. Evans and S. Edin. If a child must die. *The New England Journal of Medicine* (January 18, 1968), pp. 138–142.

Haim G. Ginott. *Between Parent and Child.* New York: Avon, 1969.
Haim G. Ginott. *Between Parent and Teenager.* New York: Avon, 1971.
Rolf E. Muus. *Theories of Adolescence.* New York: Random House, 1962.
Virginia Satir. *People Making.* Palo Alto, CA.: Science and Behavior
   Books, 1972.

21

Establishing Rapport with Hospitalized Children

John Schaefer, M. Div., Ed.
Instructor, Program in Community Mental Health
and Program Coordinator, Mental Health Administration
Continuing Education Program, Tulane University
School of Public Health and Tropical Medicine
New Orleans, Louisiana

Each child, when hospitalized, experiences trauma which will exhibit itself, depending upon age, with some regressive form of behavior. It is not uncommon for a five-year-old child, to the utter horror of his parents, to wet his bed, to ask for a baby bottle, to ask for a pacifier, or to suck his thumb. I feel that a minister can be a creative force in helping children to deal with the trauma of being hospitalized. I strongly believe that one's ministry should be primarily focused on the hospitalized child. I have yet to see parents who would not respond to my ministry once rapport had been established with their sick child.

How does one establish contact with a child? A pastor must be willing to use body language and other nonverbal techniques to establish rapport. You must assess very quickly how withdrawn a child is and you can do this by taking your fingers and making a game of walking them toward a child. By the child's reaction, you can determine whether or not physical touch is possible. Being able to touch a child and being comfortable about it yourself and having the child comfortable is very important. For the most part, the people in the hospital who touch a child do so only to "hurt" him. The child should learn that not all touching experiences are hurtful (perhaps adults also can learn that touching experiences can be pleasurable). Oftentimes a child is so withdrawn that you

205

will have to use other things besides voice and touch to establish rapport. It is most helpful to have a hand puppet with you to talk with children. At our hospital, the volunteers give each child a Pinkie puppet. Most children will carry on a most revealing conversation with Pinkie when they would not say a word to you directly. Oftentimes you can talk on the telephone or have your doll talk with their doll and get the most intimate information. It never ceases to amaze me what a four-year-old can read from a blank sheet of paper. It is time well spent to allow your own inner child to come out and play dolls, checkers, scrabble, Monopoly or chess, with a hospitalized child.

For older children, try getting them to draw pictures of the hospital, their beds, surgery, or the body organ that is sick. One child, age seven, drew a picture of the hospital in brown that had no windows. Although he said, "A hospital is a place where people get well," I wonder what his no windows or door to the hospital said about his gut reaction to being sick. Another child, who did not have a visit from his parents the eight days he was in the hospital, drew a picture of the hospital that used blacks and reds. Interestingly enough, this picture included a car which symbolized perhaps a getaway car. You know that you have "arrived" when you can get a child to draw a picture and write a story at the same time. A girl showed the story of a child being wheeled on a stretcher by a nurse to the operating room. Her story said, "This is a girl who is going to surgery for a kidney operation just like I had, she is a little scared."

Once rapport has been established, then a clergyman can do his thing whatever that may be. There are many legitimate things that he can perform, and he may at any given time do one of them. I feel quite comfortable in helping to prepare children for unusual or traumatic experiences. Often, as with adults, there is a gap in the communication between physician and parent/child, or between nurse and parent/child. The very thought of having an x-ray taken can have a child climbing the walls. The sight of blood from a slight cut can overwhelm him. Children who undergo open-heart surgery have a double whammy to deal with. Their parents oftentimes have not resolved their own guilt feelings about having a child with a physical defect. Although most of us, intellectually at least, do not believe that God causes punishment ("sickness"), emotionally it is another story. The child is caught between wondering why he is "different" and trying to be a "good child" at the same time. I think it is time well spent communicating with parents while a child is hospitalized.

During the oedipal phase of psychosexual development, children raise and deal with the most profound of religious questions: "When I die, will I become an angel?" "If Fluffy dies, will he go to heaven?" "Are God and Jesus the same person?" One young adult recently put a religious question to me this way: "I have been thinking an awful lot the past year about hell. I cannot see where God who loves me would want me to be in a place called hell. I think we create our own hell on earth. As for an afterlife, I don't know about that. I guess when I die I will know but until then I have to live life."

Often pastors feel that some of the techniques that I have described are just "playing" with kids. I feel differently. As the commercial says, "Try it, you may like it."

Suggestions for Further Reading

Warner F. Bowers. *Interpersonal Relationships in the Hospital.* Springfield, Illinois: Charles C Thomas, 1960.
William G. Hardy, ed. *Communication and the Disadvantaged Child.* Baltimore: Williams and Wilkins, 1970.
Robert L. Noland, ed. *Counseling Parents of the Ill and the Handicapped.* Springfield, Illinois: Charles C Thomas, 1971.

22

Ministry to Hospitalized Children

Harold W. Buller, Th.M.

Chaplain
Beatrice Community Hospital and Health Center
Beatrice, Nebraska

How does one see the child as "it" comes to the hospital? It could be that the wording of this question itself gives us the clue to the answer. For a man we use the pronoun "he." For a woman we say "she." But so often we lump children with chairs, chip dip, and cheetahs, saying "it."

I suspect that this way of referring to the child is not entirely a grammatical accident. It derives rather from the way children have been seen in the past—without gender, sexless creatures devoid of a basic emotional personality that needs to be respected by the adult.

An illustration of this is the relation of the child to the adult sex life in medieval times. We are told that in those days it was not unusual for the adult sex partners to engage in their love life in full view of children, since it was thought that children entertained no sexual responses and so could not be involved in what they saw. Children were "its," able to feel, think and remember only on a very superficial level. Consequently in Charles Dickens' day and much more recently a cripple was popularly considered to have a "cripple" personality—bitter, resentful and vindictive—just because he was a cripple. There was no understanding of the childhood experiences as a cripple that, together with rejecting adults around him, shaped his personality.[1]

With Sigmund Freud came the beginning of our understanding of the child as a human being, already personally and vitally related to the powerful life forces of emotion and feelings that motivate the adult. As Erik H. Erikson says, "Before Freud, man (that is, man of the male sex and of the better classes) was convinced that he was fully conscious of all there was to him, and sure of his divine values. Childhood was a mere training ground *in charge of that* intermediary race, woman."[2] As we see here, even women were not considered fully human.

The child was first discovered as a human being when Freud worked with members of precisely this "intermediary race," who were suffering from the symptoms of hysteria in the Victorian day of the domineering male—a time when children were to be seen and not heard. As Erikson explains, the majority of these symptoms proved "to lead back to events when violently aroused affects (love, sex, rage, fear) had come into conflict with narrow standards of propriety and breeding."[3] Thus, Freud "investigated memories" as representative cross-sections of a patient's emotional condition. In successive memories, he traced trends which led, like pathways, to the traumatic past; there experiences of a disruptive nature loomed like lesions interfering with growth. Thus, "the search for traumatic events in the individual's forgotten prehistory, his early childhood, replaced the search for lesions in early development."[4]

In a ministry to hospitalized children, then, there are at least two primary things that must be remembered; in other words, two ways in which we need to see the child. (1) The child is already fully human, needing to live and deal with the "violently aroused affects (love, sex, rage, fear)." (2) When we minister to the child in the hospital, we are involved with the "traumatic events" of this child's future "forgotten prehistory." This means that a ministry to hospitalized children is serious business. It means it is high time that the personhood of the child as a patient in the hospital needs to be taken just as seriously as that of the adult.

The Child in the Hospital

What happens to the child in the hospital? Let's begin with little, laughing Laura whose big blue eyes said she was three years old in every lively sense of the word. That was when I met her on her first day on the pediatrics ward. Mother was with her. Laura seemed to feel secure.

Then, the tests started—tests that involved needles and big, unpredictable x-ray machines. Before long her mother was told Laura, still little but less laughing, had leukemia. It would be fatal. Laura seemed to feel quickly that something about her mother had changed. It became necessary to cling to mother more often. Then mother needed to go home for a few days to tend to the other children. She would be back in a few days. But Laura did not understand that.

Laura tried to seclude herself in a big chair in the empty waiting room at one end of the ward, the chair where her mother used to sit. There I found her sucking her index finger and clutching a blanket from home, her fearful eyes looking about apprehensively—or closed tight in an attempt to shut out her new world. When I came and knelt beside her she nodded mutely at my comments, as I tried to reach her heart through the new shoes that had meant so much to her. Suddenly, she turned away. Then, without removing her finger from her mouth, she stammered, "Go away. I don't want to talk to you any more." Obviously, I had not been speaking to Laura where she was now.

What was happening to Laura, so fully human at her tender age? Dr. Robert E. Cook has written an excellent chapter entitled "Effects of Hospitalization Upon the Child." In it he says, "I think all of us must realize that the major disturbance a child suffers is separation, which may be divided into separation from things he is used to—home and furnishings, particularly his toys—and separation from people."[5] In place of these the child is introduced to new things, new activities, and new people. This, he says, is experienced by the child under many types of circumstances, but when the child comes to the hospital the separation is often accompanied by illness, anxiety without outlet (like play opportunity which Laura, fortunately, did have access to) and suddenness. Besides that, the new things consist of frightening laboratory equipment comparable to TV space monsters. New activities consist of strange routines like baths before breakfast, often painful procedures, and meals served in bed. "Sometimes," says Dr. Cook, "it seems that great originality has been expended to make the hospital routine as much unlike the home as possible."[6] New people consist of nurses, doctors, and others who come in large numbers. They enter the child's life suddenly, too often concentrating their impersonal attention upon a disease—an entity from which the child cannot separate himself. To add to the unreality of these relationships, as J. Vernick and M. Karon write, "Physicians and other paramedical personnel are not immune to their own feelings, fears, and anxieties concerning death. Consequently they feel obliged to 'protect' the child from anything that would cause undue concern when in reality they are protecting only themselves."[7]

Poor little depersonalized Laura! The chair, in which she curled up as though it were a womb, was only a vague reminder of another with whom she had known herself to be human. The blanket represented home and everything she felt at ease with there. So, she rolled it up and held it as closely as she could.

Unfortunately, all this is not erased as soon as the chair and the blanket are changed back into their original forms—that of mother and the home environment. In a study of more than 200 children, half of whom consisted of a control group, Dr. Dane G. Prugh found that sixty of these later had definite adaptation problems after hospitalization. A number of these were severe.[8]

Prugh, writing in still another setting, indicates that the phenomenon of "settling in"—adjustment to hospitalization and the separation—is deceptive.[9] Here he refers to a study of children up to four years of age by James Robertson that shows that elements of shock, anger, distrust, anxiety and intense emotional deprivation are the universal reactions demonstrated during the hospitalization and/or the return home. As the child seeks to cope with these feelings it is inevitable that he, if hospitalized long enough, will go through a progression of protest, despair, and denial in an anxiety reaction to the separation experience.

The first stage, "protest," with its loud cries and rejection of the nurses, is usually taken for what it is. The next two stages are the deceptives ones: "despair" with its withdrawal and apathy is sometimes confused with acceptance. This is where we see Laura. In the last stage, "denial," there is more interest in and responsiveness to surroundings. In fact, it would seem that the child has fully accepted everyone and is adjusted to the circumstances in which he finds himself. But this apparent attitude is possible only because the child has denied to himself the need for his mother and cut himself off from the emotion of love even for her, lest he be hurt again. Now severe damage has been done—just when the staff members think they have succeeded. At this point the mother is relegated to the status of an impersonal nurse, except that she may be more useful to the child as a source for toys and candy.

When the child finally returns home, it will take much patient love, permitting him to reestablish and to trust the former dependent relationships. It comes as no surprise that a child, having passed through the experience of denial of his need for parental love, may manifest symptoms of regression and insecurity long after his return home. Parents will need to be patient and understanding when the child flits about from one activity to another with an air of unconcerned independence, refusing to be cuddled as on earlier occasions by those who love him.

The Clergy's Ministry to the Child

If these, then, are some of the things that happen, or at least can happen, to the hospitalized child, how does one minister to him? It would seem that many a pastor is at a loss to know how to minister to a child, and finds it difficult to know when a ministry has been given.

Our ministry to the child, more clearly and more urgently than with the adult, needs to fall into three main areas. These are ministry directly to the child in a person-to-person relationship, ministry through the parents, and ministry through the hospital staff. The first (person to person) is almost taken for granted with adults. But it becomes a unique experience with the child where a relationship is often emotional and inward rather than defined and empirical, even on the surface.

The importance of the second area (ministry through the parents) becomes evident when one recognizes that the child standing alone and outside of a family unit, is the most pathetic sight this world has to offer. Unfortunately that is sometimes where the hospital places him. The life outlines of a child and his parents overlap and merge into each other. In a sense the parents of today (or what the parents fail to be) are already a part of the child in the future.

The third area (ministry through the hospital staff) relates to the chaplain's responsibility to the other team members as a person trained in human relationships and sensitive to the often lonely presence of personhood and humanity in an efficient, antiseptic, and disease-fighting institution.

Person-to-Person Ministry

In the pastor's ministry directly to the child, he enters the presence of a "little Laura" with all the implications of an immature life torn out of its context of security (which we hope that it had beforehand) and placed in a hospital bed. How much easier it would be to relegate the child to the status of an impersonal "it," say a few cheerful words, and move on to the adult patient. To feel this way is an indication of the minister's insecurity in the presence of the unknown that the child often presents. We will take time to listen to an adult for half an hour. He gives us words. This is something to work with even when we fail to hear the real meaning behind them. But how does one listen to a child for that long?

Sometimes our ability to listen and to hear may be a matter of attitude. We speak of "levels of communication" as though one is higher or better than another. Perhaps it would be better to say that there are types of communications. The child may not be able to use words. They have not yet become meaningful symbols to him, but he speaks eloquently with every aspect of body and soul. And it may well take just as much time to hear him out and to communicate acceptance as it does with an adult. The question is, are we willing to learn a new language?

It may be a language of silent time spent sitting beside a bed or watching a TV program with the child. Or a language of touch, "spoken" at just the right moment. It could be spoken with a pencil or a crayon. Pictures say things. The child "speaks as he colors." And the minister can answer in kind. Or, the offering of a doll by the child to the minister may be a synonym of the child herself. In a similar vein one pastor uses a puppet on his hand when he enters the room. In his case the puppet says that the pastor understands and loves the child. With it he recognizes the child's need for distance, permitting him to decide when he is ready to move beyond the puppet to the real person.[10]

It is necessary to understand that this language has many dialects—as many dialects as there are children. And the minister must listen to interpret them. Often one can enter rather easily into a child's play, but just this week the otherwise almost friendly little David could not be interrupted to include anyone. It soon became apparent that he was too busy stabbing the nurse who had just stuck his unprotected bare behind with a needle. This he had to do himself to gain relief from his frustration.

So, one could speak of the importance of play in the communication of a child. With it he expresses his anger, shuts out the unbearable, expresses his joy, tries himself out for size, and reaches toward new people asking for their friendship.

A prayer spoken at the bedside of the child prior to a tonsillectomy may also be for the benefit of frightened parents. But when it thanks God for that litter of puppies waiting back home for Jimmy, Jimmy can participate on a meaningful level. Obviously God, whoever he is, must care about Jimmy too.

Ministering to the Child through the Parent

With child and parent so much a part of each other, a ministry to the parent will help create that atmosphere in which the child may ultimately accept himself. In one specific instance it was the grandmother that ruled the family in which a four-year-old boy, an only grandson and the son of an only daughter, had a fatal form of leukemia. When this became known the young grandmother's sense of guilt, as related to many aspects of the boy's life and which had been structured primarily for her own benefit, was visited in bitter retaliation on everyone. This included God who would "exact such an unjust punishment from me for no reason at all." The child, who sensed rejection by the key figure in the family constellation, in spite of showers of gifts became an angry, rebellious terror. This continued until the grandmother could begin to accept what was happening.

Vernick and Karon sum up the concerns involved here rather succinctly when they say:

> Children are very acutely attuned to the wavelength of their environment. Consequently, when this environment signals that certain subjects are not to be discussed and may be too painful for the adult to deal with in a manner which transmits some degree of strength, the child becomes mute, outwardly accepting the adult's benign words of falsehood but inwardly feeling abandoned. He is left to cope with his fears and anxieties by himself at the very time when he needs and seeks all the strength and support himself."[11]

Under these circumstances, as these writers also indicate, the child may go elsewhere for his information, usually to other patients, or he may try to interpret chance remarks. The result is misconception and misunderstanding that can only increase anxiety. It is important for the child to know that he is in an environment where it is safe to ask questions and be completely confident of receiving an honest answer. Both home and hospital need to be—or become—just that.

Even if the illness or the circumstance is not serious the child must still use available knowledge—or lack of knowledge—to evaluate his position and react accordingly. So one little lad who had stepped on a nail in a building where he was not supposed to be was brought to the emergency room. Here, he cowered in abject fear. "Don't shoot me. Don't shoot me," he whimpered. "Who said anything about that?" asked the nurse. "The policeman said he'd take me to the hospital where they'd give me a shot," he explained.

In many cases, of course, the parents have already begun to accept the illness, but still wish to shield their child from the dire facts involved in it. The parents may think that the child is unaware of his condition. Actually, he/she quickly senses that something is seriously wrong as his/her routine is changed. He senses it in his parents' mysterious distance. The parents, too busy trying to lead the child away from the truth, do not realize that he/she is better at covering the truth than they are. The emotional energy that could be used to support the child with an encompassing, understanding love goes instead into the much more difficult task of acting as though everything was all right.

Some doctors today seek to tell the child of the illness at the same time that they tell the parents. The doctor explains what the illness is insofar as the child can understand, and what he hopes to do about it. This gains the child's cooperation, assures him/her that nothing more serious is being withheld, and permits parents and child to relate in an open, honest way.

Another area where it is important to help the child through his parents was illustrated when a mother told me, "I didn't explain a thing to Johnny about this tonsillectomy. I let him believe that he was going to have a picnic. There's no need to worry a child with fear of pain before it actually comes." Johnny was already about four years old. It was no surprise that a jolly, carefree Johnny became a vicious little tiger as soon as the laboratory technician arrived to stick his finger. Thereafter, he had to be forcibly held down for every procedure. There was no time to gain his confidence, since he was scheduled for surgery about an hour after admission. Upon awakening, he screamed endlessly. Johnny had been deceived. He did not know how much worse things might become. Nor could he trust anyone's word regarding the future. Children need to be prepared beforehand for hospitalization.

After the child comes to the hospital for a tonsillectomy, with admittance too often shortly before the hour of surgery itself, the pastor can usually do little but throw in a comment about sore throats past and present—if he gets to the patient at all. With a surgery coming up, many a parent would be most receptive to guidance in helping his child meet this shocking event.

The importance of mothers living in with their children at the hospital is seen more and more clearly. Dane G. Prugh's findings indicated that in the two-to-four-year-olds anxiety over separation from parents was more common and intense than in any other age group.[12] But we cannot ignore this type of reaction in the older child also. Dr. Alexander J. Schaffer has written a chapter on the "Advantage of Mothers Living In With Their Hospitalized Children." In it he refers to a study by David Levy indicating that 9 percent of the four-to-twelve-year-olds had severe reactions to hospitalization.[13]

The current possible magnitude of this problem is illustrated by the results of a study done by Robert H. Dombro on how often mothers are permitted to live in with their children. He found that only twenty-one of ninety-one American and Canadian children's hospitals and twenty-one out of ninety-two general hospitals with pediatric departments, also in the United States and Canada, had facilities for this. This indicates how scantily the need for parents living in is actively recognized by many—possibly outdated— medical communities. Nevertheless, studies have shown that severe emotional reactions to hospitalization can be significantly reduced when living in is permitted.

With the medical climate the way it sometimes is with regard to parents, the pastor can often do the child a favor by encouraging a hesitant parent who has been brushed off, perhaps unintentionally, by a busy nurse, to stay around as much as possible. Some nurses still feel that children cry less if the parents can be gotten to stay away. A study done by Dane G. Prugh, however, found just the opposite to be true. Those children whose parents visited frequently cried less often, in their certainty that the parents would return.[14]

We begin with the thought that the child is already fully human. He/she already begins to deal with the basic affects—love, sex, rage, fear. It is only as he is helped to cope with these in the hospital environment that his/her illness will become an experience upon which he can build. If he/she cannot control these emotions at this time he/she will be blocked from receiving and assimilating new stimuli that help him/her to grow. Consequently the hospitalization experience may well be a terrifying blank. Instead of being moved to new heights, he/she will be retarded or caused to regress.[15] Often the alert minister can help to determine the difference.

Notes

1. Leo Kanner. *Child Psychiatry.* Springfield, Illinois: Charles C Thomas, 1957, p. 52.
2. Erik H. Erikson. *Insight and Responsibility.* New York: Norton, 1964, p. 27.

3. *Ibid.,* p. 26.
4. *Ibid.,* p. 27.
5. J. Alex Haller, Jr., ed. *The Hospitalized Child and His Family.* Baltimore: Johns Hopkins Press, 1967, pp. 5–6.
6. *Ibid.,* p. 8.
7. J. Vernick and M. Karon. Who's afraid of death on a leukemia ward? *American Journal of Diseases of Children* (May 1965), p. 393.
8. Dane G. Prugh, et al. A study of the emotional reaction of children and families to hospitalization and illness. *American Journal of Orthopsychiatry,* 213 (1953): 70.
9. Dane G. Prugh. Protest, Despair, denial may be reactions to long hospitalization. *Feelings and Their Medical Significance.* Columbus, Ohio: Ross Laboratories, 3, no. 10 (1961): 2.
10. John Schaefer. Ministering to hospitalized children. *The Journal of Pastoral Care.* 19 (1965): 144.
11. J. Vernick and M. Karon, *op cit.,* p. 394.
12. Dane G. Prugh. Emotional reactions of children and parents to hospitalization. *Feelings and Their Medical Significance.* Columbus, Ohio: Ross Laboratories, 3, no. 10 (1961): 1.
13. J. Alex Haller, *op cit.,* p. 2.
14. Robert H. Dombro.
15. Dane G. Prugh, *op. cit.,* p. 2.
16. See chapter on The importance of play for the child in the hospital, by Paul Lemkau, M.D. in J. Alex Haller, *op. cit.,* pp. 43–51.

Suggestions for Further Reading

James Anthony and Cyrille Koupernik, eds. *The Child and His Family: The Impact of Disease and Death.* New York: John Wiley, 1973.
Matthew Debuskey, ed. *The Chronically Ill Child and His Family.* Springfield, Illinois: Charles C Thomas, 1970.
Irvine Redlener and Clarissa S. Scott. Incompatibilities of professional and religious ideologies: Problems of medical management and outcome in a case of pediatric meningitis. *Social Science and Medicine,* 13B (2): 89–93, 1979.

23

Pastoral Concerns for Children in Hospitals

Palmer C. Temple, M. Div.
Chaplain Supervisor
Children's Memorial and Grant Hospitals
Chicago, Illinois

These reflections come out of my experience as Chaplain at Children's Memorial Hospital in Chicago. Children's is a 240-bed pediatric hospital on the near North side of Chicago. Our patients, for the most part are very seriously ill children between one day and sixteen years of age. They include surgical, medical (cancers, cystic fibrosis, diabetes, kidney failure) and neurological patients. In my work with these patients and their parents several significant themes have emerged.

HONESTY OF FEELINGS

I am impressed with the need for honesty in relationship to children, especially very sick children. By this, I mean a personal stance toward them that is essentially open and committed to straight talk. I do not mean a technical accuracy of facts, but rather an open appreciation of the realities of the situation. We should not lie to children that procedures "won't hurt" or that they "are not very sick" when, in fact, they are. When a terminal child asks me how sick he is, I am most apt to elicit his own answer to that question. Most of the time they are quite aware of the severity of their illness and a lengthy technical explanation is not necessary. We must be honest. When a very sick child is obnoxious it is important to treat his/her behavior as you would that of an obnoxious well child. Being honest with feelings communicates respect for the patient.

NAMING OF NAMES AND TOUCH

One of the rituals that we go through in our chapel services at Children's Memorial has to do with the naming of names and touching. At the beginning of every chapel service, I name the names of all the people present. If I do not know the name of a child I will go up to him, perhaps squat down at eye level, ask his name, and then share it with the rest of the congregation. Before the service really gets too far, everyone knows each other. During the service I try to touch each child. This may be before the service starts, during the service, or afterwards as they leave. It is very important to make physical contact with children. By this I do not mean an uninvolved "patting on the head." More commitment is exacted of us than just that. By touching the shoulder or the hand or the head of a child, a person can communicate his physical presence and his desire to be close. This seems to be an important dimension of pastoral work with young persons.

ALL THE WAY

In all of our hospitals we see occasional extraordinary procedures to save life. The running of incessant IVs and blood transfusions often seems futile with older patients. We may be equally appalled when we see what seem to be extraordinary measures carried out on a child. This is not an argument for additional extraordinary means of preservation of life for terminal children. However, I am increasingly aware that we need to communicate to children that they are not going to be abandoned. We will go all the way with them. This level of commitment seems to me to be of great importance to parents and I find it imperative to help them see that they have a responsibility to go all the way. When they have done that in terms of living through critical illness and death with their child, they seem better able to move into the future, incorporating this as a real but painful part of their lives. We observe serious problems of guilt when parents feel that they quit trying prematurely.

STAFF

Part of our pastoral concern for children has to do with how we relate to hospital staff. We need to teach and demonstrate by our presence the absolute necessity of involvement with kids, even though it comes at a price. Sometimes we will react to illness and death in children with extreme anger—and so does the staff. After the death of a particularly beloved child, staff is apt to respond with uncharacteristic coldness. A part of our pastoral function may be to help them own up to this. Some staff members have adoption fantasies about every sick or distressed child, and we may be obliged to help them keep their distance from this crippling involvement. Many staff feel guilt when death comes; they did not do enough, they were helpless, or they were not present when the child died. A part of our pastoral concern for the children who remain involves our dealing with the rumblings of these leftover feelings.

DEPRESSION

We must acknowledge that working in a children's hospital or on a pediatric ward is a depressing business. It depresses us, parents, children, and the staff. We do our best for children if we can acknowledge our own sense of depression with our spouses and intimate friends—no doubt they see it anyway. But we do not need to rehearse the entire day's grief in the evening when we come home. It is enough to find somebody who can listen to us occasionally, because we are not capable of digesting it all by ourselves. If we do not attend to our own recurring depressions, our effectiveness in our daily rounds will be compromised.

Suggestions for Further Reading

Nathan B. Talbot, et al. *Behavioral Sciences in Pediatric Medicine*. Philadelphia: W. B. Saunders, 1971.
Sula Wolf. *Children Under Stress*. London: Penguin, 1969.

24

Pastoral Care for the Dying Child and His Family

Carl Rabon Stephens, B.D.
Chaplain
Walter Reed Army Medical Center
Washington, D.C.

The clergy who attempt to minister to the dying child will find that he is dealing with three distinct groups: the dying child, the family of the dying child, and those members of the hospital staff who are concerned with the care of the dying.

Before we can minister effectively to the dying (of any age) we have to come to terms with the meaning of our own dying, for not until we ourselves have worked out fully the purpose of life and of life's end can we hope to be of assistance to those who find themselves in the "valley of the shadow." Each time we stand by a deathbed we come face to face with our own departure, so we must be prepared to answer (to our own satisfaction) such questions as "Where did I come from?" "Where am I going?" In addition, the pastor who ministers to children with a terminal illness must know how to recognize and manage his own emotional defenses concerning death before he can hope to deal effectively with the emotional response of the dying child and his family.

When we attempt to minister in this crisis, our aim is not only to help the child but also to help the family to accept appropriately the loss of a child, the most profound of griefs for a parent. To do it well one must have clearly in mind one's goals and a method of achieving them. In order to establish realistic goals we must remember: (1) Each child is an individual. He is unique. There is no one else like him. (2) The child's reaction to his own death will depend upon his age, and the ego development already achieved at the time the crisis is experienced. (3) The child's reaction to a catastrophic illness is shaped by the kind and amount of emotional help available to him from the members of his family. (4) Since death is not simply a medical problem but a problem of living and humanness, it needs an interdisciplinary approach.

Now, I would like to speak to each of these issues in turn. First, I want to discuss the uniqueness of the child. There is no one exactly like the child you are attempting to minister to. That also means that there are expressions of his uniqueness, and these have to be faced and dealt with. No child lives in a vacuum. Things keep happening to him. His world is enmeshed in strong feelings. The good feelings he wants to repeat; the unpleasant ones he wants to get away from as much as possible. When things happen that are quite painful, he reacts by retreating into a world he makes more comfortable by his defenses. Some of these might be quite simple; others are more complex.

When he is faced with a big problem—he may develop a big escape and may wander far into the realm of fanciful thoughts. What he is trying to do is to match his ideas of escape with the size of the threat he experiences. Some of his escapes may be healthy and useful. Some may become a hazard that could increase with years. If he retreats from the unpleasant facts of life by trying to live in an unreal world, he may make it difficult to keep clear distinctions between what is real and what is make-believe. However, I have found that it is not always helpful to attempt to dispel these fantasies. The power to ignore a reality is a mighty force which has spared many sufferers weeks of agony. I have very often found that a process of adjustment is taking place behind this denial of reality in which the ego is gradually learning to accept the situation and ultimately discover the relief of being able to discuss it sensibly with doctor, pastor, and family.

Because he is so dependent on the adults around him, he is almost defenseless against their feelings. This makes it important for us to be both sensitive and responsive to this child so that he may know just what is happening. When this is so, the young personality can be helped to face the crisis caused by his impending death. What is needed is warmth and reassurance in simple and direct form. It is important to be able to share as much of his life with him as possible as he has experienced it in the past. The opportunity to help a child face reality and handle his deep emotions wisely is a privilege to be treasured. It invites the care and competence of one who is deeply concerned with the immediate and the long-term results.

I have found that the best way I can do this is to establish an intimate relationship with the child if he is old enough to respond. The nature of the intimacy that is appropriate will be different for different children and for different families. But an appropriate intimacy between a child and a pastor is indispensible if the pastor is to help him die appropriately. I look for opportunities to invest something of myself in him. I can invest in his feelings, his fantasies, and his associations. It is important to remember in attempting to minister in this way that we cannot deceive a child for very long. He easily sees through our falseness. Therefore, if we have not sincerely invested in him and his family we should not claim that we have.

Children respond to dying with the emotional reactions natural to a child at that age. In other words, a child lives and dies as a child. He deals with his approaching death as he comprehends the task, and he responds to the challenge with the strength of a child. However, a child has to have a definite, specific concept of himself as an individual being before he can begin to really understand that his death means the difference between "me" and "not me." When a maturing child grasps, even faintly, the reality of his existence as a unique person, he cannot avoid the questions of where he came from or where he is going. A child usually becomes aware of death as the end of life in a meaningful way at the age of five or six. Prior to this the most effective ministry we can offer a child is through a meaningful, supportive relationship with the members of his family.

For space and simplicity's sake I shall divide childhood into three phases: birth to age five, age six to age ten, age ten through adolescence. The toddler and the young child view death as a natural phenomenon but are rarely aware of their own mortality. He needs the loving care he has always known and he must not be subject to inappropriate changes in his management, so that life

can go on in as normal a fashion as possible under the circumstances. The three-year-old can be relatively untouched by discussion of his/her death. He/she knows that he is cared for, loved, and
guided. He/she can play blithely with his toys and his pets as other
family members discuss and struggle emotionally with the fact that
he/she is dying. Only when there is parental reaction of grief and
distress does the child realize that there is something to be feared.

The young child of preschool age does not understand death.
When the child of this age is faced with the prospect of his own
death he is almost completely dependent on those who are for him
and who love him for whatever understanding he has of his situation and guide him in facing this life task. He takes his cue about
how he should respond to the disease process from his parents,
from his family, and from treating personnel. His personal dying
only has meaning to the preschool child as it affects the people
around him. He has lived in the security of his parents' protection.
He should die with the same support. If he is certain that his
parents will still care for him, no matter what happens, the dying
child may be able to go to his final rest happy and comforted.

If the chaplain can help the child's family with their emotional
struggle about the approaching death, the child himself may become much more settled. It is indeed a pastoral function to encourage the parents to treat the child normally and not to spoil him,
which will be their first impulse. Happiness is based on security,
and any change in the parent-child relationship will tend to make
him insecure. They should be encouraged to live each day as it
comes, and to avoid wondering what the future holds.

During his grade-school years a child begins to move away
from his home, intellectually and emotionally, but he still continues to depend on his home for basic security and continued
stability. The grade-school child pictures death as a separation
from those he loves, with physical existence maintained "in heaven."
However, the treatment team should be aware that most young
children are not really happy to go to heaven, because this journey
means separation from their parents and family. He does not want
to leave home. He is happy with his family. Quite often the young
child from six to ten has begun to think of death and may occasionally think about his own dying. He is not likely to associate any

illness he may have with the prospect of dying and will rarely ask whether he might die from his illness. Rarely does he express his fear of death unless some personal experience of death in the family has brought him face to face with the impact of death.

The grade-school child knows that death means a final separation from life. He knows now what he will miss. He must mourn this loss as he leaves. He is sad and bitter because he does not want to go. He is lonely because he is traveling this journey alone.

The grade-school child needs to have faith in something or someone more powerful than his own certainty or his own humanity. A child of this age believes in parents and in God. He needs rules to live by. With the rules of God, society, his family, and himself, the young child, during the grade-school years, tends to organize his universe methodically. To a ten-year-old child the assurance of an adult has deep meaning. He can build on it. The pastor should keep a way open for the child to talk with him whenever he wants to. It is important that the dying child knows that he can find a reassuring and understanding adult who will talk with him whenever the need exists.

It is widely acknowledged that the adolescent lives in a transitional world. He is constantly vacillating between the role of a dependent child and an independent adult. He is trying to locate himself with respect to his past and his future, to attain a new footing as an individual and as a member of social units. He lives in an intense present: "now" is so real to him that both past and future seem pallid by comparison. Everything that is important and valuable lies in the immediate life situation or in the rather close future. The young adolescent wants to live. He is supremely able to live and to experience. Death fascinates him because it is one of the deeper experiences of life. However, while the young adolescent may be fascinated with dying as a part of living, he does not wish to stop existing. The young adolescent must emphasize to himself that he is really self-sufficient and independent. If he turns to his parents for support, understanding, and comfort he may feel that he is surrendering and submitting to their punishment.

The lonely and dying adolescent may violently reject his parents, his family, and the adult members of the treatment team—not because he does not desperately want their understanding and support but because in reality he so much longs for their caring that he cannot allow himself to admit these feelings. He wishes so much to be cared for and protected that he dreads losing control over himself. He longs for understanding but so greatly fears the loss of his new independence that he has to force people away. However, the dying adolescent between ten and fifteen years, may allow himself to be a child in the bosom of his family as death grows nearer, as long as he does not feel he is being treated disrespectfully. The minister can help the child and his family by making them understand this.

Since the young adolescent has already a tendency to feel guilty as he tries to separate himself from his parents, he frequently sees death as confirmation that he has been bad. It is sensed as merited punishment. When a dying adolescent has a secure belief in a warm, benevolent God, this belief will continue to be a source of strength and comfort. As long as he saw God only as someone or something with whom he was threatened in an inconsistent fashion he often saw death only as another threat or punishment from a vindictive deity. The pastor must be aware of what religion does mean to each child, and then he can help at the level the child can use. In order to meet the adolescent in this crisis, the chaplain must believe in his own humanity and be willing to encounter the adolescent in his, even if the youngster expresses open anger at God who is allowing him to die. God can be given the full responsibility for the child's dying, since death is beyond human understanding and control.

I have found that the best way to do this is to develop a relationship with this child in which we become important to each other. I try to discover everything I can about the child which makes him interesting to me. I encourage him to do the same thing with me. This is not a gimmick. If it is genuine; it can be a powerful means of establishing very strong ties. We cannot deceive children about important feelings, for they easily see through our falseness. Therefore, if he is not important to me I do not try to tell him he is. A child looks to the adults about him for his security in life. The problem then is how to be honest with our own feelings and at the same time continue giving security to the child. This is to say that, as clergy, we have an obligation to temper the expression of our feelings by the wisdom and judgement that characterize our maturity. We have to be in touch with our deepest emotional feelings and be able to mobilize them for a creative ministry.

Ministry to the parents should always form part of our total ministry to the child, and ideally, this relationship should be established before the terminal stage is reached. Their anxieties and their attitudes to death can easily be transmitted to the open and receptive mind of the child. Unwarranted and false promises must be avoided at all cost, for "excess of hope is presumption and leads to disaster."

The family has no option but to live through this painful experience in as productive a fashion as possible. Sometimes it is helpful if members of the treatment team can talk openly with the family about how difficult it is to deal with such a fluctuating disease and such an unpredictable situation. In this way they can help the angry, sorrowful family to channel their mourning in a productive fashion. It is much more useful if parents express their mourning and anger by battling the disease rather than attacking the treatment team. However, we ministers must provide an opportunity for an expression of deep and genuine emotions, which cannot be locked up in a closet as if they had no right to exist. Even the most uncomfortable things have to be faced openly. Depending upon the child's age, we must help the parents understand what makes for a happy child, emphasizing the need for love and security without sacrificing discipline. The treatment staff should not allow the dying child to bludgeon any member of his family, emotionally or physically. At all times the treatment team must be very aware that they are treating not only the dying child but also the mourning family.

It is very easy for the sick child to use his illness as a means of manipulating people. The parents may need a great deal of support and encouragement to deal with the youngster in as healthy and as realistic fashion as possible. One of the ways we can do this is by assuring them that they did not do anything to cause the disease and nothing they could have done would have prevented it. Many parents experience a severe guilt reaction when they discover their child is dying and they must be reassured that it is not their fault.

We should caution parents against devoting all their time to the dying child to the exclusion of the other children in the family. When the dying child is in the hospital the parents should be encouraged to go home at night if death is not imminent. This lets them maintain contact with their other children and provides some relief from the institutional setting. Regardless of whether a child has been meaningful in his family in a positive or a negative fashion, his death will mean a loss and a difference in the family. As a part of any mourning process, parents and other family members must begin to reinvest emotionally. We must "bless" this aspect of their mourning.

When a child has died, it certainly does not help the grieving family when the physician or nurse or pastor says "he is much better off now where he is." No parent, no brother, no sister, no family member likes to be told that a part of himself or herself is better dead. After the child has died, the family should be permitted to express their feelings naturally and without embarrassment. The child learned very early that there is an acceptable social pattern for dying, so family members learn that there is an acceptable way of reacting to a child's death. However, I do not feel that it is our job to impose any sort of behavior on them, but to give them absolute freedom to express the depths of their feelings.

Whatever the religious conviction of the family, the time of death is not an appropriate one at which to attempt to instill a "Christian point of view." Such education should have begun far earlier in the church school, in sermons, in classes, in seminars in which persons are encouraged to share their attitudes and feelings about death.

Since death is not a medical problem but one of living and humanness, it calls for an interdisciplinary approach. I sincerely believe that the clergy can make a major contribution in the treatment of a child who is dying by helping families and medical staff to find the courage to do what they *ought* but *fear* to do. In order to do this the minister plays different roles with each person involved. First there's the personal role in which he is involved with persons as a person. Then there is that of a professional in which he is involved with persons as a pastor. The third role of the minister is that of theologian, where it is his task to theologize about such important issues as pain, evil, dying and other human experiences. In the fourth, the minister dispenses the sacraments and provides other sacerdotal functions. Yes, for children too, symbolic acts are important. They appreciate such acts as the holding of the hand, the forming of the sign of the cross in blessing, and the touch of the laying on of hands. In all of these, our main goal is to help preserve the quality of life, even for the dying child.

Death is never a private matter, especially when it is a child who dies. In caring for the dying child, the team members will find that their roles are inextricably intertwined. The team is only as strong as each member is strong. No one, professional, or nonprofessional, has a monopoly in caring or in strength. In helping the child pass through death, the parents themselves are an essential part of the treatment team. They and other members of the family need to so interact with the hospital staff that together they give the dying child the best treatment, the finest care, and the greatest comfort. The minister can help to facilitate this creative interaction.

Nurses, social workers, laboratory technicians, dieticians, ward maids, aides, volunteers, cleaning and housekeeping personnel, school teachers and school secretaries all become involved in the death of a child. Too often they are forgotten and nobody bothers to interpret to them what is happening. Each has a job to do and would do it better if someone took the time to explain what is happening and to find out how each is coping with it. I suggest that the best person for this job is the chaplain and the time he spends with hospital and school personnel will be amply repaid.

Death is not easily dealt with (especially the death of a child) because it is not easy to look at. Throughout man's history death has remained the eternal mystery which is the core of our religious and philosophic systems. None of us can deny that our culture and our Church has done a less than adequate job of teaching about death, and assisting persons in dealing constructively and hopefully with either their own death or the death of a loved one. In attempting to minister in the face of death, we frequently use terms which side-step the reality of what has happened, that tend to avoid and deny. When we do this we allow hope to rest upon a denial of the realities that confront us. This sort of hope is empty and inadequate.

Do we have anything worthwhile to say at this critical time? Yes, I think we have, if we speak out of the strength of our faith. As

I see it, religious faith is healthy when it supports a person's efforts to face and deal with reality. It is unhealthy and destructive when it seems to avoid and deny reality or imply a reliance upon magic. Nothing is quite so reassuring as reality in a crisis.

How do we go about ministering in this way? The two most important factors in a pastor's function seem to me to be his presence and a sensitive responsiveness toward the feelings of others. He need not say a great deal. His very presence expresses more of his concern as a human being than anything he could ever say. God created persons to stand in a meaningful relationship to each other and to Him. Indeed, this is our faith. This is what ministry is all about.

Suggestions for Further Reading

Earl A. Grollman. *Talking About Death: A Dialogue Between Parent and Child.* Boston: Beacon Press, 1970.

Rachael T. Hare-Mustin. Family therapy following the death of a child. *Journal of Marital and Family Therapy,* 5 (2): 51–60, 1979.

Edgar N. Jackson. *Telling a Child About Death.* New York: Channel Press, 1965.

Oscar Lewis. *A Death in the Sanchez Family.* New York: Random House, 1969.

Marjorie Editha Mitchell. *The Child's Attitude to Death.* New York: Schocken Books, 1967.

Elizabeth L. Reed. *Helping Children with the Mystery of Death.* Nashville: Abingdon Press, 1970.

PART IV

Pastoral Care for the Aging

25

Aging with Meaning

David F. Freitag, Th.M.

Former Chaplain
The Christian Church Homes of Kentucky
Louisville, Kentucky

The crises of the aged are similar to those of childhood and adolescence. The birth of a child begins with a struggle for survival. He is totally dependent upon his mother for food, comfort, love, and toilet attention. The opposite end of life reflects these exact needs with equal dependency. When the child matures he is confronted with problems of adolescence. He must sort out values and find new goals that will maintain his motivation for change as he replaces dependence with independence. At retirement, the aging person finds himself again reflecting on new values and goals that will provide meaningful support for his declining years. And he must struggle to relinquish his independence and face inevitable dependence. This he must do with respect and dignity.

I will now embark on a case study of a Mr. West which will provide a vivid example of the crises that the aged person faces. Mr. West is eighty-five years old, a retired machinist, a widower, and has a small income from social security and pension. He was very active in church and union affairs until he lost the use of his car due to disability. All of his life Mr. West has found meaning for his existence in his successes and achievements. He had been a prisoner of success for sixty-five years. His status, his possessions, his family, his friends were all symbols of his success. Maintaining it has been his motivating force through life. Success has provided the fullness of his life. And even after retirement he has been able to feel accomplished by reminiscing about his success and using it to reinforce his ego strength.

But then something happened—a heart attack and a broken hip, a major setback—and he now realizes that old age and disability are upon him. It is a rude reminder of approaching feebleness and dependence. The "whys" of his anxiety reveal his griefs and despair for a way of life now ending. He is confronted more than ever with how meaningless and unfulfilled his life seems in the light of this crisis.

All that Mr. West has done in life to achieve and to succeed is gradually slipping from his grasp, never to be regained. And in his mind success is beginning to lose its charm and value. The "doing" and the "having" are surrendering to the "being." What becomes of supreme value to him now is not what he is still able to achieve but what he is, and at the same time, the feeling of nonbeing is the root of his despair and his sense of uselessness. Mr. West realizes he cannot recover time or recreate the circumstances of what he was. It has been twenty years since he has felt achievement. What now is his motivation to exist, as he questions, "What is the real meaning of my life outside of material wealth and success?" A truer meaning of life needs to be discovered.

I believe that we as ministers of God can supply the guidance and inspiration to help the aged person discover meaning in his declining years. Success and material wealth have supported the physical desires of life. Medicine and technology are less effective on the body and, at best, can offer only limited relief and temporary renewal but little hope for full recovery. In addition, growing old has already weakened and destroyed his sense of spiritual wellbeing: loss of work, loss of status, loss of mobility, poverty, death of respected friends, and ill health have all subtracted from the meaningful life he has known. He begins to give up to the point of showing manifestation of senile psychoses based upon his defeat and withdrawal from life.

The Christian religion fits this situation perfectly. After all, Mr. West has reached these years with a religion that has sustained him and provided strength and comfort in other crises. But in the years of solitude and descending failure his religion has been allowed to weaken through loss of contact with the church and he has all but lost his sense of anything beyond himself. He has become self-centered and his God is a part of this ingrown system. All he knows and perceives is distorted by his inward perspective.

It still remains that the personal encounter with God is the decisive experience that gives life meaning and perspective. The meaning of life is to know God's grace and mercy. To possess Jesus Christ is to fill the vacuum of inner space with new space. Mr. West claims he has known God all his life. He has recognized someone beyond himself who controls his fate or judges his deeds. But now he has lost all sense of the presence and power of God working beyond his own limited perception. To his recollection nothing new has transpired between God and his soul. His present ideas about God are based on old experiences on which he has dwelled too long. His religion has stagnated. He needs help in seeing the continuity of God's love in his present situation. Because he feels deserted, rejected, forgotten by others, he cannot be blamed for feeling that God, too, has left his unimportant life.

The minister is, in the eyes of this elderly man who has lost his ability to think abstractly, tangible evidence of God's presence; he represents concrete evidence of the God he so desires to know. Because of his isolation, God has eluded his grasp, and in losing contact with God he has lost the meaning of life. But as Mr. West encounters another person beyond himself who communicates the grace of God, he reaches out to encounter God. In Mr. West's response to acceptance and understanding he has reached out in acceptance of God.

Finding meaning in old age is not easy nor is it a commodity that the clergy can supply. It involves nurturing three elements of life. We will call these elements simply "practical," "psychological," and "spiritual." For instance, Mr. West should be permitted and encouraged to make decisions on things that pertain to his own destiny. He should be helped to find a sense of purpose through useful activity. His living in the past should be supplemented by new experiences and new memories to give life variety and spice and something to look forward to daily. All of these are movements and indicate process and progress in life. They are in drastic contrast to his static existence where stimulation comes passively through eating, hearing, and seeing.

Psychologically, the pastor can help Mr. West overcome obstacles to a meaningful existence. He can help him find relief from the grief that he has carried for ten years. He can help him conquer his fears of dependency or illness or death by supporting him as he tries to accept his old age. The pastor can bring the message of the Gospel to bear on these confused emotions and create a less threatening atmosphere in which meaning can be discovered.

But these practical and psychological efforts only provide the freedom to seek the meaning of life. Where, then, is meaning discovered? I cannot know nor can I lead him there, for I have not been there. But as long as Mr. West is eager to know and find meaning, he is in need of my support and guidance. So I journey with him.

I see myself, then, as a companion in this search, making myself available when necessary in three ways. The first crutch I offer is myself in a wholesome dependency relationship. Mr. West, unlike an adolescent, is in need of someone to depend upon. His journey has naturally brought him to dependency and it cannot be denied him. And a dependency relationship is now desirable and healthy because his needs and future dictate it. His environment is genuinely difficult and is growing more so. In this less formal relationship I am permitted to guide, support, and encourage him more than I would a troubled teenager.

I help him muster his own shrinking reservoir of strategy for adjustment. There is always slow, if any, improvement for coping with the next problem. His goals are short-term and aimed only at alleviating present frustration. Long-range changes are nearly impossible. He must learn to cope with the present. He has to discover meaning for each crisis and frustration and find that they are worth living through.

A second crutch is provided by my time to listen and understand this person who must now command my undivided attention. In the time when we encounter and experience each other in the presence of God, we encounter and experience God. As he is drawn out of his self-centered isolation, he is drawn toward Someone beyond himself and he experiences a fresh reminder that God is alive.

As I listen, he speaks in tones of grief, anger, then remorse and despair. He speaks, too, of his fears, but what I hear most is, "Why am I still alive? There isn't one thing in the world that I want to live for. I wouldn't care if I went tomorrow. All my friends are dead; my family no longer comes to visit. I'm old and feeble: what's the use?" I am there—I listen—I try to understand his feelings. After talking, we tie up the loose ends in a prayer to God. His response to me begins to express a different attitude. He says, "You've made my day—it's nice to know someone cares. Will you come back soon?"

He speaks with one breath of his uselessness and in the next of his appreciation for someone who makes him feel worthwhile. He affirms his right to live. He has chosen to live another day. For a few moments he has encountered the living God—the greatest human event.

Because I have brought some visible, concrete evidence of God's love and of God's desire to act in every situation, he has been able to embrace God. And by embracing God he has embraced the whole of life and has again affirmed his faith and hope in Him who will sustain him through life, death, and the resurrection.

What the aged person needs more than anything else that the Church can offer is to find meaning in life through encountering God. And to do that he needs another human being to lean upon and to intercede for him and to remind him that God is here. He doesn't ask the way, but only for someone whom he can depend upon to walk with him—someone who will listen and understand and be his companion. The minister is not a savior. He is only an instrument of God—a person through whom a twenty-five-year-old man can see Jesus and realize that because Jesus cares, he himself should care.

Suggestions for Further Reading

Jean B. Abernathy. *Old Age Is Not A Four-Letter Word.* Nashville: Abingdon Press, 1975.

James H. Barrett. *Gerontological Psychology.* Springfield, Illinois: Charles C Thomas, 1972.

Arthur H. Becker. Judgment and grace in the aging process. *Pastoral Psychology,* 27 (3), 1979.

J. E. Birren. *The Psychology of Aging.* Englewood Cliffs, New Jersey: Prentice-Hall, 1964.

Paul J. Brown. *Counseling with Senior Citizens.* Englewood Cliffs, New Jersey: Prentice-Hall, 1964.

Robert E. Buxbaum. The use of religious resources in the care of the aged. *Journal of Religion and Health,* 8: 143–162.

Francis M. Carp. *Retirement.* New York: Behavioral Publications, 1972.

D. Christiansen. Dignity in aging. *The Hastings Center Report,* 41 (1974): 6–8.

William M. Clements. The sense of life time in human development. *Journal of Religion and Health,* 18 (2): 88–92, 1979.

Edmund Vincent Cowdry. *Aging Better.* Springfield, Illinois: Charles C Thomas, 1972.

Elaine Cummings and Henry E. Williams. *Growing Old: The Process of Disengagement.* New York: Basic Books, 1961.

Erik Erikson. *Identity and the Life Cycle.* New York: International Universities Press, 1959.

Minna Field. *Aging with Honor and Dignity.* Springfield, Illinois: Charles C Thomas, 1968.

Edward Green and Henry Simmons. Toward an understanding of religious needs in aging persons. *Journal of Pastoral Care,* 31 (4): 273–278, 1977.

Donald H. Gustafson. On growing old . . . and dying. *Christianity and Crisis,* 31 (June 1971): 115–118.

John J. Herr and John H. Weakland. *Counseling Elders and Their Families.* New York: Springer, 1979.

Adeline M. Hoffman, ed. *The Daily Needs and Interest of Older People.* Springfield, Illinois: Charles C Thomas, 1970.

Doris and David Jones. *Young Till We Die.* London: Hodder and Stoughton, 1973.

Carrol A. Londoner. Survival needs of older church members: Implications for educational programming. *Pastoral Psychology,* 22 (May 1971): 14–20.

Henri Nouwen and Walter Gaffney. *Aging, the Fulfillment of Life.* Garden City, New York: Doubleday, 1974.

Arthur P. Rismiller. *Older Members in the Congregation.* Minneapolis: Augsburg, 1964.

J. E. Runions. Pastoral care of the elderly. *Pastoral Psychology*, 23
    (March 1972): 39–44.

Burk K. Smith. *Aging in America*. Boston: Beacon Press, 1974.

Paul Tournier. *Learning to Grow Old*. New York: Harper and Row, 1972.

W. E. Wygant. Why me Lord? *Pastoral Psychology,* 23 (October 1972):
    29–36.

26

Pastoral Care to Geriatrics

C. Raymond Probst, B.D.
Chaplain
St. John's Home
Rochester, New York

Pastoral care to the aging has been a concern of the Church since its inception, and the clergy have been ministering to the spiritual needs of the elderly in private homes, hospitals, and institutions for years. As a matter of fact, many nursing homes for the elderly were established in past years because ministers and their congregations realized a community need and worked to fulfill that need. Oftentimes a minister was appointed as the first administrator of a church-related home. Then, as nursing homes expanded and housed greater numbers, professional administrators assumed the primary responsibility for these homes and their services. Recently, many of these administrators have decided that they need a fulltime, clinically trained chaplain on their staff in order to obtain a balanced approach to the total care of the older person.

As the first director of Pastoral Care at St. John's Home in Rochester, New York, I am aware of the great need for spiritual counseling to the elderly (and I may add that I've found no ministry more rewarding). To bring hope to the hopeless, comfort to the dying, spiritual strength to the bereaved, as well as to share in the joys of celebrating birthdays and wedding anniversaries of many years, in the births of great and even great-great-grandchildren, and in the remembrances of long-forgotten friends—these make the ministry of the chaplaincy both rich and full, challenging and rewarding.

A chaplain's ministry is concerned with much the same areas of service as is any pastor's ministry, that is, regular worship services, Bible study classes, hospital calling and bedside ministry, self-growth and sermon preparation, and so on. Therefore, this ministry necessitates constant evaluation of priorities of duties and time allotments. The primary task (and one that will be discussed in this paper) is that of the supportive role that the chaplain plays in the one-to-one relationship between the older person and himself.

The minister must remember that the older person usually spends a good portion of his day alone. Due to increasing immobility, the elderly person has to adjust to new limitations which keep him from participating in social activities. His frustrations during this adjustment period often cause inward feelings that he needs to express and learn to cope with. Some of these feelings may express great hostility. As one man said to me, "I can't understand why God would let this happen to me. I don't want to hear anything more about how merciful God is. He certainly has not been to me!"

It is at these times that clinically trained clergy can support and uplift the anxious, distressed person, and be a pastor in the very best sense of the word. He must be aware of the troubles of these isolated persons, and develop good rapport. The older person needs someone to talk with, someone who will listen with interest and concern, someone whom he can trust and know, someone who will help him in any way possible. And though many older persons would not seek pastoral care, or admit that they were lonely or troubled, they nevertheless welcome and appreciate the regular pastoral visits which give them a chance to talk openly about their concerns. Indeed, without these opportunities for expression, frustrations could develop into more serious problems, to be evidenced in increased physical and mental symptoms.

From my own experiences of counseling, four major areas appear to cause anxiety in the elderly, and for each a minister's supportive role can he very helpful.

First, a person often becomes anxiety-ridden because he has

lost a sense of worth. He realizes that his increasing infirmities make him very dependent upon others; he cannot care for himself in his surroundings any longer. The loss of personal possessions with resulting financial insecurity may cause another sense of dependence, most difficult to bear for one who has long been independent. He loses his sense of personal value. This is when he needs the emotional and spiritual support of the pastor to endure and adjust through this transition. Frequent visits reassure him that because the pastor is his friend and visits him often, he must still be a person of worth, one whose company another enjoys. Convinced of this, his physical and emotional ailments may well disappear, because this helps him physically and psychologically, as well as spiritually. Sometimes he will develop new interests or hobbies, which help him to gain a further sense of accomplishment. Consequently, his self-value is greatly enhanced, as he reaps new rewards.

A second major cause of anxiety in the older resident is loneliness and depression. He is lonely because he has lost a spouse, a child, or a close friend. He is depressed because he has left his home or apartment (a familiar environment) to become a resident in a nursing home. His single room must then contain all his personal belongings. These are realistic conditions that need adjustment, and the adjustment can sometimes prove almost overwhelming. Here the need arises for the pastor to act as supportive counselor.

Neither the pastor, nor any other person can be a substitute or replacement for the deceased spouse or relative, nor can he make the new room and the surrounding environment "home" for the resident, but he may serve as a means for the older person to express his inner conflicts. He can help by being once more someone to talk with, to share memories, frustrations, lost hopes and goals with, and thus strengthen the resident during this adjustment period.

To illustrate: Two women in their late eighties, who had lived together and worked together in Christian work for more than sixty years, recently came to share a room at St. John's home. After breakfast every morning during those sixty years together, the two ladies had read portions of the Bible and shared devotions.

Last fall, one of them died very suddenly in the presence of the other. Needless to say, this was a great shock to Mrs. Blue, the one left to live alone. It was difficult for her to accept because it had happened so suddenly, and because the two had worked and lived together for so many years.

Several days following the memorial services for Mrs. Brown, I went to see Mrs. Blue. Just as she and her friend had usually shared devotions, she was continuing her daily meditations. I apologized for the intrusion, but she quickly asked if I would like to share in the devotions. I was pleased to accept, and to know that she trusted me as her friend and would permit me this privilege of sharing.

Though I can never take the place of Mrs. Blue's lifelong friend, I can give her the support she needs at such a time in making the adjustment necessary to face this time of day that had been so meaningful to both throughout their lives together. Just the presence of understanding was helpful. I shared with this woman the loneliness caused by the death of a loved one.

In contrast, very often a person who says she is lonely has not lost friends, but is lonely because she is an isolated, antisocial person who has been lonely all her life. She has never developed social relationships, and, thus, in old age, feels the emptiness deeply. She has not enjoyed social friendships up to this time and, it is not very probable that she will be able to do so now. In addition, this loneliness may be felt more as she observes other residents enjoying family and other visitors, or attending the various social activities of the home, activities in which she will not allow herself to participate. This in turn may cause abnormal behavior. She may become violently hostile toward the doctor, nurse, or some other resident for no apparent reason. She may deliberately break objects, refuse medication, or destroy property to get attention. Or she may withdraw completely for some time and refuse to respond to anyone.

Often when such unusual behavior is manifested, the chaplain can counsel this older person, because he may symbolize to her the protective understanding and security which she needs. The resident may view the chaplain as a friend (which she deeply needs) and not as a disciplinarian—not one who would make her do something that she does not want to do, as a nurse makes her take her medicine, or the doctor forces her to stay on a controlled diet, or the therapist insists that she do certain physical exercises which are often painful to her. This then places the chaplain in a unique position: he is her friend, pastor, and support. The chaplain's visits can bring security and a social relationship which often eases frustration and brings about peace of mind. This may result in patient cooperation with other staff members, which in turn will be gratifying to the lonely and depressed older person.

Anxiety can also arise in older persons from a third major cause, namely fear of death and dying. Though not every resident feels a lack of self-worth, nor an overwhelming sense of loneliness and depression, each at some time expresses a desire to know what will happen to him physically after the pronouncement of death. He wants to be secure in the knowledge that his wishes will be fulfilled. Uppermost in his mind is the matter of the funeral itself and where it will take place, open or closed casket, cremation, burial, funeral service, or memorial service, what minister will conduct the service, exactly what will be done with his personal possessions, and so on—all the immediate matters following death. As a rule, the resident has already set aside the necessary funds to cover these expenses, or has previously paid the funeral director to carry out the instructions that he has proposed. (Many fear that they will be buried as paupers, or by the county, if things have not been otherwise arranged. This to them would be a terrible disgrace.)

The chaplain should note the residents' preferences concerning these matters, and assure each resident that his wishes will be honored above all else. He should know that the chaplain will act as counsel to the family and the funeral director involved. This assurance relieves much anxiety about this matter.

Many elderly persons do not fear death, but rather welcome the idea of being at rest. As one woman said; "I've lived too long already. Even though life has been good to me, I'm ready to go at any time."

Persons who engage in frequent religious activity (or who follow a fundamentalist type of religion) oftentimes have a positive, forward-looking attitude toward death; whereas, those with little religious background or interest either evade reference to death or fear it. It would seem that in later life religion plays a very personal and important role in the individual's concept of death.

Recently this author made a study of sixty residents, both men and women, to see how their religious beliefs supported their concept of death. Thirty-two persons indicated a positive, optimistic point of view such as, "It will be wonderful." "Promise of a new and better life." "Oh, I will finally be free of pain and all my troubles will be over."

In contrast, the study revealed that twenty-six persons were evasive or apprehensive, as suggested by these comments: "Don't think about it." "Have nothing to do with it." "I feel very well. Why should I think about that now?"

Finally, only two admitted having any fear of dying or the unknown. "Death is the end of everything." "Panic overcomes me." "I hope I'm not conscious when I take that final breath—I dread the thought of it."

It appears from the above that those who read the Bible often, hold a firm belief in the future life, an expectancy of meeting loved ones, and waiting to see Jesus face to face, have few feelings of fear or depression concerning death. They seem in fact better adjusted to the reality of their own death than are those without any fundamental religious beliefs.

No two aging persons look at death in exactly the same way. Each has his individual concerns to discuss with the chaplain and/or others. Certainly the chaplain cannot always give these people the answers they are seeking, nor can he claim to have ultimate knowledge, but he can as a friend and spiritual guide help them to express their doubts and concerns and, thus face the unavoidable future with as much calm and assurance as possible.

Death itself sometimes seems to cause less concern to the elderly, however, than does the act of dying. When a resident dies rather suddenly, one hears such comments as, "Isn't that a nice way to go?" On the other hand, when death comes slowly over a period of months, there is often a concern about the suffering and pain and the loss of physical and mental capabilities. The comment is made, "Death would be a welcome relief." The elderly often fear the long-term bed care, the sometimes vegetable-like existence, or a complete unawareness of the reality of environment and people. (This may become a cause for anxiety to the patient's family, too, about which the chaplain must show concern and give counsel.)

Probably anxiety about how one will die is greatest when the resident is first confined to nursing care because of a fractured hip, a stroke, heart attack, and so on. The fear of a continuing confinement arouses real concern, to which the chaplain should bring counsel and encouragement. The manner in which the resident learns to cope with this crisis can be crucial in his recovery, both physically and mentally. He may either give up, or accept his present infirmity and gain new strengths.

The pastor will need to spend frequent time with residents during these crisis periods. However, he needs to be secure in his own philosophy of accepting death, if he wishes to help these anxious persons discover that same sense of security. The pastor's security, as much as any spoken word, can bring peace of mind and strength to a dying patient.

Finally, a fourth concern is the aging person's grief. When grief cannot be handled adequately by the psychological structure, it may find outlet in physical symptoms. The grieving person may become increasingly preoccupied with his physical functions, and frequently complain about abdominal pain or backache, and may actually develop greater physical as well as emotional problems.

The death of relatives and close friends is of great significance to older people. The loss of contemporaries can be shattering. (Even the loss of a pet can precipitate depression and grief.) When the people with whom they have shared their lives die or move some distance away, the old experience a great loss in their world, and anxiety becomes real for them. The seriousness of separation should not be underestimated.

And too many aged individuals have to suffer a succession of separations or bereavements. They may be deeply affected by the deaths of several friends and loved ones in rapid succession, and need to draw constantly upon the chaplain for strength and guidance.

Several years ago, one of our residents lost a brother and a grandson within five weeks' time. The shock was more than she could accept. She said, "I am too old to endure this terrible loss.

There is nothing left for me to live for. My life is going to be very empty." Her grief was so severe that she could not become involved with life again.

Through counsel and new insights, others find new strengths within to support them in developing a wholesome attitude toward life and death, and are able to live again successfully. Inevitably these persons learn to adjust not only to their own deaths, but to the grief caused by the death of loved ones and friends. This is the paramount adjustment the older person must make to achieve a peaceful and serene inner life, and supporting these persons through this period is one of the primary responsibilities of the chaplain in a geriatric center.

Suggestions for Further Reading

Vern L. Bengston. Self-determination: A social-psychologic perspective on helping the aged. *Geriatrics,* 28: 1973.

T. L. Brink. Pastoral care for the aged: A practical guide. *Journal of Pastoral Care,* 31 (4): 264–271, 1977.

Richard W. Hubbard. Pastoral care in the nursing home: Guidelines for communication with institutionalized elderly. *Journal of Pastoral Care,* 33 (4): 239–242, 1979.

Henri J. M. Nouwen, with Peter J. Naus and Don McNeill. Aging and ministry. *Journal of Pastoral Care,* 28 (September 1974): 164–182.

David Schonfield. Family life education study: The later adult years. *The Gerontologist,* 10 (1970): 115–30.

27

Ministry in Extended Care Facilities

John Patton, Ph.D.

Executive Director
Georgia Association for Pastoral Care
Atlanta, Georgia

And Jacob was left alone; and a man wrestled with him until the breaking of day. When the man saw that he did not prevail against Jacob, he touched the hollow of his thigh; and Jacob's thigh was put out of joint as he wrestled with him. . . . And there he blessed him. So Jacob called the name of the place Penial, saying, "For I have seen God face to face, and yet my life is preserved." The sun rose upon him `. . . limping because of his thigh.

This story of Jacob seems to me to suggest some of the concerns for ministry in an extended care facility. And, at the risk of letting my homiletical inclinations get in the way of a discussion of the central concerns of pastoral care, I submit that, like Jacob, the patient and minister in an extended care facility must find appropriate ways of dealing with *aloneness, wrestling, limping* and *blessing.* I say patient and minister because throughout this discussion there will be the assumption that it is impossible to discuss an issue which is important for the patient without also asking how the same issue affects the minister. Ministry is mediated through the person of the minister and it is inappropriate to discuss the struggles of a patient without at least acknowledging the corresponding struggles of the minister in response to that patient. The experiential basis of my remarks will be two years as a chaplain in a 160-bed extended care facility which is a part of a university medical center and which shares chaplaincy service with a 350-bed general hospital and a 100-bed children's hospital. Some of the issues which distinguish chaplaincy in the extended care facility from general hospital chaplaincy are suggested by the Jacob story.

First, there is the issue of *aloneness*. "And Jacob was left alone." His family and possessions had all been left on the other side of the stream, and he waited anxiously for an uncertain tomorrow. This can be used as an image for the life of many of the older patients in an extended care facility. Ministry to them must seek to break through this aloneness, yet at the same time accept aloneness as one of the realities of life in the older adult which, in many ways, cannot be broken.

A ministry to the grief sufferer is central in this kind of pastoral care. In whatever way the patient may present himself to the minister, a continuing theme to look for is the patient's loss of the persons and things which have meant the most to him in life. Needless to say, the patient does not always speak first about the loss which he feels most keenly, but a willingness on the part of the minister to share his feelings of loss, whether expressed or not, makes ministry possible.

Sometimes the pastoral task involves not just recognition of loss but a celebration of a brief reunion between the separated. One of our more anxious and alone students in Clinical Pastoral Education visited Mr. Warren, an eighty-five-year-old man who was confined to his bed and sometimes disoriented. The student asked Mr. Warren how he was getting along and the patient replied in a somewhat depressed manner:

Mr. W.: I'm not very well. . . . I feel quite weak, can't talk very much. . . . You'll have to excuse me.

(Unable to get through to Mr. Warren, the student chaplain sits silently for awhile. Then a volunteer brings in a letter. Mr. Warren, still feeling helpless says:)

Mr. W.: I can't see to read. You'll have to read it for me.

(The letter is read. Then the pastor hands Mr. Warren the clipping of some old friends which was referred to in the letter and asks Mr. Warren if he can get him his glasses so he can see the picture.)

Mr. W.: I can see! (becoming alert and taking the clipping without his glasses). That's the boys all right!

Pastor: (ignoring Mr. W.'s change in mood). That was nice of your niece to send you the picture of your friends.

Mr. W.: (ignoring the pastor). Yes that's the old boys.

For the moment Mr. Warren's aloneness is broken by reunion with old friends. The pastor's opportunity is to share in this and help Mr. Warren in his celebration of the event, which at least temporarily has healed his depression and corrected his myopia.

A ministry to aloneness, in addition to responsiveness to loss, involves an attempt to provide meaningful experiences in groups. Many persons in extended care facilities have a variety of visitors coming to see them, but are seldom with others in a group. Services of worship provide a natural opportunity for being in a group in a natural and familiar setting. In our institution we have also found it valuable to have a social hour immediately after the service in which volunteers from churches in the community sit in small groups with the patients, drinking hot chocolate and sharing the cookies they have brought. This is a very simple group experience, but one which has become very important to our patients. Other opportunities for ministering to patients in groups come at mealtimes in the dining room, where all who can leave their beds are encouraged to eat; in the television or reading rooms; and in rooms which are shared by more than one patient. We are just beginning our efforts to minister to the patient as a group member as well as an individual. Part of our slowness to begin had to do with our recognition of the patient's right to withhold himself from groups which he anticipates as painful. Getting him to a group may simply make him feel his aloneness more acutely—his real separation from those who have mattered most to him.

This last comment suggests what is probably the main difficulty of the patient's aloneness for the chaplain and for the other members of the institutional staff. Awareness of the patient's aloneness stirs up the anxiety of those ministering to him, so that they are tempted to manipulate the patient in response to their own needs. Because we are inappropriately anxious over the patient's aloneness, we may force him into a group for our own sake. We may become inappropriately angry with his family who has left him alone. Or we may avoid him and leave him even more alone because his withdrawal makes us uncomfortable.

One of the significant aspects of a hospital with an extended care facility is the relative absence of the physician. The patient in such a facility doesn't "need" the doctor as much as hospital patients do, so he visits the patient and talks to the staff much less frequently. This tends to make both patient and staff feel abandoned and on their own. The chaplain must deal with this aspect of the patient's aloneness, responding to the anger and depression of both patients and staff, as well as finding appropriate outlets for the same feelings in himself.

This leads us to our second concern with which ministry in an extended care facility must deal, the issue of *wrestling*. Jacob wrestled, and so do our patients and staff, and perhaps most importantly they wrestle with anger. One of the significant "feeling" dimensions in an extended care facility is anger, often experienced as a wrestling-like struggle for control of that feeling. It may be said that a chaplain in any type of institution proves his competence by the way in which he deals with anger—his own, the patient's, and that of other staff members. In an extended care facility, however, there seem to be so many more things to be angry at, particularly the chronicity of the patient's condition, and the ineffectiveness of all the staff members in doing what they want most to do—heal. Another way to describe the situation is to say that in an extended care facility the fantasies which we hold about our capacity to heal and to be healed are rudely exploded; therefore we become angry.

In the previous section I suggested that one of the persistent themes of the human situation in the extended care facility was loss and that the chaplain might at least implicitly raise the question, "How are you dealing with your loss and grief?" with every patient and staff member with whom he deals. Here I am suggesting that another appropriate question is, "How are you and I dealing with your anger?" In my supervision of introductory level students in Clinical Pastoral Education, I have noticed that this question comes into focus more clearly in the extended care facility than in the general hospital. If the student in our clinical courses learns to allow himself to feel, he feels anger—at me, for assigning him to such a depressing place, at the patient for being disoriented, at the staff for being so insensitive. The student whose anger is unavailable stands out more clearly in the extended care facility than in the hospital. Like Jacob he often appears to be wrestling an unknown man in the dark.

The wrestling of patient and minister with anger can be seen in this brief excerpt from a student interview. The chaplain is attempting to talk to one person at a time in a two-bed room, but having little success at it:

> Chaplain: Mrs. Brown, you look as though you feel better than you did the last time I saw you.
>
> Mrs. Brown: I do feel better, but I'm so weak. I've been trying to get so I can use my walker some, but I haven't been able to. If I could just get over this weakness.
>
> Mrs. Arnold (the roommate): She never will be able to walk again. Her bones are deteriorating; the doctor says they are.
>
> Chaplain (attempting to ignore Mrs. Arnold's statement and talk to Mrs. Brown): I'm glad you have the wheelchair you can use. Maybe later on when you gain your strength back you will be able to use the walker.
>
> Mrs. Arnold: I try to help her all I can, but I can't stand to see anyone suffer.
>
> Chaplain: It's good that you have someone in the room with you who looks after you.

There is wrestling for control going on between Mrs. Brown and her weak body, between Mrs. Brown and Mrs. Arnold, and between the chaplain and both of them. He wants them to be positive and deny their negative feelings. They refuse to do so; therefore, throughout the remainder of the interview he wrestles with them and returns later to the student seminar with a splitting headache which he uses as an excuse to withdraw from the group.

Along with wrestling with anger, in an extended care facility there is also a wrestling with new patterns to old relationships. Once dominant mothers may become like children, to the consternation, anger, and guilt of all concerned. These new patterns of dependency create both a great deal of anxiety and great opportunity for ministry. This can be seen in this conversation of Mrs. Conrad and her daughter with the chaplain.

> Mrs. Conrad: It's funny, my daughter always warned me to be careful if I should go outside. I only went out on the porch, but one

afternoon right in broad daylight I went out there and slipped and fell
and broke my hip. Isn't that foolish!

(The fact that Mrs. Conrad did just what her daughter warned her
against reinforces her feelings of incompetence and the hostility she
feels toward the daughter for "knowing it would happen." Mrs. Conrad
continues:)

Mrs. Conrad: I was at my daughter's. It wouldn't have happened if I
had been at home.

Daughter: Yeah, then you would have fallen down and had no one to
pick you up.

Chaplain: Do you live alone, Mrs. Conrad?

Mrs. Conrad: Yes, they all want me down here, but I want to live in
my house.

Daughter: Well, we've got you where we can keep you down here
now.

Mrs. Conrad: Oh, if I hadn't been in her house it wouldn't have
happened.

(The chaplain, recognizing the underlying anger in all that is going
on, speaks with a smile.)

Chaplain: Why is that, Mrs. Conrad? Did she push you?

Mrs. Conrad: No, I just fell down by myself.

(And, as if the chaplain's humor had finally broken through the
suppressed anger, both mother and daughter began to cry as they for a
moment relinquish the angry control they had been using on one
another.)

A third central concern for chaplaincy in an extended care
facility is ministry to those who, like Jacob, will go away *limping*.
Most of our patients will leave the extended care facility with
some kind of limp. They will not be well. If we are realistic about
the general hospital, we realize that this is true there too. No
patient, none of us, is fully healthy when we complete our period
of structured dependency. In the hospital setting however, this
may be hidden under the cloak of youth and physical strength.
In the extended care facility, many of the cloaks are no longer
available; many of our fantasies of healing are destroyed. We
must look for hope and purpose for our ministry without some
of the usual rewards.

This means that staff members may need each other more. They
need a positive response from a colleague to take the place of the

patient's continued lack of responsiveness. This means that at some points appropriate chaplaincy may be more directed toward staff than toward patients. This need has been found in what were to me somewhat surprising areas. Chaplains are, I think, used to ministering to doctors and nurses, but in our extended care facility we have found some important needs in the housekeeping and food services. Patients who are no longer aggressive enough to express themselves about medical or nursing care may have much to say about the cleanliness of their room and about the food that they eat. Their relationships with the lower-paid housekeeping and food service personnel, then, may be more genuine than with those in nursing. These personnel can appropriately receive some support and training in their relationships to patients, and some of this can best come from the chaplain. The patient who may be unsure of his competence to deal with a person in authority like a nurse or chaplain may show his feelings toward the man who mops the floor. He may feel that only such a person can now respect and honor him. To be sure, most of these feelings are not conscious, but in our facility encounters with these personnel occur too often to be ignored.

When those to whom we have tried to consistently minister go away limping, we must face our own limp seriously—and the finitude of the human resources we call upon for ministry. It should remind us of what we already know: that true ministry is always a pointing beyond oneself to a healing which is not limited by brokenness of body and is valid for "all sorts and conditions of men."

This suggests, finally, that even in the midst of loss and aloneness, wrestling and struggle, the chronicity symbolized by limping, there can be a *blessing*. Jacob's blessing was not easily won, and it is a mistake to think that we can easily offer a blessing to chronically ill patients in an extended care facility. The explicitly religious resources of prayer and Bible reading may be more useful in such a facility than in a hospital. Too easily applied, however, they may deny the painful truth of the human situation in a way which is not in accord with the realism of the Bible.

I prefer to hold on to the symbol of wrestling as an image, this time looking at its more positive meaning—the holding close, the not letting go until morning breaks. The wrestler cannot wrestle at a distance nor can the minister be distant to chronically ill patients. There can be closeness and meaningful relationship when words, the more distant symbols of relationship, no longer perform their usual function. Ministry here is a simple exchange of caring, of giving and receiving on the part of both patient and minister. One of the positive things about ministry to older persons is the relative social freedom which one has to give and receive positive feelings. Here is a place where one can enjoy the pleasures of positive transference without worrying too much about it. There are enough reality features present to keep feet rather firmly on the ground.

With this in mind, I conclude with an excerpt from the relationship of one of our students with an elderly disoriented patient. Logically and verbally, the conversation makes little sense, in terms of love, caring and *blessing* it makes as much sense as I ever hope to find.

Patient: You may not be able to find me. They change my street so often. The street has had a whole bunch of names. 430-B. 430-B (her room number) is my street. I think that's right.

Chaplain: That's dead right.

Patient: Mary Jay Davis, 430 . . .

Chaplain: B.

Patient: 430-B. Do you have a phone number?

Chaplain: Yes. Would you like to have it?

Patient: Yes, please. (She writes the name, address, phone number on the napkin she's been wiping her mouth with and asks me to sign it. I do and I'm hers.) I don't know who we are or why we're here.

Chaplain: I'm Ron Grimes. You're Mary Jay Davis.

Patient: Yes. That's who we are.

Chaplain: Why are we, Mary Jay?

Patient: Because we like each other. You and me we have fun. That's why.

Chaplain: (I'm a bit stunned and feel like I'm walking on clouds.) You're amazing—absolutely amazing. (We laugh.)

Patient: Why?

Chaplain: You know more about why we're here than I do.

Patient: Let's get some ice cream. It would taste good.

Chaplain: And I'll buy it for us. (I have some sent up. We go into another room to eat it.)

Patient: Like it?

Chaplain: You don't think I gobble like this for nothing, do you? (She grins.) (We eat in silence.)

Patient: This makes me sleepy. (She lays her head down. A nurse walks by.)

Nurse: Miss Davis, don't go to sleep on the chaplain.

Patient: (She snaps up alertly.) Don't get excited, nurse. I'm sleeping on the table not on the chaplain. (Laughter from everyone.)

Chaplain: (Kidding) Miss Davis, I'm getting out of here before you do go to sleep and someone starts scandal about both of us.

Patient: You're ice cream.

Chaplain: Why do you say that?

Patient: You taste good.

Chaplain: You do too, Miss Davis. You really do.

Suggestions for Further Reading

Vern L. Bengston. *The Social Psychology of Aging.* New York: Bobbs-Merrill, 1973.

Glen W. Davidson, ed. *The Hospice: Development and Administration.* Washington, D.C.: Hemisphere, 1978.

Carl Eisdorfer and Lawton M. Powell. *The Psychology of Adult Development and Aging.* Washington, D.C.: American Psychological Association, 1973.

Bertram B. Moss. The aging process. *Nursing Homes* (March 1971), pp. 23, 24, 48.

Charles S. Percy. *Growing Old in the Country of the Young.* St. Louis: McGraw-Hill, 1974.

Claire Townsend. *Old Age: The Last Segregation.* New York: Bantam Books, 1971.

Robert F. Willner. *Criteria for Long-term Care Placement: Referral Guidelines of the Clergy.* St. Louis: Catholic Health Association, 1979.

Index

Page numbers followed by *t* indicate tables.

Abbott, J. B., 29–37
Acceptance in drama of dying, 190, 191
Adolescent, concept of death of, 229–230
Aging
  with meaning, 237–241
  pastoral care for, 235–261
  see also Elderly
Alcoholic
  accountability of, 115
  characterization of, 112
  guilt and, 113–114, 117
  ministering to, 111–117
  responsibility of, for problem, 112–113, 114–115
  spiritual condition of, evaluation of, 115–116
Alexander, F., 142, 143
Aloneness of elderly, supportive care for, 247–249, 254–256
Alvarez, W., 143
Andrew, J., 88
Anger
  in drama of dying, 188

in response to illness, 65
of stroke patient, 169–170
wrestling with, in extended care facility, ministering to, 256–257
Anxiety
  in burned patient, 120–121, 122
  in elderly, ministerial support for, 246–252
  in emotional reactions of women, 21, 23, 24–26
  presurgical, 71–83
  see also Presurgical anxiety
Azathioprine for kidney transplant patient, side effects of, 105

Bargaining in drama of dying, 188–189
Beard, B. H., 101
Behavior, obsessive-compulsive, 31
Belgum, D., 60*t*, 133–139
Belter, E. W., 111–117
Blessing in extended care facility, 259–261
Bonhoeffer, D., 60*t*
Bouchard, R., 81

263

Bradley, N., 113
Brown, W. N., 97–108
Bruegel, M. A., 74, 78, 79
Buller, H. W., 209–218
Burned patient(s)
  anxiety in, 120–121, 122
  balm for, 119–130
  children as, ministering to,
    127–128, 129
  depression in, 121–122, 123
  guilt in, 123
  memories of, 124
  ministering to, 119–130
    body contact in, 126–128
    continuity in, 125–126
    personal reactions in, 124–125
    reactions to, 124–125
    separation of, from family, 124
    stress and, 122–123
Burns, morbidity and mortality
  from, 120
Butler, R. N., 81

Cancer as disease, 160–162
Cancer patients, ministering to,
    159–164
  clergy's ministry in, 164
  developmental age of patient in,
    159–160
  disease process in, 160–162
  personal situation of patient in,
    162–163
  spiritual dimensions of patient
    in, 163
Catharsis in drama of dying, 188
Cerebral vascular accident, 167
  see also Stroke
Child(ren)
  burned, ministering to, 127–128, 129
  dying, pastoral care for, 225–234
  and elderly parents, new relationships
    between, wrestling with, 257–258

grade-school, concept of death of,
    228–229
  hospitalized, see Hospitalized
    child(ren)
  pastoral care for, 195–234
  preschool, concept of death of,
    227–228
  to touch, 197–202
Childhood, own, in touching child,
    200–202
Chronicity of disabilities in extended
    care facility, ministering to,
    258–259
Clergy, psychosomatic approach to,
    implications of, 133–139
Clinebell, H., 173
Colitis, ulcerative, 144–147
Coma
  definition of, 179, 180
  patient in, ministering to, 179–183
Commitment in ministry to hospitalized
    children, 222–223
Communication
  problems of stroke patient with,
    167–168
  with stroke patient, establishing,
    as goal of pastoral care, 170–173
Conley, E., 73, 78, 79
Consciousness
  definition of, 179
  levels of, 179–180
  loss of, presurgical anxiety about, 76
Control, type of, in presurgical
    anxiety, 75
Cook, R. E., 211–212
Counseling, supportive, for stroke
    patient, 173
Creativity, initiative and, 17–18
Crisis of illness, 66
Crisis intervention in orthopedic
    surgery, 86–95
Curran, C., 55
Cyclothymic temperament, 31
  depression and, 33

Davis, C. E., 78, 79
Dayringer, R., 59–66
Deal, C. V., Jr., 119–130
DeArment, D., 11–19
Death
  concept of
    of adolescent, 229–230
    of grade-school child, 228–229
    of preschool child, 228
    of toddler, 227–228
    of young child, 227–228
  fear of
    of elderly, supportive care for,
      249–250
    in presurgical anxiety, 74
  see also Dying
Denial
  in child's adjustment to hospitaliza-
    tion, 212–213
  in drama of dying, 187–188
  in hemodialysis patient, 100
Dependency
  of elderly, permitting, 240
  hemodialysis patient and, 102–103
  in presurgical anxiety, 74–75
Depression
  in burned patient, 121–122, 123
  despair and, 35–36
  in drama of dying, 188–189
  in elderly, supportive care for,
    247–249
  forgiveness and, 36–37
  frequency of occurrence of, 32–34
  incidence of, 29
  in ministry to hospitalized children,
    223
  modern psychiatric interpretations of,
    31–32
  patient with, pastoral care of, 34–35
  in stroke patient, 169–170, 173
  symptomatology of, 32–34
  theological dimensions of, 35–37
Depressive reactions and pastoral care,
    29–37

Depressive temperaments, 31
Despair
  in child's adjustment to hospitaliza-
    tion, 212
  depression and, 35–36
  in drama of dying, 189, 190
Dialysis, kidney, patients on,
    ministering to, 97–108
Dickens, C., 209
Disability, physical, of stroke patient,
    168
Disassociation in message of illness, 4–5
Disharmony in message of illness, 4–5
Dombro, R. H., 218
Drug abuser
  accountability of, 115
  characterization of, 112
  guilt and, 114, 117
  ministering to, 111–117
  responsibility of, for problem,
    112–113, 114–115
  spiritual condition of, evaluation of,
    115–116
Dying
  dramas in, 187–190
  fear of, of elderly, supportive care for,
    250–251
  see also Death
Dying child, pastoral care for, 225–234
Dying patient
  basic assumptions concerning,
    185–191
  ministering to, 185–193
  pastoral concern for, reflection on,
    191–193

Egbert, L., 87
Elderly
  anxiety in, ministerial support for,
    246–252
  dependency of, permitting, 240
  depression in, supportive care for,
    247–249

Elderly (*continued*)
  in extended care facility, ministry to,
    253–261
  fear of death of, supportive care for,
    249–250
  fear of dying of, supportive care for,
    250–251
  grief of, supportive care of, 251–252
  loneliness of, supportive care for,
    247–249, 254–256
  meaning of life for, discovering,
    238–241
  sense of worth of, lost, supportive
    care for, 247
Emotional factors
  in gastrointestinal complaints and,
    141–142
  in peptic ulcer, 143
  in ulcerative colitis, 144–146
Emotional reactions of women, anxiety
    in, 21, 23, 24–26
End-stage renal failure, 98–99
English, F., 17–18
Erikson, E. H., 15, 210
Extended care facilities, ministry in,
    253–261

Faith
  justification by
    as concept in pastoral care, 49–56
    theological support for, 51–52
  loss of, as response to illness, 63
  in ministering to stroke patient, 172
  nature of, in cancer patient, 163
Family(ies)
  of dying child
    emotional reactions of, effects of,
      on child, 227–228
    ministering to, 231–232
  of end-stage renal disease patient,
    ministering to, 97–108
  of ICU patients, ministering to,
    152–153
  of stroke patient, ministering to,
    175–176

of unconscious patient, ministering
    to, 182
Faust, D., 21–26
Fear(s)
  of death
    of elderly, supportive care for,
      249–250
    in presurgical anxiety, 74
  of dying of elderly, supportive care
    of, 250–251
  helping patient face, in reducing
    presurgical anxiety, 82
  of outcome in presurgical anxiety, 73
  of unknown in presurgical anxiety,
    72–73
Feelings, honesty of, in ministry to
    hospitalized children, 221–222
Fishman, D. B., 101
Food service personnel in extended care
    facility, ministering to, 259
Forgiveness in dealing with depression,
    36–37
Frankl, V., 60*t*, 155
Freitag, D. F., 237–241
Freud, S., 14, 22, 60*t*, 176, 186, 209–210
Fuhs, M. F., 78

Garma, A., 143
Gastrointestinal complaints, pastoral
    care of patient with, 141–147
Geriatrics, pastoral care to, 245–252
  see also Elderly
Glasser, W., 53–55
God
  bargaining with, in response to
    illness, 63
  concern of, in response to illness,
    63–64
  learning on, in response to illness, 64
  strength from, in response to
    illness, 65
  will of, in response to illness, 65
"God is disciplining me" in response to
    illness, 62

"God doesn't know about me" in response to illness, 61
"God let me down" in response to illness, 62
"God is mad at me" in response to illness, 62–63
Grace, initiative and, 17
Graham, L. E., 73, 78, 79
Grantham, R. E., 167–176
Grief
    in dying patient, 187–190
    of elderly, supportive care for, 251–252
Guilt
    and alcoholic, 113–114, 117
    and burned patient, 123
    and drug abuser, 114, 117
    in message of illness, 5–7
        going beyond, 7–8
    in neurotic-depressive reaction, 32
        pastoral care and, 34–35
    in response to illness, 64

Haas, A. D., 199
Hall, J. T., 39–47
Hemiplegia in stroke patient, 168
Hemodialysis, chronic, patients on, ministering to, 100–103
Hiltner, S., 11, 13
Holst, L. E., 81
Honesty of feelings in ministry to hospitalized children, 221–222
Hope
    nature of, in cancer patient, 163
    perseverance of, in response to illness, 65
    realistic, in drama of dying, 189–190
Horney, K., 22
Hospitalized child(ren), 210–213
    adjustment of, 212–213
    dying, pastoral care for, 225–234
    establishing rapport with, 205–207
    ministry to, 209–218
        person-to-person, 214–215
        through parent, 215–218

parents living in with, value of, 217–218
    pastoral concerns for, 221–223
Housekeeping personnel in extended care facility, ministering to, 259
Hurst, D. M., 149–156
Hypomanic temperaments, 31

ICU, *see* Intensive Care Unit
Illness
    causal factors in, 59
    crisis of, 66
    as crisis of selfhood, 9
    dependency of, 66
    humanness of, 66
    as learning experience, 64, 66
    loneliness of, 66
    message of, reading of, 3–9
    theological implications of, 59–66
        faulty, 61–63
        feasible, 63–65
Initiative
    and creativity, 17–18
    and grace, 17
    pastoral, 11–19
        definition of, 13
        philosophy behind, 14–16
        prerogative for, 18
        structuring in, 13
        theological underpinnings of, 17–18
Intensive Care Unit (ICU)
    ministry in
        objectives and perspectives for, 154–155
        suggestions and warnings for, 155–156
    orientation to, for pastor-chaplain, importance of, 150
    other persons in, needing ministry, 152–154
    pastoral care in, 149–156
    pastoral role, authority, and function in, 151

Intensive Care Unit (ICU) (*continued*)
  patient in
    characteristics, feelings and needs
      of, 150–151
    ministry to, 151–152
  as setting for ministry, 149–150
  staff of, ministering to, 153–154

Janis, I., 72, 87
Johnson, J. E., 75, 78
Johnson, M. A., 72–73, 82
Justification by faith
  as concept in pastoral care, 49–56
  theological support for, 51–52

Karon, M., 212, 216
Kerney, L. G., 159–164
Kidney
  failure of, end-stage, 98–99
  removal of, patient having,
    ministering to, 103–104
  transplantation of
    convalescence from, 106–108
    finding organ for, 104–105
    nephrectomy prior to, 103–104
    patients with, ministering to,
      97–108
Kidney dialysis patients, ministering to,
    97–108
Kierkegaard, S., 35
Kubler-Ross, E., 185
Kurtz, H. P., 81

Lantz, R. B., 141–147
LeShan, L. L., 170, 174
Lethargy, definition of, 179–180
Levy, D., 217
Lewis, M. I., 81
Life, meaning of, for elderly,
    discovering, 238–241
Listening in ministering to woman
    patient, 26
Live, will to, of stroke patient,
    strengthening, 174–175

London, P., 55
Loneliness
  of elderly, supportive care for,
    247–249, 254–256
  of illness, 66
Love, nature of, in cancer patient, 163
Lurie, O. R., 199

McLaughlin, H. L., 180
Manic-depressive reaction, 31
Mason, R., 87
Mead, M., 22
Meiburg, A. L., 60t, 144
Memories in burned patient, 124
Mendenhall, E., 59–66
Menninger, K., 32, 172
Message of illness, reading, 3–9
  disassociation in, 4
  disharmony in, 4–5
  redefinition in, 8–9
  responsibility in, 5–8
Minister, role of, in reducing
    presurgical anxiety, 81–83
Ministering, *see* Pastoral care
Ministry
  ICU
    objectives and perspectives for,
      154–155
    suggestions and warnings for,
      155–156
    tasks and approaches in, 151–152
    two phases in, 152
  ICU as setting for, 149–150
Mowrer, H., 53
Myths, prevailing, in presurgical
    anxiety, 77

Names, naming of, in ministry to
    hospitalized children, 222
Needs, dependency, in presurgical
    anxiety, 74–75
Nephrectomy, patient having,
    ministering to, 103–104
Neurotic-depressive reaction,
    symptoms of, 32–33

Nighswonger, C. A., 185–193
Nurses, ICU, ministering to, 153–154
Nursing home, ministry in, 253–261

Oates, W. E., 60*t*
Obsessive-compulsive behavior, 31
Obtundation, definition of, 180
Olin, H., 169
Orthopedic surgery, crisis intervention
    in, study of, 86–95
  development of treatments in, 88–89
  discussion in, 93–95
  method of, 89–93
  summary in, 95
Outcome, fear of, in presurgical
    anxiety, 73
Owens, N. F., 81

Panic in drama of dying, 188
Parent(s)
  of dying child
    emotional reactions of, effects of,
        on child, 227–228
    ministering to, 231–232
  elderly, and children, new relation-
      ships between, wrestling with,
      257–258
  ministering to hospitalized child
      through, 215–218
Pastor-chaplain in ICU
  authority of, 151
  function of, 151
  importance of ICU orientation
      for, 150
  role of, 151
Pastoral care
  for aging, 235–261
    see also Elderly
  for burned patients, 119–130
  for cancer patients, 159–164
  for depressed patient, 34–35
  depressive reactions and, 29–37
  for children, 195–234
    in hospital, establishing rapport
        in, 205–207

for drug addicts, 111–117
for dying, 185–193
for ICU patient, 149–156
justification by faith as concept in,
    49–56
for kidney dialysis and transplant
    patients and their families,
    97–108
for patient, 69–194
  with gastrointestinal complaints,
      141–147
for presurgical patient, 71–83
psychosomatic approach in, 133–139
for sick, theory of, 1–66
for stroke patient and family, 167–176
for unconscious patient, 179–183
for woman patient, 21–26
Pastoral relationships, initiative in,
    11–19
  see also Initiative, pastoral
Patton, J., 253–261
Peptic ulcer, 142–144
Person-to-person ministry to
    hospitalized child, 214–215
Personality functioning, physical
    effects on, 138
Perspective, visual, in presurgical
    anxiety, 76
Phillips, J. B., 29
Physical disability of stroke
    patient, 168
Play in ministry to hospitalized child,
    214–215
Plum, F., 170–171, 179–180
Posner, J., 170–171, 179–180
Praying
  for sick
    dynamic concept of, 39–47
    indications for, 41
    initiating, 39–41
    techniques for, 41–47
    traditional approaches to, 39–40
  with unconscious patient, 182
Prednisone for kidney transplant
    patient, side effects of, 105, 108

Presurgical anxiety
  deleterious effects of, 71
  etiology of, 72–77
    dependency needs in, 74–75
    fear of death in, 74
    fear of outcome in, 73
    fear of unknown in, 72–73
    loss of consciousness in, 76
    presurgical preparation in, 76–77
    prevailing myths in, 77
    type of control in, 75
    visual perspective in, 76
  possible model of, 79–81
  previous hospitalization and, 73
  reduction of, minister's role in, 81–83
  relevant research on, 77–79
    on assessment, 77–78
    on individual differences in, 78–79
  religious faith and, 74
  support and information and, 93–94
Presurgical patient, ministering to,
    71–83
Presurgical preparation in presurgical
    anxiety, 76–77
Probst, C. R., 245–252
Protest in child's adjustment to
    hospitalization, 212
Prugh, D. G., 212, 217, 218
Psychosomatic approach of clergy,
    implications of, 133–139
Psychosomatic medicine
  clergy's perspective on, 136–139
  definition of, 133
  patient's perspective on, 135–136
  physician's perspective on, 134–135
Psychotherapeutic-pastoral perspec-
    tives on ICU ministry, 155
Punishment, illness as, 62

Ramsay, M. A. E., 73, 76, 78–79
Rank, 155
Rapport with hospitalized children,
    establishing, 205–207
Reactive-depressive person, 32

Reality therapy, 53–54
Reassurance in ministering to woman
    patient, 26
Redefinition in message of illness, 5–7
Reeves, R. B., 3–9
Regression of stroke patient, 168–169
Relationships, new patterns to,
    wrestling with, in extended care
    facility, ministering to, 257–258
Renal disease, end-stage, patients with,
    ministering to, 97–108
Renal failure, end-stage, 98–99
Repentence in psychosomatic medicine,
    137–138
Resignation in drama of dying, 190
Response in pastoral relationships,
    12, 13
Responsibility
  of drug abuser for problem, 112–113,
    114–115
  in message of illness, 5–8
  in response to illness, 64
Richardson, S., 52
Robertson, J., 212
Rogers, C., 155

Sacraments, administration of,
    to presurgical patient, 83
Saylor, D., 71–83
Schaefer, J., 205–207
Schaffer, A. J., 217
Schizophrenic, spiritual therapy with,
    49–56
Selling out in drama of dying, 188–189
Selye, H., 134
Separation and hospitalized child,
    211–212
Sherril, L., 160
Sick, praying for, dynamic concept of,
    39–47
  see also Praying for sick
Siirala, A., 60t
Snaith, N. H., 52
Spiegel, 94

Spielberger, C., 89
Staff in ministry to hospitalized
    children, 223
Stephens, C. R., 225–234
Strengthening will to live of stroke
    patient, 174–175
Stress
    in burned patient, 122–123
    of surgery, 72
    see also Presurgical anxiety
Stroke patient, 167–176
    anger in, 169–170
    communication with, establishing,
        as goal of pastoral care, 170–173
    communication problems of, 167–168
    depression in, 169–170, 173
    goals of pastoral care for, 170–176
        establishing communication as,
            170–173
        family guidance as, 175–176
        strengthening the will to live as,
            174–175
        supportive counseling as, 173
    physical disability of, 168
    regression of, 168–169
Structuring in pastoral initiative, 13
Stupor, definition of, 180
Suffering, viewpoints of, 60*t*
Suicide
    hemodialysis patient and, 103
    threats of, 33
Surgery, stress of, 72
    see also Presurgical anxiety
Szasz, T., 53

Temple, P. C., 221–223
Theological dimensions of depression,
    35–37
Theological implications of illness,
    59–66
    faulty, 61–63
    feasible, 63–65
Theological-pastoral perspectives on
    ICU ministry, 153–155

Theological support for justification by
    faith, 51–52
Theological underpinnings of pastoral
    initiative, 17–18
Thompson, M. S., 49–56
Tillich, P., 35, 36, 60*t*, 192
Toddler, concept of death of, 227–228
Toews, A. L., 179–183
Tolstoi, L., 101
Touch
    in establishing rapport with
        hospitalized child, 205–206
    in ministry to hospitalized children,
        222
Tournier, P., 135
Transplant, kidney, patients with,
    ministering to, 97–108

Ulcer, peptic, 142–144
Ulcerative colitis, 144–147
Unconscious patient, ministry to,
    179–183
Unconsciousness, recovery from, stages
    of, 180
Unknown, fear of, in presurgical
    anxiety, 72–73

Vernick, J., 212, 216
Visual perspective in presurgical
    anxiety, 76

Wakefulness, alert, definition of, 179
Weatherhead, L., 60*t*
Wedergren, R. B., 197–202
Will to live of stroke patient,
    strengthening, 174–175
Williams, D. D., 60*t*
Williams, J., 71, 78
Williams, R., 74–75
Winslow, E. H., 78
Wolfer, J., 78, 79

Woman (en)
   dependence of, 13
   emotional experiences of, 22
   emotional reactions of, anxiety in,
      21, 23, 24–26
   as patient, ministering to, 21–26
   psychological development of, 22
   work of, monotony of, 24

Wrestling
   with anger in extended care facility,
      ministering to, 256–257
   with new patterns to old relationships
      in extended care facility,
      ministering to, 257–258

Young, R. K., 60t, 144